Dear Mom,
   Here's a biography of
a fearless, strong, and
intelligent woman we heard
a lot about while we
were in Scotland.
   Hope you enjoy it!

      Love,
      Abby & Rey
      May 2005

For
Martha McLeod,
Roseland, Aberdeen, North Carolina,
A graduate of Flora MacDonald College,
her ancestors emigrated from Skye
at the same time as
Flora MacDonald.

FLORA MACDONALD

The Jacobite heroine
in Scotland and North America

Ruairidh H. MacLeod

*"The Captain was at some pains to
represent to her the glory and honour
she would acquire by such a worthy and
heroic action, and he hoped God would
make her successful in it.
"'You need not fear your character' said
he, 'for by this you will gain yourself an.
immortal character.'"*

Capt Felix O'Neille

SHEPHEARD-WALWYN

First published in 1995 by
Shepheard-Walwyn (Publishers) Ltd
26 Charing Cross Road (Suite 34)
London WC2H 0DH

British Library Cataloguing in Publication Data

A catalogue record of this book
is available from the British Library

ISBN 0 85683 147 6

Cover design by Alan Downs
based on Allan Ramsay's portrait of Flora MacDonald,
reproduced by permission of the Ashmolean Museum, Oxford

Typeset by Alacrity Phototypesetters
Banwell Castle, Weston-super-Mare.
Printed and bound in Great Britain by
BPC Wheatons Ltd, Exeter.

Contents

Introduction

Flora MacDonald is a name that has been mentioned in history, and yet there are few contemporary descriptions of her. Never a great writer, Flora kept no journal of her famous adventure, nor any during the remainder of her life. She made a declaration to General John Campbell, when she was captured, and gave an account, a year after the events, to Dr Burton. In the last year of her life she dictated a *Memorial* for Sir John MacPherson. This was the only source for much of Flora's life in North America.

Robert Forbes's monumental life's work, *The Lyon in Mourning* is the cornerstone of any account of the 1745 Rising, but it did not appear in full until 1895. The work contained Flora's narrative given to Dr Burton; Felix O'Neille's narrative; stories told about the Prince at Kingsburgh House; Donald Roy MacDonald's narrative and descriptions of visits to Flora at Leith. Dr Burton's short history added little more.

In North Carolina Rev Eli Caruthers was the first to collect stories in the 1830s. Rev William Foote also collected information, but it was James Banks, in 1857, who published *The Life and Character of Flora* MacDonald. James Banks's history of the 1745 Rising was inaccurate, and his account of Flora's life in North Carolina was flawed by confusing Alexander MacDonald of Cuidrach with her husband Allan.

The first Scottish publication was Flora MacDonald Wylde's autobiography — yes autobiography — of her grandmother, published in 1870. Some years later Rev Alexander MacGregor wrote a biography of Flora. His father came to be minister at Kilmuir in Skye in 1822. Rev Macgregor did not have access to *The Lyon in Mourning* and he was inaccurate in telling of the Prince's escape to Skye. He wrote that "the author was furnished, to a great extent, with the facts here given, from the lips of Flora's daughter, the said Mrs Major-General Macleod, as well as from the diction of old men in Skye. James Banks, Esq., Fayetteville, N.C., also contributed largely to the account of Flora's American adventures." But Rev MacGregor was also inaccurate in the details of Flora's life, and the North American section reflected all the errors of James Banks's book. William Jolly's *Flora MacDonald in South Uist* added little more information.

J.P.Maclean, a Cincinatti dentist, was invited, in 1909, to write a biography of Flora. *Flora MacDonald in America* copied Caruthers and Banks, and several new sources, without acknowledgement, and then improved them with speculation and dramatic writing.

A.R.MacDonald's *The Truth about Flora MacDonald* was the first book to question previous authors, and to cross check accounts and records. The author died before the book was completed, and it was edited by Rev Donald Mackinnon in 1938. Though weak on the American part of Flora's life, this was later corrected by Donald Mackinnon, who travelled to North Carolina, and met Rassie Wicker and others, who had a great interest in Flora. Donald Mackinnon had prepared a new biography, but it was never completed and published.

Since 1938, new, original material on the 1745 Rising has become available and has been published, including Flora's Memorial to Sir John MacPherson.

In 1967, the American author, Elizabeth Vining, published a biography of Flora, which was much stronger on the American episode of her life, but this was written 28 years ago. All that is available now is a reprint of J.P.Maclean's *Flora MacDonald in America* and a rehash of Rev MacGregor's *Life of Flora MacDonald* and a number of slim booklets.

There is a great deal of original material about Flora, and her husband Allan, which has not been published. Little use has been made of General John Campbell's Papers; the Duke of Cumberland's Papers; the MacDonald Papers, now in Skye; and the Mackenzie of Delvine Papers. The letters of Josiah Martin and Lord Dartmouth indicated what a central role Allan, and his son-in-law Alexander MacLeod, played in the American Revolutionary War in North Carolina. The published North Carolina Colonial and State Records conveniently contain invaluable original material. The Loyalists Claims, accessible in both London and North Carolina, contain a wealth of detail. Alexander MacDonald of Staten Island's *Letter Book* contains much MacDonald family history.

I have been to many places, met many people, written to more and consulted many manuscripts and books. My thanks to Her Majesty the Queen for allowing me to quote from the Cumberland Papers; to the Henry E Huntington Library for the Loudoun Papers; to the National Library of Scotland for the Campbell Papers and the MacKenzie of Delvine Papers and to the Clan Donald Trust for the MacDonald Papers.

Wherever possible I have used contemporary sources to describe events. I have generally kept to the original spelling, but I have added some punctuation and have divided up the text into paragraphs, for easier reading.

My thanks to Dr Alasdair Maclean, of South Uist and now Skye, for his help on Neil MacEachen; to Margaret MacDonald at the Clan Donald Centre, in Skye; and to Angus and Julia MacLeod. My thanks to the staff of the National Library of Scotland; St.Andrews University Library; Register House; Scottish National Portrait Gallery; Royal Museum of Scotland; Public Records Office and British Library.

I have been to Milton, Unasary, Nunton, Rossinish, Uiskevaig, Monkstadt, Kingsburgh, Armadale, Flodigarry and many other places in Scotland, but I have also been able to visit Cross Creek, Mount Pleasant, Barbecue Church, Glendale, Cheeks Creek, Smith's Ferry, Moore's Creek, Wilmington, Brunswick and New Bern in North Carolina. My thanks to Pinny Geffert, formerly of St Andrews Presbyterian College, Laurinburg; to the staff of the North Carolina Department of Archives and History, at Raleigh and Henry E Huntington Library, California.

My thanks to Enid MacLeod, Dartmouth, NS; Charlie Germany, Texas; Vic Clark and Bill Fields, NC. I enjoyed exploring in North Carolina with Ed Cameron, John Hairr and Dick Knight, Rassie Wicker's son-in-law. My thanks to Anne and Frank McNeill who have given me a second home in North Carolina. But this biography would not have been begun, or been completed, without the enthusiasm, interest, and hard work of Martha McLeod. To her this book is dedicated affectionately.

Finally my thanks to my wife, Anne, and daughter, Emma, for having had to live with another woman for so long, and my apologies to my son John Somhairle for having deprived him of the use of the computer!

Throughout the work, Flora's character has shone through; unassuming yet self-confident; gentle, yet resolute; an ordinary woman, devoted to her family, and yet an extra-ordinary woman, who captured a nation's imagination, and has never ceased to fascinate it since. Yet Flora was no demur matron, and at times showed a determination that drove her into warlike action.

Flora's husband, Allan, was an honest gentleman, typical of the obsolete tacksman of the Highlands, but he was hopeless with money. Their marriage was arranged, but they lived together for 40 years. There were signs of difficulties, but then Allan did ruin their lives financially in Skye, and then politically and financially in America.

I have now completed a biography of one of Scotland's most famous daughters. I have attempted honestly to explain the story of the life of a remarkable woman and her husband, who lived through dramatic times in the Highlands and North America. While thanking everyone who assisted me, I take full responsibility for my own conclusions.

Ruairidh H.MacLeod
Shetland   St Andrews Day, 1994

Persons Associated with Flora and Allan MacDonald

MACDONALD:

Alexander, 1689-1772, of Kingsburgh, Allan's father. He gave protection to the Prince, and told his story to Robert Forbes.

Alexander, b c1700, of Boisdale, half-brother to Clanranald. Lived at Kilbride, South Uist.

Sir Alexander, 1711-1746, 7th Bt of Sleat, m Lady Margaret Montgomery. Visited Duke of Cumberland, 1746. Died suddenly 1746.

Alexander, b c1720, of Cuidrach, cousin of Allan, m Annabella MacDonald, emigrated to Mount Pleasant, NC, returned to Kingsburgh.

Sir Alexander, 1744-1795, 9th Bt of Sleat. Inherited from brother, and raised rents. Created Lord MacDonald in 1776, and lived in London.

Alexander, 1755-1780, 2nd son of Allan and Flora. Emigrated to NC in 1774. Lt Royal Highland Emigrants. Lost at sea 1780.

Allan, c1722-1792, of Flodigarry and Kingsburgh. s of Alexander MacDonald of Kingsburgh. m Flora 1750. Flodigarry 1751. Kingsburgh 1764. Emigrated 1774. Returned 1785.

Ann, b 1754, elder daughter of Allan and Flora, m Alexander MacLeod of Glendale.

Annabella, b c1730, half-sister of Flora, m Alexander MacDonald of Cuidrach. Emigrated to Mount Pleasant, NC. Returned to Kingsburgh.

Anne, b c1720, sister of Allan, m1 Ranald MacAlister of Skirinish and m2 Mackinnon of Corrie. Wrote two MS accounts of the Prince.

Angus, born c1718, of Milton, brother of Flora, m Penelope d of Ranald MacDonald of Clanranald.

Charles, 1751-1795, eldest son of Flora and Allan. Lt Royal Highland Emigrants, 1776; Capt British Legion. Returned to Skye.

Donald, b c1700, of Castleton, uncle of Allan. Capt Independent Company, 1746. Arrested Flora.

Donald Roy, b c1705-1774, brother of Hugh of Baleshare. Met Prince and Flora at Portree. Emigrated to NC, died there in 1774.

Donald, b c1710, probably a cousin of Allan, major Royal Highland Emigrants, brig commanding the NC Loyalist Army, 1776.

Donald, b c1720, of Balranald, cousin to both Flora and Allan.

Donald, b c1760, s of Alexander MacDonald of Cuidrach. Emigrated to NC, lt British Legion, returned to Skye. m Fanny MacDonald.

Flora, b c1700-1759, of Castleton, mother of Allan. m Alexander MacDonald of Kingsburgh.

Flora, 1722-1790, d of Ranald of Milton, helped the Prince, m 1750, Allan; emigrated 1774, to NC, returned 1779 to Skye.

Flora, b c1733, half-sister of Flora, m Archibald MacQueen, emigrated to NC.

Frances or Fanny, b1766, younger d of Allan and Flora. Remained in Scotland, m 1790, Donald s of Alexander MacDonald of Cuidrach, Mount Pleasant and Kingsburgh.

Hugh, b c1695-1780, Flora's step-father, m Marion MacDonald of Milton. 1745 to Armadale. Arranged Prince's escape. 1753 to Camuscross. Emigrated to NC, died there.

Hugh, b c1700, of Baleshare. Met Prince in Benbecula. Brother of Donald Roy.

Sir James, 1741-1765, 8th Bt of Sleat, came of age in 1762, reviewed rents on MacDonald Estates. Wrote letters to attorney in Edinburgh.

James, b 1757, 4th son of Flora and Allan. Emigrated to NC. Remained with mother. 1779 joined British Legion. Returned to Skye.

John, 1759-1831, 5th son of Flora and Allan. Did not emigrate. 1780 went to India and retired to Exeter.

Lady Margaret Montgomery, b c1715, m Sir Alexander, 7th Bt. Thrown into a panic by the arrival of the Prince.

Margaret MacLeod, b c1700, of Berneray, m Ranald, 17th of Clanranald. Lived at Nunton, Benbecula. Provided clothes for Prince.

Margaret Nicolson, b c1720, m John of Kirkibost. Sent to Skye to warn Lady Margaret. After 1780 Flora stayed with her.

Margaret MacLeod, b c1730, of Balmeanach, m James of Cnocowe, Allan's brother. Known as Peggy. After 1781 Flora lived with her.

Marion, b c1695 d rev Angus, m1 Ranald of Milton, mother of Flora, m2 Hugh of Armadale. Died before 1771.

Penelope, b c1725, d Ranald of Clanranald, m Angus of Milton.

Ranald, c1660-1727, of Milton, father of Flora. Cousin of Clanranald. Died some years after Flora's birth.

Ranald, b c1688, 17th of Clanranald, cousin of Flora. Did not join Prince's army. Saw Prince in Uists, then left for the mainland.

Ranald, b c1720, "young" Clanranald, brother-in-law of Angus of Milton.

Ranald, 1757-1782, 2nd son of Flora and Allan. Capt of marines. In America in 1776-82. Sick, and died at sea.

MACLEOD:

Alexander, c1730-1797, of Glendale, son of Norman MacLeod, 22nd Chief. Married Ann, daughter of Flora. Emigrated to NC 1774. Returned 1778.
Donald, b c1732, 3rd son of John MacLeod, 4th of Pabbay & St Kilda. Capt Royal Highland Emigrants. Killed at Moore's Creek.
Malcolm, b 1711, 2nd son of John MacLeod, 2nd of Rigg. Guided the Prince across Skye. Returned from London in carriage with Flora.

CHAPTER 1

South Uist

Fionnghal nighean Raonuill 'ic Aonghais Oig,
an Airidh Mhuillin

At about midnight, on 21st June 1746, Neil MacEachen entered Flora MacDonald's shieling in South Uist. He introduced Capt Felix O'Neille and then Prince Charles Edward Stuart was brought into the small building. The moment was to change Flora's life.

The Prince had been appointed Prince Regent by his father, and had arrived in Scotland almost a year previously. Defeated at the battle of Culloden in April, he was being hunted as the Young Pretender by King George's troops. The Prince was desperate to escape from the Uists.

Flora was then twenty four years old. She was short and had a small pointed face, and a wide mouth. Her eyes were variously painted hazel and blue, and were described as being bright blue. She had a high forehead and dark brown hair, that showed a hint of auburn. Flora was a plain young lady, but she had a good complexion, and, in an age when so many suffered from the ravages of small pox, that made her handsome.

Flora was born in 1722 at Milton in South Uist in the Outer Hebrides. Her father was Ranald MacDonald, a gentleman farmer, holding the leases, called "tacks", of Milton and Balivanich. Ranald, who was called Milton, to distinguish him from all the other Mac-Donalds, was a first cousin of the chief of the MacDonalds of Clanranald, who held lands in South Uist, the small isles and Moidart on the mainland.

Late in life Ranald of Milton married, as his second wife, Marion, the young daughter of his cousin Rev Angus MacDonald, minister of South Uist. Ranald and Marion had three children, Angus, Ranald and Flora.

Flora was named for her mother's mother, Flora MacDonald, who had married Rev Angus MacDonald. In Gaelic, Flora's full patronimic was Fionnghal nighean Raonuill 'ic Aonghais Oig, an Airidh Mhuillin; Flora daughter of Ranald son of young Angus, Milton. The Gaelic name Fionnghal, pronounced "funeral", has been equated in English with Flora and Florence.

Gaelic was Flora's first language.

The harsh, indestructible spine of the Hebrides, made up of the oldest rocks in Britain, ran up the east side of South Uist. The tall, rounded hills were clad in heather and the lower slopes were deep in peat. To the west of these inhospitable hills lay a broad, flat, waterlogged plain, some two or three miles wide. On the western edge, it was fringed with white beaches. These beaches, made up largely of crushed shells, had acted to neutralise the acid, peaty soil to produce a narrow strip of rich fertile green meadow land called machair.

It was into this landscape that Flora was born. The old township of Milton was clustered on a low ridge between Loch Kildonan to the north and Loch Aird an Sgairbh, to the south. The white, sandy beach south of Trollaskeir was three quarters of a mile away to the west. The mill, which gave the township its name, lay the same distance away to the east, below Beinn a'Mhuillinn, which rose steeply up towards Sheaval. Between Sheaval, Trinival and Arnaval lay a large upland pasture, where in summer the Milton cattle grazed. In all the tack of Milton consisted of 2,500 acres, of which 400 acres were arable.

Most of the land on the farm was sublet to lesser folk who worked the land communally, growing bere, a type of barley, and oats, and paid their rents to the tacksman. In time of strife Ranald of Milton and his ancestors had been expected to raise men for their chief, to fight off the MacLeods or Macleans in whatever feud was brewing.

The wealth of the islands was in black cattle. These small, shaggy beasts flourished on the meagre grazing of the isles. Each summer young cattle were transported to the mainland for the long journey to the cattle market at Crieff in October. It was at the tryst that debts and rents were paid, as southern and English farmers purchased the cattle. They then drove the cattle south into England, to be fattened in East Anglia and eventually butchered at Mr Smith's Field, for the London market.

Everyone joined in the tending of the cattle. In the summer the beasts were driven up into the hills to keep them off the crops of oats and barley. They were accompanied by the women and girls who lived in huts called shielings. The womenfolk made butter and cheese. In the autumn the men helped to guide the droves of cattle to market. The people of the islands lived in low thatched cottages, with only one entrance. The cattle wintered in the lower end of the cottage, and the people lived in the upper end, around a peat fire, sleeping four or five to a bed. There were no windows or chimney, and the smoke escaped through the thatch.

On the farms some tacksmen's houses were of two storeys, but most had only one, with a thatched roof and earthen floor, little better than the smoky, windowless cottages of the lesser folk. But the cattle were wintered in a seperate building. The tacksmen and their families, however, lived in comparative style, with well made furniture, silver cutlery and linen table cloths and sheets. They were well educated and often owned extensive libraries. Many of them sent their sons to university, and younger sons often became ministers and lawyers, and soldiers. Their daughters were educated at home.

In 1879 William Jolly visited Milton, and wrote that the house where Flora was brought up had "only three rooms, one on each side of the entrance, and the other opening into the kitchen on the south. Though it was thatched and unpretentious, like all others in the islands except the castles of the chiefs, it was well furnished and eminently comfortable.

"The old farm had attached to it the usual outhouses connected with agricultural life and the dwellings of the servants; while comfortable crofters dwelt all round." [1]

Ranald of Milton died when Flora was a child. Flora's mother, Marion, was left with three small children and two farms to run twenty miles apart.

It was hardly surprising that in 1728 Marion married again. Her second husband was Hugh MacDonald from Sartle in Skye. He was a grandson of Sir James Mor MacDonald of Sleat, and was connected through his mother with the MacLeods of Raasay. Hugh had served in the French army, and had just returned to Scotland. He was reckoned to be one of the strongest men in the isles, and though he had lost one eye, he was still a great swordsman.

Hugh and Marion kept on the tacks of Balivanich and Milton, and lived at Milton with Marion's three children and with their own, two daughters and two or three sons, when they were born.

It was claimed that Marion was abducted by Hugh, and taken to Armadale in Skye. [2] Hugh and Marion did move to Armadale, but not until 1745, 17 years after they were married. The story that Flora preferred to remain with her brother in South Uist, rather than go to live with her mother and stepfather, in Skye, had no foundation. The family lived together at Milton until 1745.

It was claimed that, when Flora was 13, in 1735, Lady Clanranald "practically adopted the solitary child", and for three years schooled her with her own children. Flora had not been left alone in South Uist by her mother, and was part of a family of seven or eight children.

Flora, with her brothers and sisters, may have been educated with Clanranald's children, for they were cousins.

It was claimed that Flora crossed to Skye to see her mother, and "won the high regard of the beautiful Lady Margaret MacDonald.

"When seventeen, [in 1739], Flora was for eight months a cherished member of their circle. She also became intimate with the family of the good genial factor, MacDonald of Kingsburgh, a connection that more than any shaped her after life.

"After visits to Uist to nurse her sick brother and see her friends at Nunton, Flora was sent by Lady Margaret to Edinburgh, to complete her education."

Flora's mother did not live in Skye, so she cannot have gone there to visit her. Flora was not an intimate friend of Lady Margaret Mac-Donald, who later wrote that she had met Flora only once. Robert Forbes wrote that Flora had never been to Edinburgh, before she was brought a prisoner to Leith, in 1746.

Flora was educated at home, like all of her class, and may have shared a tutor with Clanranald's children. The stories of her precocious talents as a child should be discounted. Flora later considered her writing so poor, that, when she arrived in Edinburgh, in 1747, she immediately attended writing classes. Flora could read and write in English, and probably in Gaelic. She could play the spinet, sing and dance, and had been taught the social graces of managing a tea table. Flora could also milk a cow, and make butter and cheese. She could tend animals and walk or ride forty miles in a day.

Flora, however, did achieve a poise and polish which was to astonish her admirers, who believed that she must have been educated away from the islands. But in the first twenty or so years of her life, Flora never left the Hebrides.

Though better educated than the lesser people, Flora was not exceptional. Like many other daughters of tacksmen, she was composed and self confident, and hoped to find a husband from amongst the sons of other tacksmen. Flora was a serious, reserved, young woman. Unmarried at the age of twenty four, Flora doubtless considered herself an old maid.

Officially there were no Catholics in Britain. Clanranald, and most of his clan, remained Catholic, occasionally visited by intrepid priests, who risked their lives to minister to their oppressed people. Through the influence of her grandfather, Rev Angus MacDonald, Presbyterian minister of South Uist, Flora was brought up as a Protestant. She worshipped at the ancient church at Howmore, the parish church of South Uist, and with her family in her own home. Flora was a sincere Christian and remained a Presbyterian throughout her life.

Flora's brother Ranald, as a boy, was accidently killed on the island of Cara, off the Kintyre coast.

Flora MacDonald painted by Richard Wilson
in London in 1747
(Courtesy Scottish National Portrait Gallery)

In 1744 Flora left home.[3] Aged twenty one or two, Flora travelled south to Kintyre on the mainland, to stay with her cousin John MacDonald of Largie, and his wife Elizabeth MacLeod of the Berneray family. Elizabeth and John of Largie had a daughter, born about 1742, and Flora went to Kintyre to be company for Elizabeth. The Largies were considered wealthy, owning a pleasant house and extensive lands on the west side of the long peninsula that was Kintyre, far to the south of the Uists.

Flora stayed at Largie for 10 or 11 months and returned to South Uist in the spring of 1745.

In South Uist Flora's remaining brother Angus married Penelope, eldest daughter of his chief, Ranald MacDonald of Clanranald. Angus and Penelope were second cousins. Angus set about taking over the running of his father's farms. Flora's mother and stepfather needed to find somewhere else to live.

At Whitsun, in May 1745, the farm at Armadale, in south Skye, became vacant. Hugh and Marion, with their own children and Flora, moved to Skye. Hugh became known as MacDonald of Armadale.

In July 1745 Prince Charles Edward Stuart, Bonnie Prince Charlie, landed on Eriskay, to the south of South Uist; he sailed to the mainland and started on a daring expedition which was to bring him within 120 miles of London.

Hugh MacDonald of Armadale claimed that he met Prince Charles, when he first landed in Moidart. Flora's brother Angus had also crossed to Arisaig with his brother in law, Ranald, young Clanranald, to meet the Prince, but Angus refused to take up arms.

In December 1745 Armadale was appointed captain of one of the companies of local militia raised by Sir Alexander MacDonald of Sleat, for the defence of Skye against the Jacobites. His son James, who was only 15 or 16 years old, was appointed ensign in one of the MacDonald Independent Companies. This company, at the end of December 1745, marched to Inverness to join Lord Loudoun and the Government forces stationed there.

The house at Armadale was later described by James Boswell as a "very good tenant's house, having two storeys and garrets" and "there is really a good garden and a number or trees of age and size, mostly ash."[4] The house faced south, and had a large quarter garden behind, on a gently sloping hillside. The road from Ardvasar to Broadford passed beside the house and beyond was a little cliff above the waters of the Sound of Sleat. Across the Sound rose the steep peaks of Knoydart on the mainland.

Sleat was the garden of Skye. A milder climate and richer soil gave abundant crops, which must have seemed like Eden, after the harsh toil of the Outer Hebrides.

Hugh MacDonald of Armadale set about organising the defence of Skye for his chief, Sir Alexander MacDonald. Marion made her new home at Armadale with Armadale's daughters Flora, sometimes called Florence, and Annabella, and his sons, James and one or two other boys. Flora, Milton's daughter, had discreetly left the newly weds in South Uist and joined her mother in Sleat. It was a cold harsh winter with gales and snow.

CHAPTER 2

The 1745 Rising

In a few days, with the few friends that I have, I will erect the Royal Standara and proclaim to the people of Britain that Charles Stuart is come over to claim the crown of his ancestors, to win it, or perish in the attempt. — Prince Charles Edward Stuart.

On 10th June 1688 the course of British History was changed. At Whitehall in London, Mary of Modena, the second wife of the Catholic King James VII of Scots, and II of England, gave birth to a son James.

In 1603 Queen Elizabeth of England had died. King James VI of Scots, the son of Mary, Queen of Scots, rushed south to London and became James I of England. James's son Charles was beheaded in 1649, and left two sons, Charles and James. King Charles II left many Royal offspring but none by his Queen. When it became apparent that King Charles would leave no legitimate heirs, Parliament agreed that his brother James, Duke of York, though a Catholic, could succeed. By his first wife, James had produced two daughters, Mary and Anne, who had been brought up in the Protestant faith.

The birth of a son in 1688 altered all that. Within a year King James was forced to leave England, and his daughter Mary, and her husband William of Orange, were invited to become monarchs of both England and Scotland.

King James went into exile and, after his death, his son James became known as the Old Pretender.

Queen Mary died childless and, after the death of William, was succeeded by her sister Queen Anne. This lady had nineteen children, but none of them survived childhood. When it became clear that Queen Anne would have no direct heir, the British Parliament set about finding a Protestant one.

James VI and I had had a daughter Elizabeth, the Winter Queen, who had married the King of Bohemia. She had had a daughter Sophia who had married the Elector of Hanover. Sophia, and her eldest son George, were declared Queen Anne's heirs.

In 1714 Queen Anne died a few months after Sophia. George crossed to London and was proclaimed King.

Prince Charles Edward Stuart from a miniature
found on Culloden battlefield
Culloden Home Collection.
(Courtesy National Trust for Scotland)

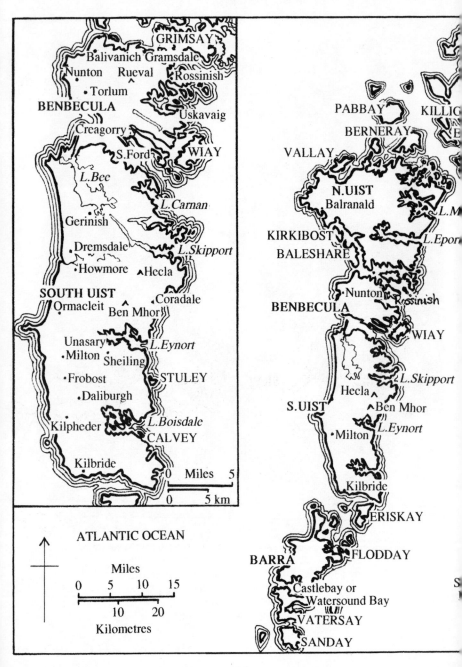

GRIMSAY
Balivanich Gramsdale
Nunton Rueval
Rossinish
Torlum
BENBECULA
Uskavaig
Creagorry
S.Ford
WIAY
L.Bec
L.Carnan
Gerinish
Dremsdale
L.Skipport
Howmore
Hecla
SOUTH UIST
Coradale
Ormacleit
Ben Mhor
Unasary
L.Eynort
Milton
Sheiling
Frobost
STULEY
Daliburgh
Kilpheder
L.Boisdale
CALVEY
Kilbride
0   Miles   5
0   5 km

ATLANTIC OCEAN

Miles
0   5   10   15

10   20
Kilometres

PABBAY   KILLIG
BERNERAY   E
VALLAY
N.UIST
Balranald   L.M
KIRKIBOST   L.Epor
BALESHARE
Nunton
Rossinish
BENBECULA
WIAY
L.Skipport
Hecla
S.UIST   Ben Mhor
L.Eynort
Milton
Kilbride
ERISKAY
BARRA
FLODDAY
Castlebay or
Watersound Bay
VATERSAY
SANDAY

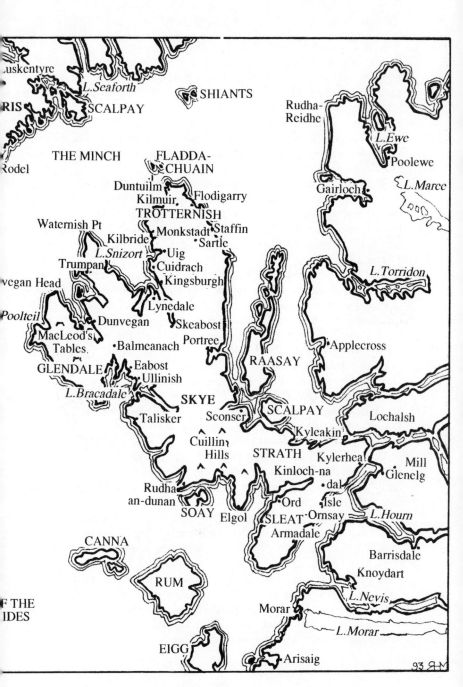

uskentyre

L.Seaforth

SHIANTS

RIS

SCALPAY

Rudha-
Reidhe

L.Ewe

Poolewe

Rodel

THE MINCH

FLADDA-
CHUAIN

L.Maree

Gairloch

Duntuilm

Kilmuir

Flodigarry

Waternish Pt

TROTTERNISH

Monkstadt

Staffin

L.Torridon

Kilbride

Sartle

L.Snizort

Uig

Trumpan

Cuidrach

vegan Head

Kingsburgh

Lynedale

Poolteil

Dunvegan

Skeabost

MacLeod's
Tables

Portree

Applecross

Balmeanach

RAASAY

GLENDALE

Eabost

Ullinish

L.Bracadale

SKYE

SCALPAY

Talisker

Sconser

Lochalsh

Cuillin
Hills

Kyleakin

STRATH

Kylerhea

Mill
Glenelg

Kinloch-na

Rudha
an-dunan

dal

Isle

Ord

L.Hourn

SOAY

Elgol

SLEAT

Ornsay

CANNA

Armadale

Barrisdale

Knoydart

RUM

L.Nevis

F THE
IDES

Morar

L.Morar

EIGG

Arisaig

93 ЯꟼM

11

It was a year before a move was made to restore James, the Old Pretender, to his father's throne. His followers were called Jacobites, from the Latin for James. In 1715 the Earl of Mar raised the standard for King James VIII and III, but was defeated at the battle of Sheriffmuir. Though James crossed to Scotland, the 1715 Rising had failed and he had to return to France.

The Old Pretender was forced to leave France and eventually settled in Rome, where on 31st December 1720 a son, Charles Edward, was born.

With France at war with Britain, in 1744, Prince Charles Edward Stuart travelled to France to join a force to invade England. The scheme failed, and eventually, in July 1745, Prince Charles Edward set sail from France with two boats, a handful of men and a little money to regain the thrones of Scotland, England and Ireland for his father.

The 1745 Rising had begun.

The Prince landed on Eriskay in July and crossed to the mainland. On 19th August the Prince raised his banner at Glenfinnan and was joined by the Clanranald and Keppoch MacDonalds and the Camerons. He marched to Perth and captured Edinburgh.

"Bonnie Prince Charlie" was a sensation. He collected a large army, consisting mostly of Highlanders, and set off south to march on London. On a fateful day in December, hemmed in by two superior Government armies, the Prince's council decided to return to Scotland. The Prince was heart broken. The Jacobite army marched safely to Scotland, and despite defeating the Government troops at Falkirk in January 1746, retired into the Highlands.

The new commander of the Government forces was William, Duke of Cumberland, the younger son of King George II.

On 16th April the two armies met at Culloden Moor. The Prince's army was devastated by accurate artillery fire and within an hour the Jacobite army was routed.

Prince Charles Edward rode off the battle field. Within a week he concluded that his cause was lost and that he must return to France. He took a boat to the Outer Hebrides, where he hoped to find a ship to carry him to France.

The Prince was on the run, with a price of £30,000 on his head. At the end of April he travelled north to Harris and Lewis but was unable to find a ship to take him to France. He was forced to return to South Uist, where for three weeks he lived in comparative comfort and safety at Corradale, on the east side of the island.

CHAPTER 3

The Prince in South Uist

This man tells us, that all the boats of the seven men of war were coming towards the land, full of soldiers, yt they were not landed when he parted from Boisedel's house, & yt he did not doubt but they were informed of the place where the Prince was. – John O'Sullivan.

It was in early June, seven weeks after the battle of Culloden, that the Duke of Cumberland first received news of the Prince's hiding place in the Outer Hebrides. The information was supplied by Sir Alexander MacDonald, who had crossed from Skye to the mainland and travelled to Fort Augustus, where the Duke had his headquarters.

The Duke wrote on 5th June "that the two Militia Companys of the Isle of Skye, who were sent thither, must either have fallen in with him or have driven him off the coast."[1]

In Skye six militia companies were commanded by Capt Alexander MacDonald of Kingsburgh, Sir Alexander's principal factor is Skye. The militia companies were locally recruited to serve in their home areas, collecting up the straggling remains of the Jacobite army as it found its way home after the defeat at Culloden.

Kingsburgh ordered two militia companies, commanded by Capt Hugh MacDonald of Armadale and Capt Alexander MacLeod of Ullinish, to cross to Barra. The companies were to search for arms and rebels and to secure all the boats. The companies were then to proceed to South Uist and Benbecula. No one was to be allowed to travel by boat from the Outer Hebrides to Skye or the mainland.

On 4th June 1746 the two militia companies crossed from Sleat to Barra. The southern isles, as far as Barra Head were searched.

In early June, Flora MacDonald left her mother's house at Armadale and travelled to the Uists to see some friends and to visit her brother Angus at Milton.

When later asked by General Campbell "if she had an Invitation from those that were there" Flora insisted that she had not, nor that she had "any knowledge where the Pretender's Eldest Son was, or ever had any proposal made to Her to take part ... in assisting Him".[2]

Flora would inevitably have given such an answer to the general, but it may not have been a coincidence that she and her stepfather left Sleat at about the same time for the Outer Hebrides. From the start Flora and her stepfather may have acted in concert, though she later showed firm resistance to helping the Prince. Even if Flora told the truth to Gen Campbell, her presence in South Uist was to prove crucial for the Prince.

Flora probably sailed to Rossinish, on the east coast of Benbecula, and then crossed the island to Nunton, the home of her cousin Ranald MacDonald of Clanranald and his wife Margaret, Lady Clanranald. Neither Clanranald nor his lady was at home.

Ranald MacDonald, the 17th chief, known as "Old Clan", had played a cautious role during the Rising. He had not joined the Prince, but had sent his son Ranald, "Young Clan", to lead his men to Glenfinnan and south to Edinburgh and Derby. After the defeat at Culloden, Old Clan retired to Benbecula, where he met the Prince at the end of April. He saw him again in May, but, warned by Sir Alexander MacDonald to submit, Clanranald had slipped across to the mainland.

Lady Clanranald was in Harris with Capt Felix O'Neille. O'Neille was a charming Italian born Irishman in Lally's regiment in the French Army. He had been aide de camp to Prince Henry, Duke of York, in Boulogne in 1745, and had been sent over from France with a special commission for Prince Charles. He had been with the Prince since his escape from Culloden.

While at Corradale in South Uist, the Prince had sent O'Neille to Lewis to take ship for France. O'Neille had been accompanied by Lady Clanranald, who had taken him to her brother in Harris. Unsuccessful in their mission, O'Neille and Lady Clanranald arrived back at Nunton about 7th or 8th June, where they found Flora.

Flora later wrote that "Collonell O'Neill, who was then along with the Prince, met her at Clan Ranald's house, and, introducing a conversation with her about him, ask'd her what she wou'd give for a sight of the Prince. She reply'd that as she had not that happyness before, she did not look for it now, but that a sight of him wou'd make her happy, tho' he was on a hill and she on another. Nothing further pass'd at the time." [3]

Flora travelled south to Milton, in South Uist, to visit her brother Angus, and his wife Penelope.

The Prince had been living in relative comfort and safety at Corradale, on the east side of South Uist, for three weeks. He had been visited by Clanranald's half brother, Alexander MacDonald of Boisdale. Boisdale had told the Prince to return to France in July 1745, but now he was gathering information for him.

Also with the Prince had been Neil MacEachen of the family of Howbeg in South Uist. Neil had been dining with Clanranald at the end of April when news came of the Prince's arrival at Rossinish. Neil ioined the Prince and became his devoted servant and intelligence gatherer. Neil was born in 1719 at Howbeg in South Uist, and was a distant cousin of Flora. He had studied in France, and may have been a French secret agent. He certainly was back in Scotland in 1747 on secret business. He later wrote a journal.

On 6th or 7th of June Neil MacEachen brought news to Corradale that the Skye militia had landed in Barra. Boisdale returned to his house at Kilbride, at the south end of the island, to gather more information. The Prince sailed north to the island of Wiay, off the east coast of Benbecula.

Lady Clanranald, having returned from Harris, went to Wiay with O'Neille, to bring the Prince supplies and to say farewell. The Prince stayed on Wiay for more than a week, but was alarmed by the arrival of William MacLeod of Hamara, to collect kelp. Hamara was a known supporter of the Government, and his son was in the Army.

Worse news was to follow, for Boisdale, on returning to Kilbride, was carried on board *Baltimore*, commanded by Capt Richard Howe. Capt Howe could get no information from Boisdale, but kept him on board to drink punch, and, in company with *Raven*, sailed south.

Fortunately for the Prince, help was at hand from an unexpected quarter. Capt Hugh MacDonald of Armadale, commanding the two Skye militia companies, had landed at Kilbride in South Uist. He was later to write that "We arrived here from Barra ye 14th Saw Mr MacDonald of Boisdale who concurred to purge this country of a few unhappy Lads yt were in rebellion & deserted that Cause before the last battle & are now willing to submit to His Royal Highness's Clemency, & would be in our custody ere now, were it not yt Boisdale was kept aboard on of ye Men of War ye day he designed to meet us wt them & not yet at liberty." [4]

Boisdale had told Armadale that he had been giving the Prince information about the movements of the militia. With Boisdale now taken out of circulation, Armadale let it be known that his militia would march steadily north, combing South Uist from shore to shore. The Prince would have to act accordingly.

When the Prince learned that Boisdale had been taken, and that Armadale was to march north to Benbecula, his party prepared to set out. They left Uiskevaig at 8pm on 15th June, and reached the mouth of Loch Skipport early next day. Pressing on, they stopped at Corradale at 5pm and rested till 10pm. Setting out again they reached Loch

Eynort in darkness where they almost bumped into *Raven* and
Baltimore, on which Boisdale was being held.

On 16th June Capt Howe had returned to Flodday, off North Bay
in Barra, and sailed northwards with *Raven*, in a freshening south
westerly gale, to the entrance of Loch Eynort.

Next morning, inside the loch, the Prince's party found that
Baltimore was still there and had to retire. The Prince's party sheltered
all day and left in the evening. They probably spent a night on the
island of Stuley. On the evening of 19th June they made for Loch Boisdale, and came to the island of Calvey late at night. Neil MacEachen
set off at once for Kilbride, where he found Boisdale's daughter and
wife asleep. They gathered provisions and promised to send information. Neil MacEachen returned to Calvey, where the Prince fell upon
the food he brought.

Armadale wrote to Lord Loudoun, from South Uist, that "Our
Marches cant but be slow here, as we are obliged to search all day &
keep Sentrys all night from Sea to Sea & having but few man for yt
purpose extreamly harasses ye Men."

Armadale had no more than 70 militia men in each company,
perhaps fewer. He marched no more than five or six miles per day, and
may have been at Kilpheder on 17th June, and Milton the next day. His
stepson Angus was there, with his sister Flora.

Armadale had lived at Milton for 17 years, until the previous year,
and knew the area intimately. His wife's first husband had been brother
to James, tacksman of Frobost, and Roderick, tacksman of Kilpheder,
and uncle of Lachlan, tacksman of Dremisdale, Bailie of South Uist.
Milton had also been uncle to Ranald of Torlum, who was Bailie of
Benbecula.

If Armadale arrived at Milton on 18th June, then this was the day
after the Prince's party almost bumped into *Baltimore*, in Loch Eynort,
only five miles to the east. The Prince had slept uncomfortably under a
sail all day, before heading south towards Loch Boisdale.

If Flora and her stepfather were in concert to help the Prince escape,
then it was at their meeting at Milton that they finalised their plans. If,
as seems more likely, Flora knew nothing of the assistance that
Armadale was proposing to the Prince, then it may only have been on
meeting his stepdaughter that the idea for the Prince's escape came into
Armadale's head. Three days later, when Armadale received news of
Capt Scott's landing in South Uist, the plan suggested itself to him
immediately.

Armadale's militia probably searched Loch Eynort on 19th June,
and may have reached Howmore in the evening, and Gerinish the

following day. On 20th June Armadale wrote that "We go this night for Benbecula to search yr till Boisdale returns, as to intelligence in this Country it must be bad as ye Inhabitants are Popish & ye Minister absent."

Armadale was thankful that the Presbyterian minister, the officious John MacAulay was absent. He had also been dining with Clanranald when the Prince first landed in Benbecula at the end of April. He had sent information about the Prince to his father, Rev Aulay MacAulay, in Harris and also to Stornoway, and it was this which had prevented the Prince from chartering a boat in Lewis.

On 21st June Armadale and his militia reached Benbecula, and he set a string of guards across the South Ford to South Uist.

General Campbell sails to St Kilda

On 10th June, the Duke of Cumberland, at Fort Augustus, ordered six Independent Companies to march from the head waters of the Spey to the Isle of Skye, under command of Capt John MacLeod of Talisker. They were to replace the militia which was to be disbanded. Three of the Independent Companies were to cross to the Outer Hebrides to seek for the Prince.

On the same day Aeneas MacDonald, the Prince's Banker, was brought to Tobermory in Mull, where he found Major General John Campbell, commanding the King's forces in the west. Aeneas Mac-Donald told the general that the Prince had crossed from Arisaig to Uist, and failing to find a boat in Stornoway, "he was forced in a hurry to return back to Clanranalds House in Uist where probably he still is or in the Isles Adjacent." [5]

Captain John Fergussone, of *Furnace*, a harsh Aberdonian, was also at Tobermory, having just captured Lord Lovat in Morar. He noted that "General Campbell Call'd all the Sea Officers together to communicate to them some Intelligence he had received of some persons of Note being on the Isle of St Kilda from the result of which the General is going for that Isle with the Terror & Furnace Sloops & 300 Land Forces." [6] The information, or perhaps misinformation, proved to be vital for the Prince, for it delayed the general's arrival in the Uists, by at least a week.

On 13th June General Campbell embarked on *Furnace*, with some regulars of Guise's, Johnstone's, and his own Scots Fusileers. *Furnace* already had one Argyll militia company, and three more were brought on board. At Kinlochmoidart a fifth militia company was added.

Meanwhile Capt Caroline Scott, a grasping Lowlander with a strong contempt for the Highlanders, had arrived at Tobermory and had just missed the general. Capt Robert Jefferys of *Scarborough* wrote that "came in the same time Captain Scott, with His Royal Highnesses Commands, Vastly wanting to joyn General Campbell Judg'd it then my Duty to forward Him in the best going Vessel with me, so Order'd Tryal in quest of the General With much impatience long to be in my Station again, for I know this is the critical time to Serve my Country. Therefore shall be as Active as possible." [7]

On 14th June General Campbell visited the island of Eigg, where Capt Scott joined him. Capt George Anderson, the general's aide de camp, noted tartly that "He had a Commission from H R H the Duke to take Captain Millers Command, which was part of those we had, and Scour South Uist." [8]

Capt Scott in *Tryal*, with Capt Miller's command, and men from Guise's and Johnstone's, sailed west to "Flotta", the island of Flodday, off North Bay in Barra. There he found Capt Howe, who had just taken Boisdale on board *Baltimore*. Next day, 16th June, the soldiers searched all the islands between Barra and South Uist, and at 2pm *Tryal* sailed for Barra, while *Baltimore* and *Raven* sailed north to Loch Eynort, where they were almost to bump into the Prince.

General Campbell sailed north about the Isle of Lewis, where he met Commodore Thomas Smith. The commodore, in command of HM's ships in Scottish waters, had sailed from Orkney on 15th June with *Eltham*, *Looe* and the *Union* cutter. He accompanied general Campbell to St Kilda, and then sailed for Barra Head. He ordered the sloops, *Baltimore* and *Raven*, to cruise in the waters to the south of South Uist, to prevent the Prince from crossing to the mainland.

Capt Anderson wrote that "The 19th we came near St Kilda & Landed part of our troops, & some Sailors, but after searching the Island found nothing but the miserable Inhabitants whose Aspect, dress and Sentiments, sufficiently denote their remote Situation & the little Commerce they have with the Continent.

"The 21st we arriv'd at Pabay a small island appertaining to the Harris, the property of the Laird of McLeod which we visited, but found nothing, from Pabay we went to Bernera another small Island contiguous to the former, on this the General disembark'd about 100 Men ... having determin'd to go himself by Land thro' the two Uists, as there was room to Suspect that the Young adventurer was yet concealed on the long Island." [8]

With General Campbell to the north at Berneray; Armadale and the Militia in Benbecula, guarding the fords, and Capt Scott and his regulars to the south in Barra; and with Commodore Smith and his ships cruising in the Minch, the net was closing in upon Prince Charles Edward Stuart.

The Prince at Loch Boisdale

Late on the night of 19th June Neil MacEachen returned to the Prince on Calvey. Next morning there was a discussion about what action to take. A plan to cross to the mainland in their flimsy boat was ruled out, and it was agreed that the party should make for the islands south of Barra.

Lady Boisdale sent information that Capt Scott had landed in Barra, and would join the Skye militia in South Uist, where he intended to be at ten next morning. Neil MacEachen wrote that "This news put them in a greater consternation than ever, which obliged them to cross over to the other side of Loch Boystile that night for more security."

Fortunately for the Prince, Capt Scott had been storm bound in Barra. Capt Howe of *Baltimore* noted on 21st June that at "7 AM Anchor'd. Found Lying here ye Tryal Sent ye Boats a Shore Mand & Armd to search ye House of ye Laird of Buisdale on Information of His Having arms & Money Conceald there." [10]

On the morning of 21st June, the Prince, on the shores of Loch Boisdale in South Uist, "sent off Rory MacDonald to learn whither Scott was arrived, and to bring back word what was passing among them. Rory returned at eight o'clock, and told the prince that the lady, her daughter, and all the servants, were tied neck and heel in one house, in order to extort a confession from them of the prince's being in the country."

Col John O'Sullivan, one of the Prince's companions, added that "This man tells us, that all the boats of the seven men of War were coming towards the land, full of soldiers, yt they were not landed when he parted from Boisedel's house, & yt he did not doubt but they were informed of the place where the Prince was.

"The first thing they saw were two men of War comeing into the Loch." [11]

Neil MacEachen wrote that "The news of the ladies ill treatment struck such terror into the minds of the timorous crew, that they immediately sunk the boat, and abandoned the prince and the few gentlemen who accompanied him. In this desperate condition there was no remedy to be thought upon, but to dismiss the few gentlemen that accompanied till then, and retire to the mountains; whereupon having left every body to shift for himself, (of whose number was O'Sullivan, who was left under a rock with the best part of the prince's baggage) the prince with Neil and MacO'Neil, made for the top of the nearest hill, that from thence they might have a better view of their enemies motion, and take further resolution how they were to dispose of themselves next.

"I forgot to tell that when Captain Scott landed in South Wist, Hugh MacDonald, who lay in Benbecula then with his party, sent one of the country gentlemen in whom he could repose a great deal of trust, to tell the prince privately that, as it seemed now impossible for him to conceal himself any longer in the country, if he would venter to be advised by him, though an enemy in appearance yet a sure friend in his heart, he would fall upon a scheme to convey him to the Isle of Skay, where he was sure to be protected by Lady Margaret MacDonald. The scheme was this; to send his stepdaughter, Miss Florence MacDonald, to Sleet, to live with her mother 'till the enemy was out of Wist. The prince at the same time was ordered to dress in women's close, that he might pass for her servant maid, and Neil was appointed to take care of both. The scheme pleased the prince mightily, and he seemed very impatient to see it put in execution." [9]

While Hugh MacDonald of Armadale, captain of the Militia was writing to Lord Loudoun about bad intelligence, he had sent a trusted local gentleman to the Prince with a plan for the Prince's escape.

The Prince, O'Neille and MacEachen spent the day on a hilltop. In the evening they ate a meal, and then set off for the north.

The Prince's own narrative, taken down on his return journey to France, stated that in the "evening we made 24 miles without stopeing, to the northward so as to attempt passing the Enemy next night about 7th in our way we met with a trusty girl whome we sent of to have intelligence of the motions of the enemy, upon which we got notice that the Enemy was imediately to march to the southward to join the other party." [12]

CHAPTER 4

Flora Meets the Prince

*"You need not fear your character," said he, "for by
this you will gain yourself an immortal character. But
if you will still entertain fears about your character,
I shall (by an oath) marry you directly, if you please."*
— Capt Felix O'Neille.

Neil MacEachen wrote that he "was informed some days before, that
Miss Flora lived with her brother in a glen near Locheynort, where they
had all their cattle a grazing at that time, and which happened to be
very near the rod they were to pass that night.

"When the prince was informed of it, he would needs go to see her,
and tell her of the message he had from her stepfather. When they were
near the little house where she was asleep, for her brother was not at
home, Neil left the prince and O'Neil at a little distance off, 'till he
went in and wakened her; she got scarcely on the half of her close, when
the prince, with his luggage upon his back, was at the door, and saluted
her very kindly; after which she brought to him a part of the best cheer
she had among the rest was a large bowl full of creme, of which he took
two or three hearty go downs, and his fellow travellers swallowed the
rest." [1]

It was at about midnight on 21st June that Neil MacEachen and the
Prince, with Capt Felix O'Neille, arrived at the shieling at Unasary. It
was barely dark and there was a bright full moon.

Flora was out tending her brother's cattle on the pasture land above
Milton. The shieling, one of several temporary huts used each summer,
had been built near a stream. It was a simple stone walled building with
a thatched roof, containing a hearth and bed. The shielings were
clustered below the crest of Bealach Sheaval, on the Milton side. Half a
mile north, down a sharp descent, was Unasary, on the shores of Loch
Eynort, where the loch cut deep into South Uist from the east.

It was not unusual for all the womenfolk to be at the summer
shielings. Flora had come to the Uists to visit her brother, but they had
gone up to the shielings together, according to MacEachen. Milton
had been called away to Milton, but Flora had other company, women
and girls from the township.

If however, Flora and her stepfather were already in concert, then it was no chance that she was in a remote glen, close to the east coast.

Neil MacEachen left a long narrative of his time with the Prince, but, although he introduced the Prince and O'Neille to Flora, he was not present during much of the critical discussions.

Capt Felix O'Neille had already met Flora at Nunton earlier in June. When O'Neille was captured he made three statements. While in prison he wrote an account of his time with the Prince, and other stories told by him at Edinburgh Castle were recorded by Robert Forbes. The five accounts showed how this charming, likeable man could change and improve his tale.

In his third statement, made to Lord Albemarle at Fort Augustus, O'Neille said that "Mr ONeill & the Pretender's Son going towards Corridale, where they was inform'd that Genl Campbell was at Bernera, and there were several Independent Companies coming into the Country in search of him, which determined them to go for Benbicula, on their way thither they met Miss Flora McDonald, to whom it was proposed to go along with the Pretender's Son to the Isle of Skye, which she at first refused, but on offering to Dress himself in Women's habit & to pass for her Servant she consented, desiring them to remain on the north side of Cerridale, & she would send him word where to meet her." [2]

When O'Neille met Flora, he knew neither that General Campbell had landed in Berneray, nor that three Independent Companies were to be sent to the Uists.

O'Neille wrote that "at midnight we came to a hut, where by good fortune we met with Miss Flora MacDonald, whom I formerly knew. I quitted the Prince at some distance from the hut. . . I told her I brought a friend to see her, and she, with some emotion, asked if it was the Prince. I answered in the affirmative and instantly brought him in." [2]

O'Neille made no mention of Capt Hugh MacDonald of Armadale, to protect him. O'Neille also made no mention, anywhere, of MacEachen. O'Neille may have been protecting him too, for MacEachenn was then still in hiding, but he was also jealous of the latter's familiarity with Flora. Felix, indeed, was a little in love with her.

Flora left three accounts of her meeting with the Prince. The first was a declaration made to General Campbell, a few days after the events. The second was made a year later to Dr Burton, and the third one many years later, in the last year of her life.

Flora told Gen Campbell that "she stay'd at a Sheilling of Her Brothers opposite to Ormaclait on the Hills, and that about the 21st of June last O'Neil or (as they called him) Nelson, came to where She Stay'd and proposed to Her that as She was going from South Uist, that the young Pretender should go with Her as Her Servant, this being agreed to by Miss McDonald, Nelson then went out and fetch'd the Young Adventurer, who was on the Hills not far off. He came & settled the manner of their going off." [3]

Flora protected her stepfather and MacEachen, stating that the plan had been conceived by O'Neille, and that she had made no demur in assisting the Prince.

More than a year later, Flora told Dr Burton that she had been brought to where the Prince was, rather than the Prince to her shieling; "she had not been long there till Captain O'Neill (by some lucky accident or other) had become acquainted with her. When the Prince was surrounded with difficulties on all hands, and knew not what to do for his future safety, Captain O'Neil brought Miss MacDonald to the place where the Prince was, and there they concerted the plan." [3]

Flora did not mention her stepfather and omitted MacEachen from the account, for she was still protecting him. In the autumn of 1747 Neil had returned to Scotland on a secret mission.

In a much later account, made in the last year of her life, Flora wrote that "the Collonel (O'Neill), some time after came to her to a shealing of her brother's where she then stay'd, and being about midnight, sent in a cousine of her own, who had been along with him and the Prince, to awake her, which he did, and told her that they were both without and wanted instantly to speak with her. She was surpriz'd and wanted to know what they had to say to her, but went out as fast as she cou'd throw on some of her cloaths, and met the Collonell at the door." [3]

Felix O'Neille wrote that, on introducing the Prince to Flora "we then consulted on the imminent danger the Prince was in, and could think of no more proper and safe expedient than to propose to Miss Flora to convey him to the Isle of Sky, where her mother lived. This seemed the more feasible, as the young lady's father being captain of an Independent Company would accord her a pass for herself and servant to go visit her mother. The Prince assented, and immediately propos'd it to the young lady, to which she answered with the greatest respect and loyalty; but declined it, saying, Sir Alexander MacDonald was too much her friend to be instrument of his ruine. I endeavoured to obviate this by assuring her Sir Alexander was not in the country, and that she could with the greatest facility convey the Prince to her mother's, as she lived close by the waterside." [2]

Felix O'Neille was never one to hide the importance of his own part in the Prince's escape. He suggested that it was he himself who had conceived the plan, but then cunningly allowed the Prince to propose it, as though the Prince had thought of it.

Flora may well have wished to protect Sir Alexander MacDonald, but she was not the close friend that O'Neille claimed him to be. Nor did O'Neille know that Sir Alexander was not in Skye. O'Neille did not know his geography, either, for though Flora's mother lived by the waterside, it was a very long way from Benbecula, on the inner coast of Sleat.

While in prison at Edinburgh Castle, Felix O'Neille had time to improve his story, and he proved to be a master craftsman, providing some of the most memorable lines written about Flora. With the help of hindsight, he produced the first of his memorable 'Arguments,' writing that "I then remonstrated to her the honour and immortality that would redound to her by such a glorious action, and she at length acquiesc'd, after the Prince had told her the sense he would always retain of so conspicuous a service." [2]

Flora had no thoughts of immortality when she finally acquiesced, and the Prince, who had a delightful turn of phrase, used less haughty terms to kindle the flame of adventure that flickered in the young woman's eyes.

While imprisoned at the Castle in Edinburgh, O'Neille said a good deal more than he wrote. Others told Robert Forbes that O'Neille had stated that he "had very great difficulty to prevail upon Miss Mac-Donald to undertake being guardian to the Prince. She was not only frighten'd at the hazards and dangers attending such a bold enterprize, but likewise insisted upon the risque she would run of losing her character in a malicious and ill natured world." [2]

O'Neille's reported account exaggerated his powers of argument, and Flora's fears of the hazards and dangers of the project. Flora knew little of the malicious and ill natured world, but perhaps Felix O'Neille could not resist suggesting that she did, so that he could conclude by stating that "the Captain was at some pains to represent to her the glory and honour she would acquire by such a worthy and heroic action, and he hoped God would make her successful in it. 'You need not fear your character,' said he, 'for by this you will gain yourself an immortal character. But if you will still entertain fears about your character, I shall (by an oath) marry you directly, if you please.'" [2]

Whether true or imagined, Felix O'Neille's statement proved to be prophetic, for Flora, by saving the Prince, did gain herself an immortal character.

O'Neille's offer of a handfast marriage was not taken up by Flora.

Many years later, Flora left a full account of her meeting with the Prince. She wrote that "Leaving the Prince behind the hut, he (O'Neill) immediately propos'd to her (as he knew she had a desire to come to

Sleat in Sky, where her mother then lived, and did not like to stay longer in Uist, as all there were then in confusion) to take the Prince along with her as her servant, dress'd in women's cloaths. She told him as there were so many dangers to encounter, it wou'd grieve her more that he shou'd be taken along with her than in any other way and begg'd he wou'd not insist on her undertaking that piece of service. He answered that there was no other method to extricate him out of his present danger, and that, tho' she deny'd him, he was sure she wou'd not deny himself as soon as she saw him. 'Don't think, Sir,' said she, 'that I am quite so faint hearted as that comes to.'" [3]

Felix O'Neille knew more of the world than Flora, for she proved to be as faint hearted as Felix had predicted.

"He then whistled. The Prince appeared. He indroduc'd him to Miss Macdonald, and spoke to him in Italians, telling him her scruples, and that she had deny'd him her undertaking the proposed scheme. The Prince himself then spoke to her, being previously perfectly well known to the situation of the country, and told her she wou'd be quite safe in undertaking what he wanted, as her stepfather, Hugh Macdonald of Armadale, was commanding officer there, a gentleman he knew himself, and waited on him personally when he landed first on the mainland, and was sure he wished him well, and that he wou'd give her a pass in to Sky. She still insisted on the danger, but her former resolution fail'd her, and undertook the voyage provided she got her stepfather's pass." [3]

Though she had met her stepfather only a few days previously, Flora knew nothing of the plan to help the Prince's escape, nor that it was Armadale's plan. She was astonished by the proposal. For all Felix O'Neille's arguments, and the Prince's charm, it was the fact that her stepfather, Capt Hugh MacDonald of Armadale, had agreed to give her a pass, which made up Flora's mind.

If Flora had been in concert with her stepfather all along, then she feigned her surprise very convincingly.

"After taking a little refreshment," Flora wrote later, "and fixing an appointment to meet at Roshinish in Benbecula, the Prince and the Collonel went to the hills, and Miss Macdonald went to her stepfather to procure his pass, he being in the way to Benbecula." [3]

Once Flora had agreed to help the Prince, she quickly took charge. The Prince, O'Neille and Neil MacEachen were given something to eat, and were then sent on their way into the hills north of Loch Eynort. In the early hours of Sunday, 22nd June 1746, Flora left her shieling, promising to send a message to the Prince. Flora returned to Milton, where she had time to pack her trunk, which was to cross with her to

Skye. Flora saw her brother Angus, and sister-in-law Penelope, and told them what she had engaged to do. Flora then "set out for Clanranald's house" at Nunton in Benbecula, some 20 miles away, "and at one of the fords was taken prisoner by a party of militia, she not having a passport. She demanded to whom they belonged? And finding by the answer that her stepfather was then commander, she refused to give any answer till she should see their captain. So she and her servant, Neil MacKechan, were prisoners all that night." [3]

Flora's account was not quite accurate. Neil MacEachen wrote "she was ordered immediately away to Benbicula to consult with her stepfather and Lady Clanranald, to get everything in readiness as soon as possible, and to send them word back again next day how all was going on with them." [1]

Neil MacEachen took the Prince and O'Neille and plunged over the pass down to Unasary and skirted the head of Loch Eynort, and then climbed up round the flanks of Beinn Mhor to a rock in Glen Dorchy. Neil knew the area from his childhood.

The Prince was impatient for an answer, and sent off Neil MacEachen to Benbecula. Neil was immediately stopped at the South Ford, and held all night. Next morning, at low tide, he was taken to "the captain of the guard on the other side, who happened to be Hugh MacDonald; when Neil went in he found Miss MacDonald, who was stopped in the same manner by another party of the MacLeods, who had guard two nights before, with some other gentlemen at breakfast with Mr MacDonald. Neil call'd miss aside, and ask't if every thing was ready, she told him as it was put out of her power to go the length of Lady Clanranald, that nothing was as yet done, but that she was going off within half an hour to consult with the lady, and designed to go to Roshiness, both of them, that same afternoon, and carry along whatever clothes or provisions was requisite for the voyage, and she begg'd of Neil to make all the haste possible to return to the prince, and, without losing one moment of time, to make the best of his way to Rosshiness, where he would be sure to find them without fail." [1]

Flora recorded that "Her stepfather, coming next day, being Sunday, she told him what she was about, upon which he granted a passport for herself, a manservant (Neil MacKechan), and another woman Bettie Burk, a good spinster, and whom he recommended as such in a letter to his wife at Armadale in Skye, as she had much lint to spin." [3]

Capt Scott came to South Uist on Saturday 21st June and the Prince walked to Unasary that night. Flora left the shieling early on Sunday 22nd June and reached the fords, where she was captured. Her stepfather arrived next day, Monday 23rd June.

Donald Roy MacDonald recalled that the letter stated that "I have sent your daughter from this country lest she should be anyway frightened with the troops lying here. She has got one Bettie Burk, an Irish girl, who as she tells me is a good spinster. If her spinning pleases you, you may keep her till she spin all your lint; or if you have any wool to spin you may employ her. I am, Your dutyful husband, Hugh Macdonald."[4] Flora added "I have sent Neil MacKechan along with my daughter and Bettie Bourke to take care of them."[5]

Flora later wrote that "She told him (Hugh MacDonald) what she had undertaken, what the Prince said of himself, and that he knew him, which Mr Macdonald acknowledged, and immediately gave her the pass, with a letter to Mrs Macdonald, his wife, telling her that her daughter had accidently met with with [sic] & fee'd an Irish girl an excellent spinstress, Burke by name, and wou'd be very useful to her. This letter was design'd to be shown to any that might happen to meet them by sea or land to prevent any closer search.

"If her stepfather had not granted Miss a passport, she could not have undertook her journey and voyage. Armadale set his stepdaughter at liberty, who immediately made the best of her way to Clanranald's house and acquainted the Lady Clanranald with the scheme, who supplied the Prince with apparel sufficient for his disguise, viz. a flower'd linen gown, a white apron, etc., and sent some provisions along with him."[3]

Hugh MacDonald of Armadale's role was central in the escape of the Prince. When Armadale had landed at Kilbride in South Uist on 14th June he had consulted with Boisdale about the Prince's movements. When Boisdale was taken next day, Armadale announced that he would march his companies to Benbecula. It was probably when Armadale met Flora at Milton that the idea for the Prince's escape suggested itself to him. As Armadale marched north so the Prince moved from Benbecula, down the east side of the islands to Loch Boisdale.

With the arrival of Capt Scott in South Uist on 21st June, Armadale proposed to the Prince that he should move back to Benbecula, since the militia companies were due to march south to join Capt Scott. Armadale's role in suggesting the escape plan to O'Neille and the Prince, and his willingness to give his stepdaughter a pass, was crucial. Without his help the plan would not have been undertaken. Flora was aware, however, of her stepfather's vulnerability, should the plan fail. Armadale was, after all, in command of the Skye militia in the Uists, and had been sent there to flush out rebels and the Prince.

On parting with Flora and Neil MacEachen, Armadale made it clear that he was moving his militia men south towards Loch Boisdale. The militia would make a rapid march and a fruitless search, thus removing themselves from the area where Armadale knew the Prince to be. He had, however, delayed long enough, in his march towards Capt Scott, to allow the Prince to return to Benbecula.

Armadale parted with Flora and Neil on the morning of Monday 23rd June. Armadale did not know that General Campbell had landed on Pabbay on 21st June and crossed to Berneray the next morning. He marched instead resolutely southwards towards Loch Boisdale, to meet up with Capt Scott, and away from the Prince, and the general.

Neil MacEachen wrote that, on parting with Flora, he "posted off immediately, and arrived at the prince at the hour he had appointed, and found him under the same rock where he had left him; he no sooner saw Neil come in sight than he ran to meet him, and took him by the hand asking what news he had from Miss Flora; Neil told him what orders he had from the lady (as he called Miss Flora), after which they set out for Roshiness." [1]

O'Neille told the story differently. In his first statement he said that, having not heard from Flora for two days, the Prince "determin'd to send O'Neil to general Campbell to Let him know he would Surrender himself Prisoner but while in this thought a Message Came from the younge Lady Desiring us to Come to the Point of Rushnish where she would wait us." [2]

O'Neille did not know that General Campbell had landed at Berneray. The messenger was MacEachen.

In his written journal, however, O'Neille made no mention of the Prince's despair and the plan to give himself up to General Campbell. Neil MacEachen was still referred to as a messenger. He wrote that "Next day at four in the afternoon we received a message from our protrectress, telling us ALL WAS WELL. We determined joining her immediately, but the messenger informed us we could not pass either of the fords that separated the island we were in from Benbecula, as they were both guarded." [2]

The Prince's narrative stated that "we got notice that the Enemy was imediately to march to the south ward to join the other party, we hapen'd luckily to get a small boat which carry'd us to Benbecula att the same time they crossed the sands to go south which agreed with the intelligence we had.

"He came to a hutt there where he refreshed himself, & made to northward that evening where he had given an appointment, but those he expected unluckily failing to be there, he was obliged to wait there the whole night & next day during all wch time it poured most heavy rain, & had neither meat or drink of any kind. he staid there 3 days." [6]

Neil MacEachen and Felix O'Neille left longer accounts of the journey to Rossinish, and the Prince's uncomfortable stay there.

Flora hurried to Nunton, the substantial residence of the chief of the Clanranald MacDonalds in the Uists. The house had two storeys, a pitched roof, and large windows.

Clanranald had slunk away to the mainland at the end of May, where he was later to refuse to help the Prince. But his wife was made of sterner stuff. She was Margaret, elder daughter of William MacLeod of Luskentyre. Born about 1700 on the island of Berneray, her grandfather was the redoubtable Norman MacLeod of Berneray, who had fought for King Charles II at the Battle of Worcester in 1651, and had been knighted by him at the Restoration.

Lady Clanranald took charge of the arrangements to save the Prince, and never once did she shirk her responsibility. Later she never denied her part in the affair.

Flora, with clothes for the Prince, was due to meet him at Rossinish on the afternoon on Tuesday 24th June. But Flora's short stay at Nunton became protracted. Flora, Lady Clan, and the women in the household made the clothes for the Prince, but this cannot have taken them three days to complete.

There now occurred a delay, which could have proved fatal. Flora stated that she "stay'd three Days at Lady Clan Ranald, in which time O'Neil came frequently from the young Pretender to inform Her where he was, what steps had been taken for their leaving the Island & at the same time to hasten her to get her affairs in readiness for going off." [5]

Flora later indicated that during her "stay at Clanranald's house, which was till Friday, June 27th, O'Neil went several times betwixt the prince and Miss, in which interval another scheme was proposed, that the Prince should go under the care of a gentleman to the north wards, but that failing them, they behoved to have recourse to that agreed before:"

Neil MacEachen wrote that the Prince, at Rossinish, "resolved to return Neil to Nuntown to inform Miss MacDonald that he was arrived, and to hasten her to come without any longer delay.

"Neil, who foresaw clearly the danger he would be exposed to, if he was left with a man who knew but one step of the country, or where to retire to in case of necessity, absolutely denied to part with the prince upon any account, and so Mr O'Neill was obliged to go upon that expedition; who was mighty well pleased to be entrusted with that embassy, not so much to further the prince's affairs, as to be in company with Miss Flora, for whom he professed a great deal of kindness at that time.

"The guide, who went with O'Neil the night before to Clanranald's house, returned towards evening, who brought along with him a roasted fowl, and a couple of bottles of wine, and a letter from O'Neil to the prince, the contents of which I could not find out, though it's very probable he excused himself for not returning, under pretence to hasten all matters for leaving the country." [1]

Felix O'Neille wrote that from Rossinish "The Prince ordered me to go to the lady and know the reason she did not keep her appointment. She told me she had engaged a cousin of hers in North Uist to receive him in his house, where she was sure he would be more safe than in the Isle of Sky.

"But the gentleman absolutely refused receiving us, alleging for a motive that he was vassal to Sir Alexander MacDonald." [2]

Hugh MacDonald of Baleshare was the man who refused to take in the Prince. At the time, he was setting up an alternative escape route for the Prince, with the help of Lady Margaret MacDonald in Skye.

Baleshare, on learning that the Prince was in Benbecula, despatched a boat to Skye, with a letter for his brother Capt Donald Roy Mac-Donald, with the information that "the Prince intended soon to quit the Long Isle (such a strict search being there), and to land upon a small grass island called Fladdachuan, belonging to Sir Alexander Mac-Donald, and having only one tenant upon it, and lying to the north of Troternish, about two leagues distant, that therefore he should be careful to keep a sharp look out, ... and to meet the Prince upon Fladdachuan and to provide him with necessaries." [7]

Capt Donald Roy MacDonald received this letter on 24th June, or 25th at the latest. In his own account, Baleshare neither mentioned this scheme for sending the Prince to Fladdachuan, nor that he had refused to take in the Prince. Baleshare was not even aware that General Campbell was on Berneray, only a few miles to the north. He wrote that "The prince sends for me to consult how to behave.

"My advice was this, that as he lay in the view of the chanell, if the chanell was clear of ships he should go of in the afternoon to give him a long night, to keep closs by the land of Sky, that he might have the opportunity of running ashore in case of the wors, and desir'd him shou'd go to Kulin hills in Sky, where he cou'd get to the Laird of McKinnon, who woud see him safely landed on the mainland.

"But advis'd him if he shoud not get to McKinon, that he shoud without loss of time go in to Sir James McDonald's country of Slet, and apply to Donald McDonald of Castletoun, to Hugh McDonald of

Armidell, to Alexander McDonald of Kingsborrow, to Archibald McDonald of Tarsquivaig, and Rory McDonald of Camiscross, all cadents of Sir James McDonald's family."[8]

This was strange advice for Armadale was in the Uists. Kingsburgh, Tarskavaig and Camuscross were all militia captains in Skye. Baleshare's visit to the Prince was not mentioned by Neil MacEachen.

On the failure of the North Uist scheme, Lady Clanranald reverted to Armadale's plan that the Prince should cross to Skye, as Flora's servant. It was agreed that Margaret, wife of Capt John MacDonald of Kirkibost, in North Uist, should cross to Skye the day before the Prince, to warn Lady Margaret MacDonald of his arrival.

O'Neille wrote that "The Prince sent me to acquaint Miss Flora of our disappointment, and to intreat her to keep her promise as there was no time to be lost. She faithfully promised next day. I remained with her that night, the Prince remaining at Rushness attended by a little herd boy."[2]

Neil MacEachen, described by O'Neille as a guide and messenger, and here as 'a little herd boy', was scathing about the Irishman.

"Next morning the prince wrote a letter to O'Neil by the same post that brought the former, desiring him to come to him that night; but O'Neil contented himself to return him an answer by the same bearer, telling him he could not come by reason that he waited Miss McDonald and Lady Clanranald, who was to come next day without fail.

"The prince seemed very uneasie that night that neither Mr O'Neil nor the ladys did not come according to promise.

"The next day Rory McDonald, and one John McDonald, who were to be two of the crew, arrived in the morning, and told that both boat and crew were ready whenever he pleased . . . Whereupon Neil carried the prince to the same hill where they had sculked the day before, and leaving him in the hands of the two McDonalds before mentioned, posted off himself to hurry the ladys from Nuntown."[1]

The Prince's Departure from Benbecula

*The company being gone, the prince, stript of his
cloaths, was dressed by Miss Flora in his new attire,
but could not keep his hands from adjusting his head
dress, which he cursed a thousand times.*
— Neil MacEachen

The Prince had expected Flora to meet him at Rossinish, on Tuesday
24th June. Three days later, he was still waiting for her arrival. With
Felix O'Neille away at Nunton, the Prince was understandably
anxious about his own safety.

In the comfort of Nunton House, and with the purposeful efficiency
of Lady Clanranald, Flora did not need to control events. Others were
helping to set up the exciting adventure. The arrival of Capt O'Neille
should have concentrated the minds of the ladies at Nunton, but
instead Felix O'Neille appeared to be more interested in spending his
time flirting with Flora. Flora's brother, Angus of Milton, and his wife
also arrived at Nunton.

The weather had been severe all week, with fresh south easterly and
south westerly gales each day, with occasional hail, and strong winds.
In the warmth of Nunton, it was easy to put off going out into the cold,
wet and boggy lands of Rossinish.

But at last Lady Clanranald took action. The arrangements for the
escape were in place and the dress was ready. On Friday 27th June,
Flora set off to join the Prince. It was not before time.

Flora stated that she "went from Lady Clanranald's accompanied by
Her and Her Eldest Daughter Fryday July 27th to a place call'd Whea
but not finding the young Pretender there, they went to Roychenish (a
shielling) where he was. John McLane who had acted as Cook to the
Young Pretender also went with Lady Clan Ronald." [1]

Lady Clanranald's eldest daughter, Penelope, was married to Angus
of Milton. Flora later added that her brother Angus of Milton
accompanied her as well. Milton was later made prisoner and, in a
declaration, gave an unlikely story that "Lady Clan Ranald said she
was a going to the Isle of Whea, to see a grazing Park she had there, and
desir'd the Declarant to accompany Her thither, but when they were in
Whea, she proceeded on to Roschinish." [2]

32

John Maclean, Clanranald's cook, was later made prisoner, and confessed to having cooked for the Prince at Corradale. He declared that "lady Clan Ranald order'd the Declarant to take the Victuals he had dressed & go with her, she being accompanied by Her Eldest Daughter, McDonald of Milton and Miss Flora McDonald, that they went to a place call'd Rosschnisch where they met the Young Pretender, O'Neil, and Neil McCachen." [3]

Neil MacEachen wrote that, leaving the Prince with two Mac-Donalds, who were to act as boatmen, he posted off to hurry the ladies from Nunton, and sent O'Neille to the place where he had left the Prince. He then took the ladies by another road, "where they were to have the conveniency of a boat to Roshiness." [4]

Flora, with her companions, might have walked or ridden to Creagorry, at the South Ford, and then taken a boat to Wiay. Travel by sea was much easier than by land over rocky ground, so interspersed with lochs. From Wiay Flora's party crossed by boat to Rossinish.

Milton declared that, having arrived at Rossinish, "they went into a Shieling (the property of Lady Clan Ranold but inhabited by another person at this time one Duncan Campbell) where the Declarant saw the Young Pretender O'Neill & Duncan Campbell, and Roderick McDonald they stay'd there part of the night, and then the Declarant returned with lady Clan Ranald, & went to His own House in S Uist." [2]

Neil MacEachen added that "The prince, who arrived first, welcome them ashore, and handed the Lady Clan to the house, while O'Neil took care of Miss Flora. There they passed some hours very hearty and merry till supper was served." [4]

Flora told Dr Burton that the Prince was "in a very little house or hut, assisting in the roasting of his dinner, which consisted of the heart, liver, kidneys, etc., of a bullock or sheep, upon a wooden spit. O'Neil introduced his young preserver and the company, and she sat on the Prince's right hand and Lady Clanranald on his left. Here they all dined very heartily." [5] It was so dark and smoky in the cottage, that Flora could not distinguish bullock from sheep.

Rossinish formed part of the tack of Nunton, and was a natural grazing park, with good grasslands and a large sand dune to the north east. The peninsula was joined to the rest of Benbecula by a narrow neck of land, less than half a mile wide. It was here that Duncan Campbell had his house. An old cottage, and a more modern shepherd's cottage, now abandoned, still survive, with a cleared slipway on the shore to the south.

Neil MacEachen wrote that "supper was served, which was scarce began, when one of Clanranald's herds came with the news that General Campbell was landing his men within three miles of them. The supper thus ended, which was hardly begun all run to their boat in the greatest confusion, everyone carrying with him whatever part of the baggage came first to his hand, without either regard to sex or quality, they crossed Lochisguiway, and, about five in the morning, landed on the other side, where they ended the supper." [4]

Flora told Dr Burton that "Next morning, June 28th, they heard of General Campbell's arrival at Benbecula, and soon after a man came in a great hurry to Lady Clanranald and acquainted her that Captain Ferguson with an advanced party of Campbell's men was at her house, and that Ferguson had lain in her bed the night before."

This obliged Lady Clanranald "to go home immediately, which accordingly she did, after taking leave of the Prince. She was strictly examined by Ferguson where she had been? She replied she had been visiting a child which had been sick, but was now better again. Both the General and Ferguson asked many other questions, such as where the child lived, how far it was from thence? etc., but they could make nothing out of the lady fit for their purpose." [5]

Neil MacEachen, Flora and O'Neille all stated that General Campbell's arrival had been a surprise. It indicated that Lady Clanranald's intelligence had been so poor that she had not even known that the general had landed at Berneray, a week before, let alone that he had crossed to North Uist that day. General Campbell, who suffered from a gouty foot, had been delayed from leaving Berneray by the same bad weather.

The company crossed Loch Uiskevaig by boat, and landed on the southern shore of the loch. The small island of Oronsay, joined to the main island at low tide, provided a secret anchorage for concealing the boat. On the hillside above the anchorage there were commanding views of the hills of South Uist; the Minch and MacLeod's Tables in Skye; the islands to the east of Benbecula; the hills of North Uist, and Rueval in Benbecula. Any ships in the Minch could be seen.

With Lady Clanranald gone, responsibility for the Prince now rested firmly with Flora. She prepared the Prince for the journey to Skye, but before that she faced a stern trial.

Flora recorded that "O'Neil would gladly have staid with the Prince and shared in his distresses and dangers, but Miss could by no means be prevailed upon to agree to that proposal." [5]

Armadale's pass was, after all, for Flora and only one man and one maid servant.

Neil MacEachern wrote that "Great was the debate betwixt Miss

Flora and O'Neil upon this occasion, who insisted strongly to leave the country with the prince; but Miss McDonald would never condescend, because he being a stranger, and consequently did not speak the language of the country, would readily be taken notice of by the common sort, and so took leave of the prince and Miss, made the best of his way to South Wist along with Milltown." [4]

In his third statement O'Neille declared that "they could not prevail upon Miss Flora to take Mr ONeil along with them, as he did not speak the Language of the Country & as he had (as she said) a Foreign air, Upon which he was obliged to part with them, with a promise to join them as soon as the Boat which carried them would come back." [6]

Felix O'Neille himself wrote that "The Prince intreated the young lady that I should accompany him, but she absolutely refused it, having a pass but for one servant. The Prince was so generous as to decline going unless I attended, until I told him, if he made the least demur, I would instantly go about my business, as I was extremely indifferent what became of me so that His person was safe. (With much difficulty and after many intreaties) he at length imbarked, attended only by Miss Flora MacDonald." [5]

Flora saw the danger to the Prince, and perhaps even to herself, of allowing O'Neille to travel without a pass. Flora, though attracted by O'Neille's charm, was unmoved by his smooth talking manners. She was a resolute lady. Flora would not yield and O'Neille had to remain behind in Benbecula. Instead Flora took the dependable Neil Mac-Eachen as her manservant, and 'Bettie Burke' as her maid.

The Prince, Flora, Neil MacEachen and the boatmen spent the rest of the day hiding. It was an agonisingly anxious day of waiting for Flora. Being involved in preparing the dress, finding the Prince, and even dashing across Loch Uiskevaig, had filled Flora's time. Now she had all the time in the world to reflect on why she was undertaking a scheme which could end in the Prince's capture, and her own arrest and imprisonment, even in a trial of treason for her own life. Rain and midges added to her anxiety. She doubtless missed the company of Felix O'Neille. During the day Hugh MacDonald of Baleshare claimed that he saw the Prince again.

Capt Alexander MacDonald, a cousin of Flora, though not present, wrote that "The Lady Clanranald begged of his royal highness to try on his new female apparel, and after mutually passing some jocose drollery concerning the sute of cloaths, and the lady shedding some tears for the occasion, the said lady dresses up his royal highness in his new habit. It was on purpose coarse as it was to be brooked by a gentlewoman's servant. The gown was of caligo, a light coloured quilted petticoat, a

Prince Charles Edward Stuart as Betty Bourke
by J Williams
(Courtesy Scottish National Portrait Gallery)

mantle of dun camlet made after the Irish fashion with a cap to cover his royal highness whole head and face, with a suitable head dress, shoes, stockings, etc." [5]

If indeed Lady Clanranald dressed the Prince, it was before dinner, for she certainly had no time to do so after the meal, once the news of General Campbell's arrival had been given.

Flora told Dr Burton that "When all were gone who were not to accompany the Prince in his voyage to the isle of Sky, Miss MacDonald desired him dress himself in his new attire, which was done." [5]

Robert Forbes collected a story that Flora had revealed that "when the Prince put on women's cloaths he proposed carrying a pistol under one of his petticoats for making some small defence in case of attack. But Miss declared against it, alleging that if any person should happen to search them the pistol would only serve to make a discovery. To which the Prince replied merrily: 'Indeed, Miss, if we shall happen to meet with any that will go so narrowly to work in searching as what you mean they will certainly discover me at any rate.' But Miss would not hear of any arms at all, and therefore the Prince was obliged to content himself with only a short cudgel, with which he design'd to do his best to knock down any single person that should attack him." [5]

Later in life, this mildly naughty story became one of Flora's favourites.

The Prince's pistols were given to Angus of Milton, and were taken from him by Armadale and brought to Skye. The Prince gave Flora the gold and paste buckles from his shoes, and a quarter of one of these survived into this century.

Neil MacEachen added that "The company being gone, the prince, stript of his own cloaths, was dressed by Miss Flora in his new attire, but could not keep his hands from adjusting his head dress, which he cursed a thousand times." [4]

The Prince was a strange sight. At almost six feet he was tall for a man, and huge for a woman. His face was weather beaten and he had not been shaved since his stay at Corradale, three weeks before.

The Prince and Flora had been extremely fortunate. General Campbell had arrived in Benbecula on the evening of Friday 27th June. The next day he had been at Nunton, where he interviewed Lady Clanranald, had dinner, cooked by John Maclean, and spent the night. On Sunday 29th June, Capt Anderson wrote "we march't to Kilbride the House of McDonald of Buisdael brother to Clanranold, but in all this march we could get no Intelligence of any Person of distinction being on the Island, tho' there is great reason to think the Young Pretender is yet there, for 'tis certain He was once on the islands, and there does not appear to have been any opportunities for His getting off, therefore I believe we shall in a day or two, or when the weather permits (which at present is, & for some days past has been very stormy) pay these islands a second visit."[7]

In South Uist the general met Capt Hugh MacDonald of Armadale. The general later wrote that "this villain met me in South Uist, and had the impudence to advice me against making so close a search, and that if I should for Some Days a little desist. He made no doubt of my Success. I suspected Him at the time."[8]

Armadale had not only misinformed General Campbell, but had also persuaded Capt Scott to leave South Uist for the southern isles.

The Independent Companies arrive in Skye

During the week military matters had altered in Skye as well. On 20th June Capt John MacLeod of Talisker, with five of his six companies, had reached Glenelg. Talisker was senior cadet of the MacLeods of Dunvegan, a friend of the Macleod chief, and half uncle of Sir Alexander MacDonald. At once he reduced the Skye Militia companies. He also commandeered a Glasgow kelp boat to take three of his own companies to the Outer Hebrides. He left Capt Donald Mac-Donald of Castleton with his company to secure the crossings from the mainland to Skye. By 24th June he had moved the rest of his men to Eabost on Loch Bracadale, on the west side of the island.

Three companies prepared to cross to South Uist. These were commanded by Norman MacLeod of Berneray, and Capts James and John MacDonald. Allan MacDonald, Kingsburgh's son, was lieutenant in John MacDonald of Kirkibost's company. James MacDonald, Armadale's young son, was ensign in James MacDonald of Airds' company.

"Tomorrow, I send my Lieutenant wt twenty men to Trotternish my Ensign wt the like number to Polteel & shall go myself wt the remainder to Vaternish; these three being the places of this Island in which any body Comeing from the Long island are likeliest to land."

Talisker's lieutenant was Alexander MacLeod of Balmeanach. His ensign was John MacAskill of Rudha an dunan.

"Our numbers at present are too small to prevent the landing of Rebells upon the whole of this Island & will be so after Vaterstein joins us, but as we dont fear any numbers of them that may land together, & that I take it to be our Principal Bussiness to gett intelligence of any that land in order to apprehend them. I believe I may venture to scatter out men pretty thin upon the coast."[9]

The Militia in Skye was reduced on 20th and 21st June. Capt Alexander MacDonald of Kingsburgh, who had been in command of all the Skye companies at Kinlochnadale, returned home to Kingsburgh House in Trotternish.

On 25th or 26th June Talisker's three detachments were in position at Loch Pooltiel, Waternish and Trotternish.

Lady Margaret MacDonald wrote, on 27th June, that "Buyness is quite Lay'd aside Here. King[sbu]r[gh] has been Station'd at the Kyle, for some months Past but has now gott Leave to Retourne Home. How Soone Everything is in Peace and quietness I shall begin agen to lett you Hear Regularly from Me." [10]

On Saturday 28th June Mrs MacDonald of Kirkibost crossed from "North Wist, and who was so strictly examined by the party upon the point of Waternish (taking her to be the prince in disguise), that she was at all pains imagineable to keep off the soldiers' hands from examining her person too closely." [4]

Talisker was stationed at Waternish Point with 30 men. He knew Mrs MacDonald well, for she was the wife of Capt John MacDonald of Kirkibost, one of Talisker's company commanders. His ostentatious searching of Mrs MacDonald was a cover, and she probably warned Talisker not to stop any boats from the Uists, in the next few day. She did not join her husband, but instead continued across Loch Snizort to Monkstadt.

Flora and the Prince had one alarm before they departed from Benbecula. Flora told Dr Burton that "at a proper time they removed their quarters and went near the water with their boat afloat, nigh at hand for readiness to embark in case of alarm from the shore. Here they arrived, very wet and wearied, and made a fire upon a rock to keep them somewhat warm till night. They were soon greatly alarmed by seeing four wherries full of armed men making towards shore, which made them extinguish their fire quickly, and to conceal themselves amongst the heath." [5]

The wherries were the four boats that General Campbell had had at Berneray and then at Gramsdale. Viewed from the hillside at Uiskevaig, the four wherries appeared amongst the cluster of islands and rocks to the east of the point of Rossinish. They were heading for Loch Boisdale and Barra, and their course took them a mile east of Uiskevaig, to pass outside Wiay. Flora and the others were alarmed by the sight of the boats, but it was unlikely that they passed very close to the shore.

At last, as the day was dusking into evening, it was time to depart. Flora stated that "the Boat they Embark'd in was one the Young

Pretender had constantly kept with him to transport Him from place to place to place. There was one Man that was constantly kept with the Boat & for this Expedition She procured four more in South Uist."[1]

Neil MacEachen noted that the boat was "managed by the following persons Rory McDonald, John McDonald, John McMurich, Duncan Campbell, and Rory McDonald of the Glengarry family."[4] This last was probably Garryfliuch in South Uist, rather than Glengarry.

Lachlan MacMhurrich, under duress, later gave the same names, adding that John MacDonald, who lived with MacDonald of Dremisdale, had not been captured; that Duncan Campbell had been taken by Capt Fergussone; one Rory MacDonald by Capt Scott and the other by Capt Campbell of Skipness. John MacMhurrich of Boranish Uachbrach had also remained uncaptured.[11]

Duncan Campbell, alias MacIver, also spelt 'McKievre,' later declared that "on Satturday the 28th June being a Servant to Clan Ranold, the Lady obligd Him to go into a Boat and help to Row the Young Pretender from South Uist to Skye."[12] Duncan Campbell was Clanranald's cattleman at Rossinish.

The skipper of the boat was Lt John MacDonald, living at Dremisdale. His brother was 'little' Rory MacDonald. John and Rory were the sons of Dremisdale. There was a second Rory MacDonald, an ensign in Clanranald's Regiment, described as of the Glengarry family by MacEachen. He may have been Roderick, third son of Alexander MacDonald of Garryfliuch, in South Uist.

The Prince's narrative stated that "waiting the glooming of the evening to get away, and for his comfort he had the men of warr cruising before him, who luckily towards night fall sailed off, wch gave him the opportunity of making for Mungaster in Skie, Lady Margaret McDonalds house."[13]

Flora recalled that "At eight o'clock, June 28th, Saturday, 1746, the Prince, Miss Flora MacDonald, Neil MacKechan, etc., set sail in a very clear evening from Benbecula to the Isle of Sky.

"They had not rowed from the shore above a league till the sea became rough, and at last tempestuous, and to entertain the company the Prince sung several songs and seemed to be in good spirits.

"In the passage Miss MacDonald fell asleep, and then the Prince carefully guarded her, lest in the darkness any of the men should chance to step upon her. She awaked in a surprise with some little bustle in the boat, and wondered what was the matter etc."[14]

Robert Forbes wrote that Flora "likewise us'd to tell that in their passage to the isle of Sky a heavy rain fell upon them, which with former fatigues distressed her much. To divert her the Prince sung several pretty songs."[6] Flora recalled that the songs the Prince sang, included "The King shall enjoy his own again" and "The twenty ninth of May," Jacobite songs of the 1715 Rising.

"She fell asleep, and to keep her so, the Prince still continued to sing. Happening to wake with some little bustle in the boat she found the Prince leaning over her with his hands spread about her head. She asked what was the matter? The prince told her that one of the rowers being obliged to do somewhat about the sail behoved to step over her body (the boat was so small), and lest he should have done her hurt either by stumbling or trampling upon her in the dark (for it was night) he had been doing his best to preserve his guardian from harm."[5]

In answer to Robert Forbes questions, Flora wrote that "Lady Clanranald did furnish them with some bottles of milk, and the Prince (in the passage) putting the bottle to his head, drank in common with those on board *Jock-fellow-like*. Lady Clanranald had but one half bottle of wine (there being so many demands upon her, particularly from parties of the military) which she likewise caused to be put on board the boat. The Prince in the passage would not allow any person to share in this small allowance of wine, but kept it altogether for Miss MacDonald's use, lest she should faint with cold and other inconveniences of a night passage."[5]

Neil MacEachen added that "The weather proving calm in the beginning of the night, they rowed away at a good rate; but, about twelve, there blew up a gale of westerly wind, which eased the Rowers not little, but at the same time there came on such a thick mist as robbed them of the sight of all lands: great was the debate among the boatmen upon this occasion, some asserted that they lost their course, while others maintained the contrary, till their dispute end'd at last to cease rowing till day would decide their error. In the morning, the weather being quite clear, they rowed along the coast of Sky, but the wind, shifting about to north, blew at nine o'clock so strong in their teeth, that for an hour and a half it was impossible to discern whether they made any way or not.

"The prince, who, all this time, was not in the least discouraged, encouraged them to row still better, saying that he would relieve him that was most fatigued. The poor men, almost ready to breathe out their last, at length made the point of Watersay [Waternish] on the north corner of the Isle of Sky, where, having got into a cliff in a rock, they rested themselves an hour, and at the same time revived their drooping spirits with a plentiful repast of bread and butter, while the water that fell from the top of the rock furnished them drink".

"This gave them fresh vigour for to undertake the remaining part of their labour, the weather being quite calm again, they rowed round the point close by the land. They had not gone far on the other side, when they spyed two centrys upon shore, one of whom approached nearer, and ordered them to put to, but they rowed the faster; which he observing, advanced as far as the sea would permit him, bad them put to, a second time in a more threatening manner, and seeing them like not to obey, he cocked his piece, which he thought to fire upon them, but, as Providence ordered it, she misgave, and so he was disappointed. The other who look'd on all this time, made to heels to a neighbouring village, about a cannon shot off, to acquaint their officer (if there was any) of what had happened.

"The boatmen, justly judging what he was going about, made them row for dear blood. They very soon saw the event of their conjectures, for a body of about fifteen men, full armed, marched straight from the village to the rock, where their centry was post'd, and if they had the presence of mind to launch out one of their boats (of which they had two close by them) we must have been inevitably taken.

"The prince by this time was sensible of his error in not allowing the men at parting from Uist to have any arms in the boat, which if they had had, were fully resolved to fight it out to the last man, notwithstanding the inequality of numbers. The enemy seeing it quite out of their power to execute their design in coming thither, as we got fairly out of reach, took a walk along the shore, without giving the prince or crew any uneasiness, further than to gaze at them." [4]

Flora reversed the attack and eating, and later wrote that "she was afraid they wou'd be now taken. 'Don't be afraid, Miss,' said the Prince, 'We will not be taken yet. You see it is low water, and before they can launch their boats over the rough shore, we will get in below those high rocks and they will lose sight of us.' which they did. They then slept and took a little refreshment before they went further to sea." [14]

Capt MacLeod of Talisker's sentry, from his detachment of thirty militia men, had fired on the boat which would not put into the shore, but Talisker had then made no effort to have the boat followed.

CHAPTER 6

Flora and the Prince Ashore on Skye

The lady, in great perplexity, was at a loss how to
behave on this occasion ... sent for Kingsborough, to
whom she disclosed the whole secret. Kingsborough,
without being in the least discomposed, explained to
her the danger the prince and her would be exposed to
if she insisted to have him brought to her house, where
she was to entertain one of the King's officers that day.
— Neil MacEachen.

Flora had reached the Isle of Skye with the Prince, and had only to deliver him to Sir Alexander MacDonald, and his wife, Lady Margaret. Flora could now turn to others, who were more influential, to conceal and care for the Prince.

But in her declaration to Gen Campbell, Flora took full responsibility for arranging the Prince's journey through Skye, stating that "The 29th about 11 of the Clock they got to Sky near Sr Alexander McDonald's House. Here McAchran & Miss McDonald Landed, leaving the Young Pretender in the Boat they went to Sr Alexander's House & from thence Miss McDonald sent a person for one Donald McDonald who had been in the Rebellion but deliver'd up His Arms some time ago. Miss McDonald told him to get a Boat to Carry the Young Pretender to Raasay after acquainting Him of their late voyage & where He was. Miss McDonald stayed & din'd with Lady Margaret McDonald & McAchran return'd to the Boat to acquaint the Young Pretender what steps they had taken for procuring a Boat to go to Raasay." [1]

A year later, Flora told Dr Burton that they landed at Kilbride. "There were also several parties of militia in the neighbourhood of Kilbride. Miss left the Prince in the boat and went with her servant, Neil MacKechan, to Mougstout, Sir Alexander MacDonald's house, and desired one of the servants to let Lady Margaret MacDonald know she was come to see her ladyship in her way to her mother's house. Lady Margaret knew the errand well enough by one Mrs MacDonald, who had gone a little before to apprize her of it." [2]

This Mrs MacDonald was the wife of John MacDonald of Kirki-bost, captain of one of the MacDonald Independent Companies.

Neil MacEachen wrote that "In the neighbourhood of this place was another party of the Sky militia, who was post'd there to examine all boats that came from the isles, as they were pretty well assured that the prince was there at that time. Miss and Neil having kept the prince in the boat as well as they could, went to the house, leaving strict orders with the boatmen not to stir from it till they came back, or some word to them, and in case their curiosity led any body thither, who might perhaps take the liberty to ask who was the person kept in the boat, to answer Miss McDonald's maid, and to curse her for a lazy jade, what was she good for, since she did not attend her Mrs.

"When they were come near the house, they were informed by a servant that Sir Alexander was gone for Fort Augustus some days before to wait upon Cumberland, and that there was no company with the lady but two gentlemen, to wit, McDonald of Kingsbourg, and Lieutenant McLeod, commander of the party before mentioned, and one Mrs McDonald who came the day before from North Wist, and who was so strictly examined by the party upon the point of Waternish (taking her to be the prince in disguise), that she was at all pains imaginable to keep off the soldiers' hands from examining her person too closely, which must have been the Prince's fate had he fallen into their hands.

"Miss Flora having met with one Miss McDonald, Lady Margarate's gentlewoman, sent her to acquaint her lady that she wanted to speak to her, who came back and carried Miss Flora to the lady's apartment, where she told all the circumstances of the prince's escape from the isles, and that she must harbour him as he came now under her protection." [2]

Flora met Lady Margaret in her spacious apartment at Monkstadt House. It was also called Mugstot, a large two storeyed building, which had been completed a few year's earlier by Sir Alexander, as his principal residence in Skye. Despite prior notice, Lady Margaret, one of the elegant daughters of the Earl of Eglinton, was in a panic.

Neil MacEachen wrote that "The lady, in great perplexity, was at a loss how to behave upon this occasion, for her hurry and impatience hindered her to fall upon proper means to get the prince conveyed privately to the house, especially at such an improper hour as eleven o'clock of the day."

Fortunately for Lady Margaret, Flora and the Prince, assistance was at hand.

Neil MacEachen added that Lady Margaret "sent for Kingsborough, to whom she disclosed the whole secret. Kingsborough, without being in the least discomposed, explained to her the danger the prince and her would be exposed to if she insisted to have him brought to her house, where she was to entertain one of the king's officers that day, who could not miss to see and take notice of the person in disguise, as well as every body else about the town." [2]

Flora was later to write that she "went to the house, where Mr Macdonald of Kingsburgh and several other government officers were. Sir Alexander being at Fort Augustus, the secret was discover'd to Kingsburgh, who chearfully undertook to convey him to his own house." [4]

Kingsburgh had been a Government officer until 21st June, only a week before.

Flora had told Dr Burton that "As Mr Alexander MacDonald of Kingsburgh was accidently there, Lady Margaret desired him to conduct the Prince to his house; for it is to be remarked that Lady Margaret did not see the prince in any shape. Kingsburgh sent a boy down to the boat with instructions whither to conduct the prince about a mile, and he (Kingsburgh) would be there ready to conduct him." [2]

Flora stated that Kingsburgh was at Monkstadt House 'accidently', but his presence there was more than good fortune. Kingsburgh had only recently returned to his house, having been released from the militia, and Lady Margaret knew that he had come home. She had been warned the previous day, by Mrs MacDonald of Kirkibost, that the Prince was soon to arrive, and Lady Margaret had sent for Kingsburgh.

Neil MacEachen wrote that Kingsburgh, "having got the lady at last to yield, though with great reluctancy, he ordered Neil to return to the prince, and to carry him to the back of a hill, a long mile from the house of Mungstot, and there to wait till he came to join them." [2]

Meanwhile Lady Margaret sent Mrs MacDonald of Kirkibost with a letter to Donald Roy MacDonald. Donald Roy had been one of the few of Sir Alexander's tenants to join the Prince's army, and had been wounded in the foot at Culloden. He had received information from his brother Hugh MacDonald of Baleshare, and had crossed to Fladdachuan, where he had expected to find the Prince. He had returned to Monkstadt on 26th or 27th June and had gone back to his quarters.

Donald Roy borrowed Dr John Maclean's horse, and "when near Mouggistot he spied Lady Margaret and Kingsburgh walking together, and talking in a serious way, above the garden. When he came near them he dismounted, and Lady Margaret, upon seeing him, stept aside from Kingsburgh to meet the Captain and to speak with him, spreading out her hands and saying, 'O Donald Roy, we are ruined for ever.'

Upon this, he asked what was the matter? Her ladyship answered that the prince was landed about half a quarter of a mile from the house."

What "made the case the more perplexed, and made her altogether at a loss how to behave in the matter, which was that Lieutenant MacLeod was at that very instant in the dining room with Miss Flora MacDonald (she having left the prince in women's cloaths on the spot where he had come ashore): and, which still rendered the case worse and worse, that the Lieutenant had three or four of his men about the house with him, the rest of his command being only at a small distance from the house." [2]

After a long discussion, in the garden, it was agreed by Donald Roy and Kingsburgh that the Prince should be sent to the Isle of Raasay, not by sea round the north end of Trotternish, which was now well guarded, but by land to Portree. Donald Roy was sent off to find John MacLeod, young Rona, the Laird of Raasay's son, to make arrangements.

Kingsburgh took some wine and biscuits and set off to find the Prince. Neil MacEachen had, meanwhile, been sent by the Prince to fetch his knife canteen, which had been inadvertently left in the boat. The Prince was alone when Kingsburgh found him, and Neil rejoined the two men a little later.

Flora had passed on responsibility for the Prince to Lady Margaret and Kingsburgh, but she still had a difficult task to carry off. She had somehow to dissuade or prevent Sandy MacLeod of Balmeanach, lieutenant in Talisker's Independent Companies, from searching the boat.

In the composite account that Robert Forbes received from London, the first he entered into *Lyon in Mourning*, he noted that the officer "enquired of Miss Flora MacDonald who she was, and who was with her, which she answered as she though proper. The officer, however, would not be satisfied until he had searched the boat. In the meantime the prince was hid on shore so near as to hear what passed." [3]

Kingsburgh denied that the boat had been searched, but the story had been put about as a cover for Sandy MacLeod, who should have searched the boat. Flora may well have hinted to Lt MacLeod not to make a search.

Flora told Dr Burton that "the commanding officer of the parties in search of the Prince ... asked Miss whence she came, whither she was going, what news? etc., all which Miss answered as she thought most proper, and so to prevent any discovery of what she had been engaged in." [3]

Robert Forbes added that Flora "could not help observing Lady Margaret going often out and in as one in great anxiety, while she in the meantime endeavoured all she could to keep up a close chit chat with Lieutenant MacLeod, who put many questions to her, which she answered as she thought fit." [3]

Flora was no longer responsible for the Prince, and had prevented Sandy MacLeod from searching the boat. She could have retired gracefully from the scene, by remaining at Monkstadt, but she did not.

Flora stated that "Lady Margaret pressed Miss very much in presence of the officer to stay, telling her that she had promised to make some stay the first time she should happen to come there. But Miss desired to be excused at that time, because she wanted to see her mother, and to be home in these troublesome times. Lady Margaret at last let her go." [3]

Flora, with Mrs MacDonald of Kirkibost, and her maid and man servant, "overtook the Prince and Kingsburgh. Mrs MacDonald was very desirous to see the Prince's countenance; but as she went along he always turned away his face from Mrs MacDonald to the opposite side whenever he perceived her endeavouring to stare him in the countenance." After several comments from the maid about the Irish woman, Flora had to ask Mrs MacDonald "to step a little faster and leave those on foot, because, as there were many parties of militia in the great roads, it was necessary for the prince to cross the country, and it was not proper to let Mrs MacDonald's man or maid servant see it. So on they went, and the Prince and Kingsburgh went over the hills and travelled south south east till they arrived at Kingsburgh's house, which was about twelve o'clock at night, and they were very wet. But Miss MacDonald, who had parted with her companions and her man-servant on the road, arrived some short time before the Prince." [3]

Neil MacEachen wrote that "About an hour before sunset they set off for Kingsborough, where they were to be that night." He recounted how comments were passed on Betty Burk walking and talking with Kingsburgh, and paying no attention to Flora MacDonald; on her long strides and the way that she lifted her skirts when crossing streams. Eventually "Neil told them that he knew nothing about her further than to hear she was an Irish girl who met with Miss MacDonald in Wist, and upon a report of her being a famous spinster of lint, engaged her for her mother's use." [2]

Three lines later Neil MacEachen's narrative ended.

The Prince's narrative stated that "that Evening he walked 8 miles to a Gentns house where he was to meet the young Lady again, but being unused to petty coats he held them in walking up so high that some common people remarked an awkwardness in wearing them, wch being told, he was obliged to change his habit again next day." [6]

Flora told General Campbell that "After dinner Miss McDonald set out for Portree, where they proposed being that night but on the Road overtook McAchran & the Young Pretender who had been joined by Kingsbury she told them she was to call at Kingsbury's House and desir'd they would go there also they proceeded There. Miss McDonald was taken sick & being ask'd to Stay all Night, Miss desir'd the other two to stay also." [1]

Once again Flora took full responsibility for the Prince, and stated that it was her idea to visit Kingsburgh House, and that it was her sickness which had forced the party to stay the night there.

Donald Roy MacDonald had gone in to Portree to arrange for the Prince to cross to Raasay. He received a note from Kingsburgh indicating that Flora was so fatigued that she would stay a night at his house. "The Captain took the hint." [3]

Flora and the Prince at Kingsburgh House

Robert Forbes collected a substantial account of the Prince's stay at Kingsburgh House from Alexander MacDonald himself, and his wife, Flora. Anne MacAlister, Kingsburgh's daughter, wrote two accounts of the Prince's visit, and her son left a third account.

"When the Prince came to Kingsburgh's house (Sunday, June 29th) it was between ten and eleven at night; and Mrs. MacDonald, not expecting to see her husband that night was making ready to go to bed. One of the servant maids came and told her that Kingsburgh was come home and had brought some company with him.

"What company?" says Mrs. MacDonald. 'Milton's daughter, I believe,' says the maid, 'and some company with her.'

"'Milton's daughter,' replies Mrs MacDonald, 'is very welcome to come here with any company she pleases to bring. But you'll give my service to her, and tell her to make free with anything in the house; for I am very sleepy and cannot see her this night.'

"In a little her own daughter came and told her in a surprize, 'O mother, my father has brought in a very odd, muckle, ill-shapen-up wife as ever I saw! I never saw the like of her, and he has gone into the hall with her.'

"She had scarce done with telling her tale when Kingsburgh came and desired his lady to fasten on her bucklings again, and to get some supper for him and the company he had brought with him.

"'Pray, goodman,' says she, 'what company is this you have brought with you?'

"'Why, goodwife,' said he, 'you shall know that in due time; only make haste and get some supper in the meantime.'"

Lady Kingsburgh sent her daughter to fetch the keys in the hall, but on seeing a 'muckle woman' striding up and down, she returned." Mrs. MacDonald went herself to get the keys, and I heard her more than once declare that upon looking in at the door she had not the courage to go forward.

" 'For,' said she, 'I saw such an odd muckle trallup of a carlin, making lang wide steps through the hall that I could not like her appearance at all.'

"Mrs. MacDonald called Kingsburgh, and very seriously begged to know what a lang, odd hussie was this he had brought to the house; for that she was frighted at the sight of her that she could not go into the hall for her keys.

" 'Did you never see a woman before,' said he, 'goodwife? What frights you seeing a woman? Pray, make haste, and get us some supper.'

"Kingsburgh would not go for the keys, and therefore his lady behov'd to go for them. When she entered the hall, the Prince happen'd to be sitting; but immediately he arose, went forward and saluted Mrs. MacDonald, who feeling a long stiff beard, trembled to think that this behoved to be some distressed nobleman or gentleman in disguise, for she never dream'd it to be the prince, though all along she had been seized with a dread she could not account for from the moment she had heard that Kingsburgh had brought company with him. She very soon made out of the hall with her keys, never saying one word.

"Immediately she importun'd Kingsburgh to tell her who the person was, for that she was sure by the salute that it was some distressed gentleman. Kingsburgh smiled at the mention of the bearded kiss, and said: 'Why, my dear, it is the Prince. You have the honour to have him in your house.'

" 'The Prince,' cried she. 'O Lord, we are a' ruin'd and undone for ever! We will a' be hang'd now!'

" 'Hout, goodwife,' says the honest stout soul, 'we will die but ance; and if we are hanged for this, I am sure we die in a good cause. Pray, make no delay; go get some supper. Fetch what is readiest. You have eggs and butter and cheese in the house, get them as quickly as possible.'

" 'Eggs and butter and cheese!' says Mrs MacDonald, 'what a supper is that for a Prince?'

" 'O goodwife,' said he, 'little do you know how this good Prince has been living for some time past. These, I can assure you, will be a feast to him. Besides, it would be unwise to be dressing a formal supper, because this would serve to raise the curiosity of the servants, and they would be making their observations. The less ceremony and work the better. Make haste and see that you come to supper.'

" 'I come to supper!' says Mrs. MacDonald; 'how can I come to supper? I know not how to behave before Majesty.'

" 'You must come,' says Kingsburgh, 'for he will not eat a bit till he see you at the table; and you will find it no difficult matter to behave before him, so obliging and easy is he in his conversation.' " [3]

Kingsburgh's daughter Anne and her husband Ranald MacAlister of Skirinish were staying in the house. In her second account Anne MacAlister wrote that "he was brought up stairs to the best room in the house, your mother came in with a pair of candels as no servant was admitted, he turned about to Flora McD. and said, he was sure she [Anne] was no servant. She told him she was the landlord's daughter, saluted her very kindly no less than with a kiss." [6]

In her earlier account Anne MacAlister wrote that "Your grandmother [Lady Kingsburgh] sat by him the whole night but while he was shifting which he greatly required. Supper was got, your mother attended, which gave him great pain always begging of her to sit down. He at last got up and drew a chair for her. Your grandmother told him she must not sit long, that no servant woud be admitted to the room while he was in the house. There was some fine English beer in the house which regaled him greatly, he always called for the other drink. He ate and drank hearty. He chose rum punch rather than wine." [6]

Kingsburgh added that "The Prince ate of our roast eggs, some collops, plenty of bread and butter, etc., and (to use the words of Mrs MacDonald) 'the deel a drap did he want in's weam of twa bottles of sma beer. God do him good o't; for, well I wat, he had my blessing to gae down wi't.'

"After he had made a plentiful supper, he called for a dram; and when the bottle of brandy was brought, he said he would fill the glass himself; 'for,' said he, 'I have learn'd in my skulking to take a brandy dram.'

"He filled up a bumper and drank it off to the happiness and prosperity of his landlord and landlady." [3]

At dinner Anne MacAlister later recalled that "I forget the conversation they had at supper. Miss Flora, said he, you was much afraid this day when they were firing upon us from the point. I am not free of fear yet said she. They may come for us here. O Fie Miss Flora youl never see a Mac Leod dare to search a Mac Donald house. Do you know that my crab stick that lies in the corner there has a charm that no enemy dars attack me while I have my crab stick. I wish it may be so said she, as it is not unlike, but you may be in greater danger than you have been this day. After this passed Miss Flora retired and went to bed." [6]

Robert Forbes recorded that "The Prince and Kingsburgh turn'd very familiar and merry together, and when the Prince spoke to Kingsburgh, he for the most part laid his hand upon Kingsburgh's knee and used several kind and obliging expressions in his conversation with the happy landlord.

"Kingsburgh became so merry and jocose that putting up his hand to the Prince's face, he turned off his head dress which was a very odd clout of a mutch or toy; upon which Mrs. MacDonald hasted out of the room and brought a clean nightcap for him." [3]

When the Prince insisted on another bowl of punch, and Kingsburgh refused, the two men grabbed the bowl and it fell and broke, thus ending their carousing. The broken and repaired punch bowl, with a Chinese pattern was passed down to Col MacAlister's descendants. Another punch bowl is at the Royal Museum of Scotland.

Flora said nothing of the evening to General Campbell. To Dr Burton she stated that "here the Prince got his most material refreshment, and was very much fatigued, Yet he was very merry till the company parted to go to rest." [3]

Later Flora recalled that "The worthy landlady of the house was very happy with her guest, and he himself was so well pleas'd with his reception and lodging that he took a chearful glass with his landlord, and having got a good clean bed (which he was a stranger to for some time) sleep'd soundly till ten o'clock next morning." [3]

Flora slept in a room by herself, and Neil MacEachen slept in the same room as the Prince.

Robert Forbes recorded that "Next morning Mrs. MacDonald went to Miss Flora's bedside before she got up and asked of her an account of the adventure. Miss (among other things) told her that there was not any other probable way of saving the Prince but that single one which had been used, and that it had the appearance of a desperate attempt at best; that Lady Clanronald provided them with women's cloathes for the disguise, and that she had contributed all in her power for preserving the Prince out of the hands of his enemies.

"Mrs. MacDonald desired to know what was become of the boat and rowers.

"'They returned directly,' said Miss Flora, 'to South Uist.'

"Mrs. MacDonald declared great concern to hear that, because upon their return they would immediately be seized by the military and harshly used to tell what they knew.

"'I wish,' said Mrs. MacDonald, 'you had sunk the boat and kept the boatman in Skye where they could have been concealed, and then we would have known the better what to have done with the Prince, because his enemies by this means would have lost scent of him.

But all will be wrong by the returning to South Uist.'

" 'I hope not,' said Miss, 'for we took care to depone them before they parted from us.'

" ' 'Alas!' replied Mrs. MacDonald, 'your deponing of them will not signifie a farthing. For if once the military get hold of them they will terrifie them out of their senses and make them forget their oath.' "

Flora told Dr Burton that when morning was far advanced, she became anxious about the Prince's still being in bed, in case he should be discovered by his enemies. She went to Kingsburgh, who wanted the Prince to rest as long as he could. "Accordingly Kingsburgh went into the Prince's bedchamber and found him in so profound a sleep that he could not think of awakening him, and so retired softly out of the room." [3]

"After Miss Flora had got up," Robert Forbes noted, "Mrs Mac-Donald told her that she wanted much to have a lock of the Prince's hair, and that she behoved to go into his room and get it for her. Miss Flora refused to do as she desired, because the Prince was not yet out of bed.

" 'What then,' said Mrs. MacDonald, 'no harm will happen to you. He is too good to harm you or any person. You must instantly go in and get me the lock.'

"Mrs. MacDonald, taking hold of Miss with one hand, knocked at the door of the room with the other. The Prince called, 'Who is there?'

"Mrs. MacDonald, opening the door, said, 'Sir, it is I, and I am importuneing Miss Flora to come in and get a lock of your hair to me, and she refuses to do it.'

" 'Pray,' said the Prince, 'desire Miss MacDonald to come in. What should make her afraid to come where I am?'

"When Miss came in he begged her to sit down on a chair at the bedside, then laying his arms about her waist, and his head upon her lap, he desired her to cut out the lock with her own hands in token of future and more substantial favours. The one half of the lock Miss gave to Mrs. MacDonald and the other she kept to herself." [3]

Flora later recalled that "Mrs Macdonald apply'd to Miss Mac-donald to get a lock of the Prince's hair, which he instantly comply'd with." [4]

This was the only occasion in which Flora and the Prince were alone together. Flora's modesty had made her hesitant about going into the room while the Prince was still in bed, but the Prince had reassured her of her safety. The Prince was always gallantly concerned about Flora's welfare, but he remained impassively cool about her while they were together. Flora, like any young woman suddenly introduced to a handsome and engaging man, who was a Royal Prince, was affected by his presence. This did not influence Flora's resolution, however, in acting calmly, and efficiently, in arranging matters to ensure the Prince's safety. She even resisted his arguments, when the Prince had insisted that O'Neille must accompany him to Skye.

But there was no spark of romance between Flora and the Prince. Flora had been much more taken with Felix O'Neille, whom she had been forced to abandon in Benbecula.

Anne MacAlister insisted that "Flora McD was not present when the Princes hair was cut, she was off for Portree to meet him there, it was your mother that cut his hair, it was your grandmother that proposed cutting his hair, which he was very happy to give her, his hair was very short it was at the back of his head they coud get any length, he always wore a wig." [6]

The word of neither Flora nor Anne MacAlister can be doubted, and they both cut a lock of the Prince's hair. Flora's family certainly had a lock of his hair. Anne MacAlister's descendants still have a ring containing strands of the Prince's hair. Both ladies agreed that it was Mrs MacDonald of Kingsburgh who instigated the project.

Both Flora and Anne also agreed that the sheets in which the Prince had slept were reserved by Lady Kingsburgh, and used at her funeral, when she died in 1759. Flora repeated this to James Boswell in 1773, after the funeral.

Flora was asked by General Campbell "while they stay'd at Kingsburgh house, if any of the Family inquired who the disguised person was Miss McDonald answers that they did not ask Her or McAchran but that She observ'd the people of the family whispering as if they suppos'd Him to be some person that desir'd not to be known & from the servants Miss found they suspected Him to be Bernera a person that had been in Rebellion." [1]

In her statement Flora attempted to protect Kingsburgh. Bernera was Donald MacLeod of Berneray, one of the few MacLeods who joined the Prince. He was well known to both Flora and Kingsburgh.

Unknown to Flora, Kingsburgh had, the day before she made her statement, admitted to General Campbell that he had known that the disguised person was the Prince.

Ranald MacAlister, once his wife retired to bed, had got up, thrown on some clothes and fled from the house. Next day Anne MacAlister dressed the Prince in her husband's best coat and vest. When these were thought to be too good, she changed them for her husband's second best suit.

Malcolm MacLeod later conveyed the Prince across Skye. The Prince passed as Malcolm's servant, but Malcolm felt that his vest was too grand for a servant. The two men exchanged garments, and Malcolm hid MacAlister's vest under a stone and recovered the remnants of it on his return from imprisonment in London. The pieces were given to Robert Forbes. The tartan has incorrectly been named MacDonald of Kingsburgh.[7] The tartan was MacAlister of Skirinish.

Flora stated that "Though the Prince was determined (from the observations and persuasion of Kingsburgh) to cast off his disguise, yet it was necessary he should leave the house in the female dress he came in, which would, if enquiry happened to be made, prevent the servants telling the particular dress he had put on when he stript himself of the gown, petticoats, etc., and therefore in Kingsburgh's house Miss put on his cap for him."[1]

Anne MacAlister added that "The Prince dress was a printed goun, a coarse stuf petticoat and an old Camlet cloak, a linen apron, a musline cap and a ribon, and a coarse napkin, and cotton gloves your grandmother made a bed cover of the goun, your mother got the gloves, Flora McD got the apron which I myself saw. There was bits of the ribbon and cape sent to different families in the South, your grandfather kept the shoes. There was as many demands upon bits of them, your grandfather gave him a pair of his own shoes."[6]

Flora also told the general that "The 30th Miss McDonald went on Horseback for Portree, having first desir'd McAchran to have the young Pretender Dress himself in Mens Cloaths, some where on the Road betwixt Kingsbury's & Portree as notice had been taken the day before that Womans Cloaths rather made him more suspect.

"Miss McDonald got to Portree about 12 at Night."[1]

Flora stated that she left Kingsburgh at about the same time as the Prince. Anne MacAlister, however, recalled that Flora had set out for Portree, when the Prince's hair was cut. She added that the Prince put on his wig again, "after he left the house when he dressed himself at the side of a hill near the house in your Fathers cloths.

"Your grandfather went a good way from the house with him till the boy caught up with them that was to conduct the Prince to Portree."[8]

The Prince's nose bled when he parted from Kingsburgh. "The female attire was deposited in the heart of a bush and afterwards carried to Kingsburgh house; where upon the alarm of a search it was burnt, except only the gown which Kingsburgh's daughter insisted on saving as a precious relick. It was stamped linen with a purple sprig.

"The Prince attended by Neil MacKechan and having Kingsburgh's boy Macqueen of about eleven years old for a guide, went ten Scots miles, got safe, though very wet to Portree."[6]

CHAPTER 7

The Prince and Flora Part at Portree

On Monday Evening the 30th past Miss McDonald
Daughter to Milton came to His House & several
hours after McAchran & another person unknown
Join'd them ... there was one Donald McDonald who
had been in Rebellion but before had surrendered His
Arms this person supp'd with the Lady before the
arrival of McAchran & the unknown person.
— Charles Macnabb, Innkeeper, Portree.

Flora told General Campbell that she "got to Portree about 12 at Night, where She found Donald McDonald who was sent before to prepare a Boat to carry him to Raasay & the young Pretender & McAchran arriv'd about an Hour after. Here he took some refreshment, chang'd a Guinea paid the Reckoning took his leave of Miss & went out with Donald McDonald but who after seeing him to the Boat Return'd." [1]

Flora added little more for Dr Burton. "Miss MacDonald went thither on horseback by another road, thereby the better to gain intelligence and at the same time to prevent discovery. They were very wet, it having rained very much, and staid about two hours." [2]

Later Flora recalled that "she arriv'd at Portree before him, where she found Mr Macdonald commonly call'd Donald Roy Macdonald, waiting for the Prince by appointment. The Prince arriv'd afterwards, and the night being short, he stay'd no longer than to take a little refreshment, Mr Macdonald hurrying him to a boat waiting for him from Raasay at a little distance from the house, where he deliver'd him." [3]

The Prince's narrative stated that "being advised that Rasay was the best place to go to, he walked that Evening Eight miles in pouring rain all the while to get to the shoar at xxxxx [sic] there being in mens Cloaths he parted wth the young Lady and embarked in a little Boat for Rasa being told the Enemy was still on the main land." [4]

The longest account of the parting at Portree was written by Donald Roy MacDonald. He had been called to Monkstadt on Sunday, 29th

June, and then despatched to find young Rona and to arrange a passage to the Isle of Raasay for that evening. Late at night Kingsburgh had sent him a message that Flora had been taken sick and that she would stay at Kingsburgh house.

Donald Roy wrote that "In the journey from Kingsburgh, Miss Flora MacDonald on horseback came first to Portree, and immediately notified to Donald Roy MacDonald privately that the Prince was on his way in such a road; upon which he stept out to meet him, and staying about twenty minutes, could not see him." [2]

A little while later young MacQueen appeared and took Donald Roy outside, where, in the pouring rain, he met the Prince and Neil MacEachen.

"When the Captain happened to express his concern that he had got such a stormy night, the Prince said 'I am more sorry that *our Lady*' (for so he used to name Miss MacDonald) 'should be all abused with the rain.'

"Then they went into the house, the Captain stepping in first, the people of the house (an inn) not knowing anything of the matter at all. The Prince no sooner entered the house than he asked if a dram could be got there, the rain pouring down from his cloaths, he having on a plaid without breeches, trews, or even philibeg.

"Before he sat down he got his dram, and then the company desired him to shift and put on a dry shirt, Captain Roy MacDonald giving him his philibeg. The Prince refused to shift, as Miss Flora MacDonald was in the room; but the Captain and Neil MacKechan told him it was not a time to stand on ceremonies, and prevailed upon him to put on a dry shirt. By this time they had brought some meat into the room (the Prince having called for it before he would think of shifting), which consisted of butter, cheese, bread, and roasted fish. The landlord's name is Charles MacNab.

"The Captain was still urging him to be gone in as discreet a manner as possible, but the Prince was desirous to stay all night in Portree as the rain was still heavy.

"In paying the reckoning the Prince got change for a guinea, upon which he desired to have silver for another guinea, but the landlord having no more than eleven shillings, the Prince was for giving him the guinea for them, for that (he said) eleven shillings would be much more useful to him than a guinea in gold could be. But the Captain would not hear of this at all, as this piece of generosity might tend to raise a suspicion in the breast of the landlord about the real character of one who was so liberal in paying a small reckoning, and therefore the captain made a shift to change the guinea for him." [2]

The Prince asked Donald Roy to accompany him, but Donald Roy excused himself because of his wounded foot. The Prince said that he liked to be with MacDonalds. When Donald Roy suggested that he had been quite safe amongst Sir Alexander MacDonald's people, and that Lady Margaret was willing to give him money, the Prince was distinctly cool about both Sir Alexander, who had not joined his army, and who was then with the Duke of Cumberland, and Lady Margaret, who had not sheltered him at Monkstadt.

"The Prince now began to bid farewell to Miss MacDonald and Neil MacKechan (the captain being always begging him to depart), and, turning to Miss, he said,

"'I believe, Madam, I owe you a crown of borrowed money.'

"She told him it was only half-a-crown, which accordingly he paid her with thanks. He then saluted her, and expressed himself in these or the like words,

"'For all that has happened I hope, Madam, we shall meet in St James's yet.'" [2]

When questioned by Robert Forbes, at their first meeting in Leith, in January 1748, Flora stated that the Prince's "farewell to her was in these words:

"'I hope we shall meet in St James's yet, and I will reward you there for what you have done.'" [2]

The Prince owed his safety to Flora, a young woman who had been selected by the chance that she was the stepdaughter of the captain of Militia in South Uist. The Prince's parting words to her were no more than a formal farewell. He did remember to settle his account, and he did salute her — embrace her — but he did not thank her for risking her character and life for him, nor mention that she might still risk her life for him if she was arrested and brought to trial.

Though Donald Roy could only recall that the Prince had said "For all that has happened I hope, Madam, we shall meet in St James's yet", the Prince's parting words engraved in Flora's memory were "I hope we shall meet in St James's yet, and I will reward you there for what you have done."

The Prince knew, and Flora certainly knew, that the Old Pretender would never be restored to his palace at St James's in London. The Prince's promised reward was a chimera. His words were an empty, meaningless pleasantry, signifying nothing. The Prince never again thought of, asked after, wrote to or met Flora. In his narrative, written down only two months later, the Prince never mentioned her by name, referring to Flora only as a trusty girl and a young Lady.

Flora did not repeat the Prince's parting words in the Memorial that she wrote in the last year of her life. By then the Prince was dead, and Flora knew that she would never receive any reward from him.

Donald Roy MacDonald concluded that the Prince "then bad farewell to honest MacKechan, who stayed that night with Miss MacDonald at Portree, and attended her next day to the place she intended to go to." [2] The Prince was loaded with provisions, and Donald Roy took him out of the inn and found Malcolm MacLeod, who took him directly to the boat for Raasay.

Donald Roy returned to the inn, where he slept the rest of the night. Charles MacNabb, the inn keeper, was inquisitive, but Donald Roy told him that the visitor had been a fellow Jacobite MacDonald, discreetly visiting friends, who had decided to move on elsewhere. Donald Roy could not resist adding that "The landlord said he had entertained a strong notion that the gentleman might happen to be the Prince in disguise, for that he had something about him that looked very noble." [3]

Flora concluded to General Campbell that "She thinks the Pretender went to Raasay but after leaving him at Portree Miss McDonald does not know what became of him." [1]

Charles MacNabb, the inn keeper at Portree, was interviewed and declared "that on Monday Evening the 30th past Miss McDonald Daughter to Milton came to His House & several hours after McAchran & another person unknown Join'd them ... The Lady & McAchran stay'd behind went to bed, and did not leave his House till ten the Next day viz 1st July.

"They solicite to have a Boat to go to Broadford, but were refus'd however he gave them his Boat to ferry them over Loch Portrie which was immediately return'd ... The reason of their wanting a Boat to Broadford was to transport their Baggage, because no Horse could be got ... They were supplyd with Horses for the baggage on the other side of Loch Portrie."

Charles Macnabb added that "the people at Penefeler who furnish'd Horses for the Lady & McAchran must know where they went to." [5]

Flora told Dr Burton that "Miss MacDonald took leave of the Prince, and from thence went to her mother, after a fatiguing journey cross the country." [2]

At Penifiler Flora and Neil MacEachen found a horse to carry their baggage and set off for Armadale, forty miles away. They perhaps reached Armadale on the evening of 2nd July. Flora "never told her mother or indeed anybody else, what she had done." [2]

Robert Forbes recorded that "When she returned to her mother in Sky, the honest old woman was surprised to see her, and asked the reason why she had made such a short stay with her brother. Miss replied that things being in a hurry and confusion in South Uist, with such a number of mility folks, she was uneasy till she got out of it; but she never once hinted at the adventure she had so successfully managed, of which the mother knew nothing at all till a party came to take the daughter prisoner, although Miss had been with her mother eight or ten days before she was taken." [2]

Having seen Flora and Neil MacKechan off by boat, Donald Roy MacDonald turned north. "The Captain left Portree the same day (July 1st) and went directly to Kingsburgh, informing him and his lady how the Prince had got off in a very private way to Raasay.

"Kingsburgh and his lady said they had reason to think it was not known that the Prince had been in their house; only there was a suspicion among their servants that yon person might be a man in women's cloaths, because so monstrous and tall.

"From Kingsburgh the Captain went to Mouggistot and informed Lady Margaret how safely and privately things had been managed, There he met with Lieutenant MacLeod (son of Donald MacLeod of Balmeanagh, and the very person that had been in the dining room with Miss Flora MacDonald when the Prince was sitting upon the shore) who was very fond to see Donald Roy as they were very well acquainted together. The Lieutenant would not part with the Captain that night, but would needs carry him to his quarters about a long mile from Mouggistot.

"He lay in the same bed with the Lieutenant that night ... The Captain finding that the Lieutenant by his expressions knew nothing at all of the Prince's late motions, began to be afraid that he had been only dissembling the matter with him; and therefore he got up pretty early in the morning and went to the guardhouse to pump the common fellows, for he was well acquainted with some of the command.

"In a joking way they called him rebel and he again called them rebels. Then he asked if they knew anything about his young master, for that he longed much to hear something about him, and they could not fail to know somewhat of him, as the army was so extraordinarily diligent, both by sea and land, to find out and watch his motions.

"With an air of assurance they told him that the young Pretender was still somewhere in the Long Isle, and that certainly he would be very soon catched, if he was not in the hands of the army already. This gave great inward pleasure to the Captain, as it was a plain proof that they knew nothing about the Prince's being in or about the Isle of Skye at all." [2]

This elaborate tale from Donald Roy suggested that he too was covering for Sandy MacLeod. Lt MacLeod had probably guessed what had happened, though his men knew nothing of the Prince's whereabouts.

CHAPTER 8

Flora Arrested

9th [July] *in the evening I received a letter from Talisker of 8th from Mugstote with orders to apprehend Miss MacDonald Milton's Daughter, which was executed.* — Capt Donald MacDonald of Castleton

Capt Felix O'Neille parted with the Prince on Saturday 28th June. He wrote pompously that "I now could only recommend him to God, and his good fortune, and made my way amidst the enemy to South Uist, where we had left Colonel O'Sullivan. Next day I joined O'Sullivan, and found (four days after the prince parted) a French cutter, commanded by one Dumont, who had on board two captains of the Irish brigade with a number of volunteers." [1]

It was the Prince's ill fortune to have missed, once again, a French ship, which had been sent to find him. Capt Dumont and *Le Hardi Mendiant*, (the sturdy beggar), had already been in West Highland waters that summer but had returned to Dunkirk. Sailing north about Scotland, on 3rd July the boat anchored off Ormaclett in South Uist.

John O'Sullivan had made his way to Benbecula, and with Felix O'Neille went to Torlum house on the evening of 4th July. Within a few hours *Le Hardi Mendiant* sailed into the sound between Benbecula and South Uist. The two Irishmen agreed that O'Sullivan should go on board, and that they should meet up in Applecross, opposite the isle of Raasay, where O'Neille hoped to find the Prince.

The Italian Irishman's journal now took a flight of pure fantasy. O'Neille wrote that "After having seen my friend on board, and after innumerable difficulties, I got a boat and went round the Isle of Sky to the Isle of Rasay, place of rendezvous; but at my landing had intelligence that the Prince was returned to the Isle of Sky, whereupon I hasted to said Isle of Skye again, and there too had the grief to learn that he had departed that island, but for what place nobody could inform me in the least. I then repaired to Loch Nammaddy in North Uist, where by our agreement Colonel O'Sullivan was to come to me in case that in eight days I did not join him at Loch Seaforth; but not meeting my friend there, after delay of four days I returned to the island of Benbecula, where I promised myself greater safety than any where else; but I met with a quite different usage. For the very person in whom

I had entirely confided, and under whose care I was, betrayed me to Captain Macneal (induced thereto by a great sum of money offered for me), who was in that country under the command of Captain Ferguson of the *Furnace Bomb* I was taken by this Captain MacNeal in a rock over a loch, where I had skulked for four days." [2]

O'Neille's tale was directly contradicted by other accounts.

It was the arrival of *Le Hardi Mendiant* in South Uist which began a series of events, that ended in the arrest of Flora.

On 4th July General Campbell, off the Isle of Barra, heard of the French ship. Capt Fergussone was sent to Berneray in the cutter, and some Argyll militia were landed in South Uist. The two parties were to march through the islands and meet at Benbecula. General Campbell met up with Commodore Smith to discuss plans. Next day the general returned to Vatersay Bay.

"The party with Captn Fergusone," wrote Capt George Anderson, "got to the west of South Uist and Visited Several of the Small Islands at Night they got to Bernera but mett with Nothing, the 6th the party Set out in the Cutter for Benbicula where they Arrived about 5 in the Evening & took several Prisoners for Information, One of which Inform'd Capt McNeil that O'Neil who had hitherto accompanied the Pretender was Concealed in a Shelling 7 Miles from any House. He March'd a party Immediately to the place & took O'Neil & brought Him Prisoner to Clan Ranalds House the same night.

"The person who gave information of O'Neil, Being immediately put into Barrisdale, confessed that the Younge Pretender Left South Uist Satturday the 28th of Last Month. That he was gone to Trotness a place in Sky belonging to Sr Aler McDonald."

The Barrisdale was an unpleasant torture machine, which forced a heavy stone onto the prisoner's chest. Designed by Coll Macdonald of Barrisdale, Capt Fergussone had found it at Barrisdale House in Knoydart.

"This person allso Inform'd of one that was part of the Crew that conducted the Young Pretender to Sky, who being taken Prisoner says that the young Pretender Left South Uist in Womens Cloths accompanied by one Miss McDonald Daughter to Milton & Neil McAuchran of Hobeg in South Uist.

"Sunday the 29th the Boat with the Young Pretender being got Neigh Sr Alexrs House McAuchran went on Shore the Rest Staying in the boat. He Returned in about a Quarter of an hour and ordered the Rest to Disembark. After which the Boat return'd to Benbecula leaving the Young Pretender in Sky." [2]

The person who gave information against O'Neille and Duncan

Campbell, the crew member, was Lachlan MacMhurrich. On 12th July he told Capt Campbell of Skipness that "the Crewes names which fferryd the Pretender to Skye are John Mcdonald Living wt Lauchlan Mcdonald in dremisdale S Uist duncan Campbell Prisoner wt Capt fferguson Rory Mcdonald Prisoner wt Capt Scot Rory Mcdonald Prisoner wt Skipness — Persons names not taken that were carrying off the Pretender's Son John Macdonald who stayes with at the Baily of S Uist, John McVurich in Boranish Uachbrach."[3]

O'Neille was made prisoner two days after he had parted with O'Sullivan and Capt Dumont. He could not have travelled to Raasay, Skye and back again. This whole interlude, widely believed and quoted, was pure fiction. O'Neille never left Benbecula.

Flora told Dr Burton about the French boat and that "O'Sullivan went immediately on board, while O'Neil made haste to find out the Prince before he might have left the island. But finding that the Prince had left the island about two days before, immediately he returned to the place where he had left the cutter. But unhappy for him, he found that timourous Sullivan, having a fair wind, and not having courage to stay till O'Neil's return, being resolved to take care of Number One, obliged the captain to set sail directly, lest he should be taken and should lose his precious life. O'Neil returned in the compass of three hours after Sullivan had set sail, and was taken prisoner soon after."[4]

Flora remembered O'Neille fondly. She was irritated that O'Sullivan should have denied O'Neille the opportunity of escaping. But hers was an unkind assessment of John O'Sullivan's motives.

Capt Fergussone thought that he could still get information from O'Neille, who claimed to be a French officer, though he did not have his commission with him. If accepted as an officer O'Neille would be treated as a prisoner of war, and not as a rebel. O'Neille, however, languishing in the dungeons at Edinburgh Castle, could not resist attacking Capt Fergussone.

O'Neille wrote that he was "brought to Captain Ferguson, who used me with all the barbarity of a pirate, stripped me, and had ordered me to be put into a rack and whipped by his hangman, because I would not confess where I thought the Prince was. As I was just going to be whipped, being already stripped, Lieutenant MacCaghan of the Scotch Fusileers, who commanded a party under Captain Ferguson, very generously opposed this barbarous usage, and coming out with his drawn sword threatened Captain Ferguson that he'd sacrifice himself and his detachment rather than see an officer used after such an infamous manner."[1]

In Skye, Capt John MacLeod of Talisker had remained at Waternish. His three Independent Companies had sailed to Loch Eynort in South Uist on 29th June, the day the Prince had crossed in the opposite direction. Hugh MacDonald of Armadale arrived at Eabost from South Uist, with his militia company, on 5th July. He gave his news to Talisker, and handed over his company's guns. Armadale slipped away home on 6th or 7th July. He and Alexander MacLeod of Ullinish were no longer under military orders.

On 7th July, wrote Capt Anderson, "Capt Ferguson with his Party of about 50 Men imbark'd again in the Cutter (which they had got thro the Long Island to the east Side thereof) and made sail for Sky where they will undoubtedly meet with the Young Pretender if He is not allready got to the Continent." [2]

Another, unnamed account added that "fferguson Immediately Sett out for the isle of Skye in the Cutter & General Campbell followed in the ffurnace as soon as he got the News. fferguson arrived first at Sir Alexanders & the Genl soon after. Lady Margaret was Surpris'd att the business told us most frankly upon our Enquiry that Miss McDonald had dined at her house on sunday the 29th with a good deal of Company, that tho' She pressed her to Stay all night, yet she could not prevail with her, and that She had a man and Maid Servant with her, it appeared to me pretty plain that her lady Ship knew nothing of the Maid's Quality." [5]

Lady Margaret was to write that "This fatell Visitant, Occastioned The Troops Under Genl Campbells Command together with Capt fferguson off the Furnace to Come Here Early off a Morning and Surrounded this small Habitation you may guess my Astonishment when I was Call'd out off Bed at four O'clock, and had my House Surch'd. I must however do Capt fferguson the justice to Say He Show'd all imagineable Civility and allow'd none off his People to Comit the Least Outrage which they were abundently inclin'd too had they gott the Smallest incourragement." [6]

Alexander MacGregor wrote that Capt Fergussone, having left Monkstadt, on meeting a dairymaid at Kingsburgh, invited her on board *Furnace*. "Here the maid was treated with great kindness, and was flattered by receiving several nice presents. Captain Ferguson spoke Gaelic to her, and she thought him the nicest man she had ever seen. She was asked all the country news.

"The poor girl, ignorant as to who her entertainer was, told him, with an air of pride, that she had seen Prince Charles, that he was a night at her master's house, and that his appearance pleased her much." [7]

According to Robert Forbes' account, "Captain John Ferguson

searched Sir Alexander MacDonald's house for the Prince, and in quest of him he came to Kingsburgh, where he examined Kingsburgh and his lady and their daughter, Miss Nanie MacDonald, alias Mrs MacAllaster, for she was married. Kingsburgh told his lady that Captain Ferguson was come to examine her about some lodgers she had lately in her house, and desired her to be distinct in her answers.

"Mrs MacDonald looking Ferguson broad in the face said, 'If Captain Ferguson is to be my judge, then God have mercy upon my soul.'

"Ferguson asked for what reason she spoke such words.

"'Why, Sir,' said she, 'the world belies you if you are not a very cruel, hardhearted man; and indeed I do not like to come through your hands.'

"Ferguson had nothing else to say for himself but the common saying, viz, That people should not believe all that the world says.

"When Ferguson asked Kingsburgh where Miss MacDonald and the person along with her in woman's cloaths lay all night in his house, he answered, 'I know in what room Miss MacDonald herself lay, but where servants are laid when in my house, I know nothing of that matter, I never enquire anything about it. My wife is the properest person to inform you about that.'

"Then he had the impertinence to ask Mrs MacDonald, Whether or not she had laid the young Pretender and Miss MacDonald in one bed?

"To which she answered, 'Sir, whom you mean by the young Pretender I shall not pretend to guess; but I can assure you it is not the fashion in the Isle of Sky to lay the mistress and the maid in the same bed together.'

"Then Ferguson desired to see the different rooms where their late lodgers had slept; and after seeing them he said, it was pretty remarkable that the room in which the maid slept seem'd to look better than the one where the mistress had been laid; and this behoved to confirm him in the belief that it was the young Pretender in woman's cloaths who had been along with Miss MacDonald." [8]

Capt Fergussone had known that the visitor was the Prince in women's clothes, but he had failed to shake the confidence of Kingsburgh and his wife. Lady Kingsburgh, however, in recounting the story to Robert Forbes, had had fourteen months in which to think up her robust and witty answers.

On 8th July Talisker hurried from Waternish to Monkstadt where he wrote that "By the Boat that came yesternight from Harris I had some surmise that the young Pretender had landed in this Country which made me come here early This morning to make all the search about this Surmise that It was possible where I found Capt Ferguson of Furnace before me.

"It is now certain that upon Sunday was eight days he landed not far from this house in disguise along wt Miss McDonald daughter to McDonald of Miltoun or brother sister to the present Miltoun a Gentleman of S.Uist for whose waiting woman and was so sick that she chose to step slowly before up the country. The Young Lady woud by no means accept of a Invitation given her by Lady Margaret to stay all night.

"I have not yett had time to enquire what road they have taken through this Country, but I have sent orders to Castletoun & the officer at Broadford to apprehend the young lady & bring her here." [9]

Talisker was fortunate that his letter, sent to Lord Loudoun, was the first information seen by the Duke of Cumberland.

The Prince had spent two uncomfortable days on Raasay, and had then returned to Portree. He had walked from Portree to Strathaird, with Malcolm MacLeod, disguised as Malcolm's servant. Malcolm delivered the Prince to John Mackinnon of Elgol, and John Mackinnon, the 'old' Laird of Mackinnon. On 4th July the Prince had left Elgol in Mackinnon's boat for the mainland. Malcolm MacLeod had returned to Trotternish, where he told John MacLeod, Raasay's son, what he had done. "The 8 [July] I was going to Kingsborrow, how mett me within a mile of her house, but the Mrs of Kingsborrow, and her daughter, and some women servants with them. So the Mrs of Kingsborrow and I sat near the rod. We began to speak a litle of my servent and master.

"What did we see going by in great haste but six of the McLeods under Sandy McLeod of Balmainach command, who did command a party of the McLeods of Harries near Mogstote. Then as the soldiers was going by, Mrs McDonald asked what news they had. They did answer, Very cold. They had no news. Only that General Campbell and Captain Ferguson landed at Moystote with fifteen hundred soldier with them."

Malcolm MacLeod wrote, "Says I, its time for me to turn." [8]

Whether or not Talisker had guessed that the Prince had passed by Waternish on 29th June, he now had to be seen to act decisively to apprehend Flora. He sent lt Sandy MacLeod off to Sleat to arrest her.

Early on 8th July, General Campbell, off the Isle of Barra, sent Capt Colin Campbell of Skipness and 50 of the Argyll militia ashore, and ordered him to arrest Lady Clanranald. At noon *Furnace* weighed anchor, but ran into a severe gale. Capt Anderson wrote that on 9th July at "12 a Clock General Campbell went on Shoar at Kingsbury where Sr Alexrs Factor Lives . . . but not withstanding that they Did not suspect who was their Guest, being Acquainted with Miss McDonald & McAuchran and the 3rd person pass'd for Miss's Maid by the name of Betty Burk." [2]

Anne MacAlister, in her second account, wrote that "General Campbel came next day, they were all happy to see him, he never asked a single question of her, or of any in the house tho your Father [Ranald MacAlister] was in company all the time he was in the house and accompanied him from the house a good way. He never made a single mention of the Prince's name.

"He said to your grandmother he was realy sorry to see the Distruction that was done everywhere, burning good houses and cornyards which woud be no advantage to Government. She said it was a pity so good a man as he was did not come sooner to prevent these mischiefs. If I had, Mrs McDonald, I would not have allowed a house or cornyard to have been burnt. He passed the day with them set off for Portree in the evening." [10]

Ranald MacAlister, a staunch Whig, and acting as Sir Alexander's Chamberlain in Skye, did his best to repair his father-in-law's indiscretion. His wife's benevolent portrait of General Campbell was tinged with hindsight, for he was to become Duke of Argyll.

Capt Anderson continued that "The same Night we went to Sr Alexr McDonalds House first sent of Capt McNeil & Lieut Hope with about 22 Fuziliers & 14 Argyle Levies with Orders to go to Armadael where Miss McDonald's Father in Law Lives, to Apprehend her & McAuchran if possible.

"The General stay'd all night at Sr Alexanders where we mett Capt Ferguson & Lieut McGachan with the Men they Brought in the Cutter from South Uist." [2]

On 10th July, *Furnace* weighed anchor and sailed to Kilbride, below Monkstadt. General Campbell came on board and *Furnace* sailed north about Trotternish. Next morning it was off Raasay. Here the general met Capt Scott, with his independent command. Capt Anderson wrote that "He after speaking with General Campbell made sail for McKinons Country in Hays Brig; having hear'd that the Younge Adventerour was gone that way which was Allso agreeable to some Information General Campbell had Recvd, & in Consequence thereof Ferguson was to march there allso . . . but as they go by Land it is Possible Capt Scot may get theither before them" [2]

That day, Kingsburgh, on being re-interviewed, admitted that Bettie Bourke had been the Prince. He was hurried to Portree and then out to *Furnace*, where he made a statement to General Campbell that "the young Cheval went from His House Monday June 30th about 2 o'clock in the afternoon in Compy with McAchran to Portree from Portree Mr McDonald is certain they went to Raasay And does not know how they procured a Boat Miss McDonald parted with them at Portree.

"The 2nd or 3rd of July the young Chevalier came from Raasay with Malcolm McLeod who left him in John McKinnon's House in Aird in McKinnon Country."[11] David Campbell added that "Kingsborough Sayes we must not reveal by Information to any person but you, being afraid to be known as such."[12]

With Capt Scott's information, it confirmed General Campbell's plans. He hurriedly sent Capt Fergussone and Kingsburgh back to Skye to Mackinnon country. *Furnace* sailed south towards Sconser.

On 11th July, Capt John MacLeod of Talisker wrote again to Lord Loudoun, concluding that "the Change keeper wt whom they lodged that night, being examined declares that late that Evening the Young Lady came to his house, & that after She had supp'd there came two Gentlemen to the house, on of whom, McAchrin, he knew, the other whom he took to be the Young Lady's Brother after Putting on dry linnens & taking some thing along wt the other Gentleman to supper went to the Door as every Body thought to return again but did not, & has not been seen or heard of.

"However we are now in such a way of getting distinct & pointed information that I hope in a few days to be able to send your Lordship an account of his being taken a thing next to inevitable if he is hitherto upon this Island & if he has left we will in all probability be able to trace out distinctly where he has gone."[13]

Donald Roy MacDonald had been busy since parting with Lt Sandy MacLeod and his guard at Bornaskitaig, on 2nd July. He went to Monkstadt, where he saw Lady Margaret MacDonald, and then Toterome, where he found John MacLeod, Raasay's son. At Camustianovaig he received an unmarked letter from the Prince. Donald Roy returned to the inn at Portree.

On Tuesday, 8th July, having got news that Lt Sandy MacLeod was on the march, Donald Roy left in a hurry. Despite his wounded foot he travelled over 40 miles in two days, and wrote disingenuously that he "happened to be at Armadale when the message came to Miss Flora MacDonald from Donald MacDonald of Castleton (by the contrivance of Taliskar MacLeod), inviting her to come to his house. The Captain was of opinion that Miss should not venture upon complying with any such message at any rate, for that he was afraid there might be a snare laid for her. But when he found her resolved to go, he desired her to deliver up to him the letter which Armadale had sent along with her to his wife in the way of a passport, and in favour of Bettie Burk, alleging it was to no purpose (except a bad one) to carry that along with her whatever might turn out to be the matter. She acknowledged the wisdom of the advice, and accordingly delivered up the letter to him." [8]

Capt Donald MacDonald of Castleton, commanding an Independent Company in Sleat, based at Kinlochnadale, wrote that on "9th in the evening I received a letter from Talisker of 8th from Mugstote with orders to apprehend Miss MacDonald Milton's Daughter, which was executed." [16] On 10th July Castleton sent a message to Armadale, inviting Flora to call on him.

Flora told Dr Burton that "About eight or ten days after, she received a message from one of her own name, Donald MacDonald of Castleton in Sky, who lived about four miles from Slate or Armadale, to come to his house, an officer of an Independent Company (one MacLeod of Talisker) having desired him so to do.

"She, a little suspicious of what might happen, thought proper to consult some of her friends what she should do in the matter. They unanimously agreed she ought not to go, at least till next day; but go she would. Then she was instructed what to say upon an examination; and accordingly, when that happened, she said she had seen a great lusty woman, who came to the boatside as she was going on board and begged to have a passage, saying she was a soldier's wife. Her request was granted, and when she landed in Sky, she went away, thanking Miss for her favour. Miss added withal that she knew nothing of what became afterwards."

With all the innocent courage of a heroine in a romantic novel, Flora parted with Donald Roy, and left Armadale.

"Miss set forwards, as she proposed, to her friend's house, whither she had been desired to come, and on the road she met her father (Armadale) returning home; and soon after she was taken by an officer and party of soldiers, who were going to her mother's house in pursuit of her." [4]

Flora never told anyone about what passed at her meeting with her stepfather. Armadale had taken his time in returning home. He had landed at Eabost on 5th July, and had left there before 8th July. The officer who arrested Flora was Lt Sandy MacLeod, whom she had so successfully prevented from searching her boat at Monkstadt. He had travelled over 60 miles in two days to find her.

Flora was taken to Kinlochnadale where she was interviewed.

Castleton wrote to his chief, Sir Alexander MacDonald, that "I examined the Girl concerning what passengers came in the same boat with her, She told me there were none in the boat, besides the crew, but herself, & Neil MacEachin son to MacEachin of Howmore, and a young woman who called herself Bettie Bourk;

"That this Bettie Bourk told her in Benbecula, That She was one of those Irish persons ordered to be transported to America, and was landed in Lewis and made her escape, and was a married woman and was told that her husband was in the Isle of Sky, and begged that She (Miss Macdonald) would be so good as give her passage which she consented to.

"That upon their landing at Mugstot, Bettie Bourke went off, but that she did not know whither, neither had she seen her since that time which was Sunday 29th June.

"She said she never saw the young Pretender, tho she often heard of that person, and had been told of his being in different places; & that since she came to Sky heard he had been in Strath.

"I advised her to be ingenuous and to tell the whole truth and that it would fare be better wt her. She answered that she knew no more. This was all I could get from her. But when she meetes General Campbell I hope more can be made of her." [15] Flora stuck to her story, concocted by Donald Roy, but Castleton did not believe it.

This same day, 10th July, Castleton received further information that Neil MacEachen had crossed to Morar, and sent Capt MacNeill after him. He also wrote of the Prince that "I hope a little time shall discover whither he went, and it is the general report that person has left this Island, but by what passage I have not yet learned with any certainty, tho it is said to be by the Aird of Strath, but pretty certain I am that he came not to Sleate." [8]

Flora told Dr Burton that she was "taken by an officer and party of soldiers, who were going to her mother's house in pursuit of her. They carried her on board ship, and would not suffer her to return home to take leave of her friends." [4]

Robert Forbes added that, having been seized "Immediately Miss Flora was hurried on board of a sloop of war without being allowed the priviledge of taking leave of her mother, or telling her anything of the matter, or taking along with her one stitch to change another." [10]

Flora had probably spent the night at Kinlochnadale. Castleton did not treat her harshly, but he did not allow her to return to Armadale. Castleton was the brother of Flora, Lady Kingsburgh, and was a neighbour of Flora at Armadale. He wrote that "I sent my Ensign and a party with her to Talisker." [15] Next day Flora set off for Monkstadt with Lt Sandy MacLeod, and Castleton's ensign, Donald MacLeod of Mill.

Travelling north through Skye the party met Capt Fergussone, heading south into Mackinnon country. Capt Fergussone took charge of Flora, and retraced his steps to Sconser where a boat could carry the party to *Furnace*, which was expected off Raasay. Flora told Dr Burton that "she was carried on board the *Furnace*, commanded by Captain John Ferguson, a sloop of war where General Campbell happened then to be, who orderd Miss MacDonald to be used with the utmost respect." [4]

Capt Anderson noted that "The same evening Miss MacDonald was Brought on Board the *Furnace* having been taken by a Party of McLeod of Tallesker's Men at Her fathers House, At the request of Captn Ferguson & the party the General sent with him to Sky.

"Capt Ferguson after Delivering Miss McDonald on board went again to Portree in the Cutter to search McKinnons Country." [2]

Capt Scott had parted with General Campbell earlier on 11th July, and wrote that he was "going with my Brigantine to Armiedale.

"I am sorry to be obliged to suspect those who Eat His Majesty's Bread Should not be true to their Trust but I fear my suspicions are too true and you will see by the Enclosed from South Uist that theres comp to believe it. also I have it by other people that the Skye Militia and inhabitants are not the most faithful of His Majestys Scotts subjects; among the very few who have not stray'd from allegiance."

Capt Scott sailed through the narrows at Kylerhea to Isle Oronsay. He wrote that "I got here to Anchor and landed and March'd forth with to the House of Armiedale where we found Nothing Flora Macdonald having been taken the day before and was carryd away to Major General Campbell.

"On my arrivall att Armidale the laird was within half a mile of Hiss own House but did not choose to be seen by me, Whither as the old saying, Guilty Conference needs no accuse, be the case with him or not I Can't Say." [16]

On Saturday 12th July, on board *Furnace*, Flora was brought before General Campbell. She gave an honest account of all that had happened to her. Flora stated that O'Neille had proposed the scheme and that Lady Clanranald had helped to prepare the dress for the Prince. Both had been made prisoner. She also mentioned Lady Clanranald's cook, John Maclean, who had also been detained. Flora introduced McAchran — Neil MacEachen — for the first time, when landing at Monkstadt, but did not say who he was. Neil was safely on the mainland.

Flora protected Lady Margaret by taking responsibility for sending for Donald Roy MacDonald, and protected Kingsburgh by stating that it was her idea to call at the house, and that it was her sickness which caused the party to spend the night at Kingsburgh house. Flora concluded that the Prince "took His leave of Miss & went out with Donald McDonald but who after seeing him to the Boat Return'd. She thinks the Pretender went to Raasay but after leaving him at Portree Miss McDonald does not know what became of him."

When cross questioned Flora added that "Milton went with Lady Clan to see them off & that Her father in law hearing of Her having engag'd to go along with the Pretender advis'd Her very much against it, she ask'd Her Father in law for a Pass which he gave specifying it was for His Daughter & an Irish Girl Her servant, this Pass McDonald Baylie of Benbecula saw." [17] Flora protected her stepfather to the last.

Meanwhile, Donald Roy wrote that "the day after Miss MacDonald was made prisoner Captain Roy MacDonald was careful to deliver up the above letter into Armadale's own hands, who immediately destroyed it, By this time Donald Roy had destroyed the Prince's letter to himself, and Lady Margaret's letter to the Prince, not knowing what might happen. Armadale, immediately upon Miss MacDonald's being made prisoner, began a skulking, because a report had gone about that he had given a pass to her, though it consisted with his knowledge that the young pretender was in company with her in disguise as a woman servant. General Campbell upon this account was much in search of honest and brave Armadale, being not a little chagrined that Armadale should have outwitted him, to say no more of it.

"When Miss MacDonald was made the captive lady, Donald Roy MacDonald was obliged likewise to go a skulking, the cripple foot notwithstanding, information having been given against him that he had been with the Young Pretender at Portree." [8]

On 10th July, at Fort Augustus, the Duke of Cumberland had received the first information from Capt MacLeod of Talisker that the Prince had crossed to Skye. The Duke wrote to General Campbell and Commodore Smith congratulating them on their vigilance in pursuing the Prince to Skye. "I send Captain Hodson one of my Aide Camp that I may be better imformed how he be taken or kill'd in the attempt & desire you'll let him know all that concern it & trust him as one that come from me ... Sir Alexander Macdonald goes with Capt Hodson." [18]

Capt Hodgson went on board *Furnace* on the evening of 12th July. Sir Alexander wrote from Portree to the Duke of Cumberland at midnight that "in rideing a few Miles I was inform'd of the pretender's whole Progress since he landed in the Iland." [19]

On 13th July, the Duke of Cumberland wrote again, commending General Campbell for the "Diligence you have used in tracing the pretenders son. You will use all possible Means to prevent anybody getting off from the Island.

"You will take Care of what Prisoners you have taken & put them under that of Commodore Smith, when you may separate. O'Neil may be of use . . . You have done very well to secure Lady Clan Ranold, & you will upon leaving that Country dispose of her as you may judge her Behaviour may require, & that People may know & feel that it is not altogether indifferent whether they support & assist the rebels or not. I send you a copy of the proclamation I have ordered to be published." [20]

The proclamation announced that "whosoever shall harbour, conceal resort to or keep company with Any Person or Persons who have notoriously been engaged in the Rebellion or with any Persons in disguise without giving immediate Notice of such Persons to the nearest officer of His Majesty's or Party of the Kings Troops, shall be treated as Rebells, by burning their Houses seizing or destroying their Effects, driving their Cattle & the utmost rigore exercised against their Persons, of which all People are to take notice." [21]

Anne MacAlister wrote that "The Duke of Cumberland gave orders to burn the house at Kingh and take up the cattle. Sir Alexander told him that woud be a greater loss to him than to Kingsborrow, that he had the whole management of his Estate and had *not cleared with him for two years*. I shall go myself and bring him here and deliver him up to your royal Highness. There was a small party came with Sir Alexander and Kingsborrow met them at Sconser." [10]

On 13th July Sir Alexander MacDonald came on board *Furnace* with Kingsburgh. Whereas Flora had truthfully admitted to the general her part in the Prince's escape, Kingsburgh had pretended not to know whom the stranger had been. Despite all his valiant words, as the prospect of imprisonment loomed, so Kingsburgh's nerve failed. He gave evidence against others who had assisted the Prince, and finally admitted that he had only helped the Prince because the latter had been in such a miserable physical condition.

The general treated Kingsburgh courteously, protecting him as best he could, and wrote a letter to the Duke of Cumberland stating that the Young Pretender had "got from Sky to the Continent the 4th of this month . . . I have hinted to Capt Hudson several things I observed, with some that I suspect of being Wanting in their duty." [22]

Capt Hodgson, Sir Alexander and Kingsburgh set off for Fort Augustus, which they reached on 17th July. When Kingsburgh arrived, freely riding his horse, the Duke of Cumberland was furious. He added in a postscript to the Duke of Newcastle in London that "Since I had finished my letter, Captain Hodgson & Sir Alexander MacDonald are returned from the isle of Skye & given me but a bad account of the pretender's Son's Escape, who was conceald at Sir Alexr MacDonald's Chief Factor's House 'till they got him safely conveyed to the mainland of Scotland, where we have him left to hunt. I hope to God that they may take him; for else this Country never will be quiet."

He enclosed General Campbell's letter and "the Deposition of the girl who accompanied him ... In the meantime I have seized the Harbourer." [23]

Kingsburgh was thrown into the common gaol and shackled.

The Duke of Cumberland left Fort Augustus on 18th July, and made a rapid journey to London, where he received a rapturous welcome. Command of the army in Scotland passed to the Earl of Albemarle.

General Campbell wrote to Lord Albemarle that "I am afraid it will appear that many have been employ'd who are very unworthy. Hugh McDonald of Armadael, one of the Militia Captains, and Stepfather to Miss McDonald my Prisoner, has escaped me & gone off, I discover'd Him to have been very active in the Young Pretenders Escape, and was so indiscreet as to give His Daughter a Pass for Herself, and one said to be an Irish Girle Her Servant, this villain met me in South Uist, and had the impudence to advice me against making so close a search, and that if I should for Some days a little desist. He made no doubt of my Success I suspected Him at the time, & have given it in charge to the officers in Skye to apprehend Him, plainly telling some of them, that if he was not taken, I should have reason to suspect them likewise." [24]

General Campbell knew that the Young Pretender had left Skye and had crossed to the mainland, and yet he turned away, because *Furnace* needed to be resupplied. The morning's gale moderated into hazy weather, and at 1pm, on 13th July, *Furnace* set sail. At 7pm *Furnace* anchored in Gairloch, one mile from the Laird's house.

CHAPTER 9

Flora a Prisoner

*Be careful to make all your conduct of a piece. Be not
frighten'd by the thoughts of your present circumstances either to say or do anything that may in the
least tend to contradict or sully the character you are
now mistress of, and which you can never be robbed of
but by yourself. Never once pretend (Through an ill
judg'd excess of caution and prudence) to repent or be
ashamed of what you have done.*
— Capt Felix O'Neille

Flora began her imprisonment on board *Furnace* on 11th July. On 12th
July she was interviewed by General Campbell, and the following day
Furnace sailed. In the evening the ship anchored in Gairloch, 25 miles
north of Applecross Bay and 40 miles from Sconser in Skye.

Flora was well treated by General Campbell, but was no longer able
to influence the fate of the Prince. She had ample time to consider what
might become of herself. Other prisoners on board were treated much
less kindly. In a harsh age, the prisoners were confined below decks
without bedding, and allowed out on deck only for one hour a day.

On 17th July *Furnace* sailed out of Gairloch, and next morning
passed Ruadh Reidh to cruise in the entrance of Loch Broom. On 19th
July supplies were transferred on board. A boat from South Uist found
Furnace and delivered some prisoners. They had been sent by Capt
Colin Campbell of Skipness. He wrote asking what should be done
with Lady Clanranald, and General Campbell ordered him to leave a
trusted officer to guard her.

One of the prisoners was Capt Felix O'Neille. Robert Forbes
collected a series of 'Remarks etc, and particular sayings of some who
were concerned in the Prince's preservation', in July 1747. He recorded
a meeting between Felix O'Neille and Flora. The account of the
meeting had been given by O'Neille, while he was a prisoner at
Edinburgh Castle, and had been retold by someone else. The story bore
the marks of having been improved with telling.

"When Miss MacDonald was a prisoner she happened in coursing
about from place to place to fall in luckily with Captain O'Neil, then a

prisoner likewise, to whom she made up, and giving him a gentle slap upon the cheek with the loof of her hand, said, 'To that black face do I owe all my misfortune.'

"The captain with a smile replied, 'Why, Madam, what you call your misfortune is truly your greatest honour. And if you be careful to demean yourself agreeably to the character you have already acquired, you will in the event find it to be your happiness.'

"She told him she was much afraid they designed to carry her to London, which she could not think of but with the utmost uneasiness, not knowing what might turn out to be the consequence.

"Upon this O'Neil told her that he would take upon him to commence prophet in the case, and to foretell what would happen to her.

"'For,' said he, 'if you are carried to London I can venture to assure you it will be for your interest and happiness; and instead of being afraid of this you ought to wish for it. There you will meet with much respect and very good and great friends for what you have done.

"'Only be careful to make all your conduct of a piece. Be not frighten'd by the thoughts of your present circumstances either to say or do anything that may in the least tend to contradict or sully the character you are now mistress of, and which you can never be robbed of but by yourself. Never once pretend (Through an ill judg'd excess of caution and prudence) to repent or be ashamed of what you have done, and I dare take upon me to answer for the rest.

"'I do not think (added he) that the Government can be so very barbarous and cruel as to bring you to a trial for your life, and therefore I hope you have nothing to fear, and that things will happen to you as I have said.'"

Whether or not Felix O'Neille made this stirring speech, and it certainly had his style, Flora deserved to have it addressed to her.

"Captain O'Neil was wont to tell those who visited him in the Castle of Edinburgh that he had been at the same pains as a parent would be with a child to lay down rules to Miss MacDonald for her future behaviour under the misfortune of being a prisoner, and that it gave him infinite pleasure to find that things had happened to her hitherto according to his words, and to hear by all the accounts he could learn that she had sacredly observed the advices he had given her. He frequently expressed his heartiest wishes that she might get free of all her troubles, and arrive at that which so justly she deserved."[1]

Felix O'Neille had claimed that he had offered to marry Flora, at their meeting at Unasary in South Uist. He was much taken with her, when they were both at Nunton, before the Prince escaped from

Benbecula. Flora had resisted O'Neille's demand to accompany the Prince to Skye, but she had been relieved to see him on board *Furnace*, and her playful slap may have indicated more than mere friendship.

Flora and O'Neille remained prisoners together for another ten days, but then were never to meet again. Felix O'Neille, once Flora became a national heroine, enjoyed the reflected glory of having acted as parent to a famous child.

On 24th July, at Monkstadt, Lady Margaret MacDonald wrote to Duncan Forbes of Culloden, that "your Lordship can't yet be a Stranger to the trouble which has been lately brought upon this Island by the indiscretion of a foolish Girl, with whom the unhappy disturber of this Kingdom landed at this place; tho' I cannot but look on myself and family as peculiarly favoured by Heaven, in drawing that unlucky Visitant so quickly away from the place of his landing, that there was no room for considering Him as a Person in Disguise; far less my knowing anything of it."[2]

On the same day Lady Margaret wrote to John MacKenzie of Delvine that "The News off the Pretender having Landed at this Place which had like to give Me a good dell of trouble, Millton's Sisr from South Uist, who I never Saw, but once, thought fitt to bring him from that Country in disguise, She had not just Asurence Enough to Bring her To this House, but came by Here Self And dind Here, Among a Croud which luckily for Me was Here that day She went off after dinner, but sent her Servt Betty, Emediately upon his landing, Along with a fellow She had with her to King[sbu]r[g] where they intruded themselves that night."[3]

Lady Margaret wrote that she had met Flora only once before, which contradicted the tradition that Flora was a particular friend of Sir Alexander and Lady Margaret, and that Flora had lived at Monkstadt for nine months. Lady Margaret described Flora as a foolish girl, when Flora landed on her door step, and yet Lady Margaret had been willing enough to send information, money and her husband's shirts to the Prince at a distance. Flora had done all she could, in her declaration, to protect Lady Margaret. Lady Margaret now showed no concern for Flora. She lied about not "knowing anything of it."

Lady Margaret continued that "I must, at the same time, not only look upon myself, but the whole Country, as greatly suffering from the hurt it is likely he has done to the Man into whose House he intruded himself that night; I mean Kingsborrow; a man well known for his singular honesty, integrity and prudence, in all occurancies of Life, before that unhappy night; a man of such consequence, and so well lik'd in this Country, that if the Pretender's Son had done no other hurt to it but the ruining this single Man, it could not but render him odious to their posterity." [3]

It had been Lady Margaret, in a panic, who had asked Kingsburgh to join the Prince, and he had done so willingly, even joyfully. Kingsburgh had felt honoured to be able to invite the Prince to stay in his house. Neither Flora nor the Prince had intruded themselves upon him.

Lady Margaret begged Duncan Forbes to plead for Kingsburgh "both on account of his own Merit, and the use he is of in Sir Alexrs Affairs," and added that "The gypsy that brought that unwelcomed guest to this country is taken up and on board the Furnace." [3]

Lady Margaret had enjoyed being a Jacobite at a distance, but when she was faced with having the Prince in her own house, she had panicked. Her condemnation of Flora, as a gypsy, was despicable; condemnation for a young woman who had protected her so gallantly. Lady Margaret never forgave Flora for the part she played in bringing the Prince to Skye, or for the fame that Flora later acquired.

Lady Margaret's letter was directed to her husband at Fort Augustus.

Sir Alexander wrote to Duncan Forbes that "One thing I will venture to give you a minute detail of; the misfortune of Kingsborrow, now sent a prisoner to Edinr. When the young Pretender made his unhappy visit to Skye, from South Uist, in a small boat, he landed near my house, in woman's clothes, by way of being maid servant to one Florence Macdonald, a Girl of Clanranald's family, now a prisoner with General Campbell. Miss Macdonald went and made a visit to Lady Margaret, dined with her, and put her into the utmost distress by telling her of the Cargo that she had brought from Uist. She called on Kingsborrow, who was at Mugstot, accidentally, and they had a very confused consultation together; and it was agreed to hurry him off the Country as fast as possible."

At least Sir Alexander was honest about Lady Margaret's knowledge of the whole affair.

"So they went to Kingsborrow's house, where he lay that night; and he furnished him a horse to carry him seven miles next day to Portree. There he found, accidently, a small Rasay boat, into which he put foot and disappeared all at once."

"Kingsborrow chose to come to this place ... On arriving here, the Duke ordered Sir Everard Fawkener to examine him; and since, he has been confined and now sent to Edinr. I used my little Rhetoric with the Duke; but he stopt my mouth by saying, that this man had neglected the greatest piece of Service that could have been done; and if he was to be pardoned, you have too much good sense to think this the proper time; as it would encourage others to follow his example.

"I need not tell your Lordship how much I am concerned for the man's misfortune; nor need I beg your assistance in a thing I have so much at heart as the Safety of this man, because I have always found you friendly in everything that concerns me."

Sir Alexander added that "Along with this is a scrawl from my Wife, who does not know that her name has been mentioned." ²

Sir Alexander showed genuine concern for his friend Kingsburgh. It passed through his mind that Kingsburgh was suffering in his place. What would Sir Alexander have done if he had not been at Fort Augustus with the Duke of Cumberland, but at Monkstadt with his wife on 29th June?

Furnace returned to Skye waters, but then contrary winds prevented her from passing through the narrows at Kyle. *Furnace* reached Glenelg on 24th July. General Campbell called at Bernera Barrack, where he learned that the Duke of Cumberland had left Ft Augustus for London. Next day *Furnace* crossed to Isle Oronsay, on the Skye side of the sound. The weather turned foul, with gales from the north west. Here the general found Capt Campbell of Skipness, who had crossed from South Uist with the remainder of his men, and more prisoners.

Flora told Dr Burton that "About three weeks afterwards, Miss, in cruising about, being near her stepfather's house, the General permitted her to go ashore and take leave of her friends, but under a guard of two officers and a party of soldiers, with strict orders that she was not to speak anything in Erse, or anything at all but in the presence and in the hearing of the officers. And therefore she stayed only about two hours, and then returned again to the ship." ⁴

Furnace was storm bound at Isle Oronsay on 25th and 26th July, and it was on one of these days that Flora was allowed ashore. She travelled the six miles to Armadale house, where she saw her mother, 16 or 17 days after she had been made prisoner.

Robert Forbes recorded that "It was Miss MacDonald's good fortune to be soon removed out of the hands of Ferguson into those of the polite and generous Commodore Smith, who in the coursing around, obtained leave of General Campbell to allow Miss to go ashore to visit her mother and to seek a servant to attend her in the state of confinement. Then it was that poor Kate MacDonald generously made an offer to run all risques with the captive lady, who gladly accepted." ⁴

Flora did not join Commodore Smith on *Eltham* until 13th August, and that ship did not cruise past Armadale.

On 27th July *Furnace* weighed anchor and next morning was at Canna, and the following day in Loch nan Uamh. On 31st July *Furnace* rounded the Point of Ardnamurchan and sailed down the Sound of

Mull. At 11am on 1st August *Furnace* came to in Horseshoe Bay, in a spectacular setting between the island of Kerrera and the mainland, a mile south of Oban. Already at anchor were *Eltham*, *Looe* and *Glasgow*. General Campbell found Commodore Smith on board *Eltham*.

Flora was to be transferred from *Furnace* to the commodore's more spacious *Eltham*, but it was not to sail for several days. On 1st August General Campbell wrote to Neil Campbell, Captain of Dunstaffnage, in command of a garrison in the ancient castle at the mouth of Loch Etive.

"Make my compliments to your Lady and tell her that I am obliged to desire the favour of her for some days to receive a very pritty young Rebell; her zeal and the perswasion of those who ought to have given her better advice, have drawn her into a most unhappy scrape, by assisting the younge Pretender to make his escape. I need say nothing further till we meet ... I suppose you have heard of Miss Flora McDonald." On the reverse the general added, "If Dunstaffnage is not home, his Lady is desired to open this letter." [6]

Flora welcomed being sent to Dunstaffnage. The huge castle, sitting on a massive pillow of conglomerate, had thick, high walls built by the MacDougalls in the 13th century. The castle passed to the earls and dukes of Argyll, who had appointed an hereditary keeper. In 1685 the castle had been burned, but during the 1715 Rising it had been garrisoned. In 1725 the Captain of Dunstaffnage had built himself a small dwelling inside the crumbling courtyard. In 1745 the castle was once more garrisoned. A later visitor wrote that "the portion of (the castle) which was habitable was very limited, situated on the north side of the interior square, consisting of a sitting room and bedroom; and, on the east side, were some habitable bedrooms, over hanging the battlements, to which you ascended by a circular stair." [7] These latter rooms were in the tall tower that stood over the gateway.

In July, when the Duke of Cumberland first heard that the Young Pretender had crossed to Skye, he wrote to General Campbell that "O'Neil may be of use, and you will endeavour to draw from him all the Information you can for preventing the Escape of the Persons you are in Search after. He must be well instructed where the French Vessells, which are sent to take them off, will chiefly endeavour to lay themselves in their Way." [5]

Felix O'Neille, however, knew as little about the French plans to recover the Prince, as anyone else. General Campbell received two declarations from O'Neille, but did not learn anything further about what the Young Pretender might do in the future.

General Campbell wrote to Lord Albemarle that O'Neille claimed to be a French officer, but did not have his commission. "All I can say of Him further, is, that He seems to be a person acquainted with Service, & to have what the french call du Monde, your Lordsp from Examining Him will be best able to Judge what treatment he merits." [8]

On 5th August Capt O'Neille, in company with Capt Lachlan MacNeil, who had found him in Benbecula, set off for Fort William and Fort Augustus.

Next day Lord Albemarle replied to the general that O'Neille had arrived "& I believe him a Dangerous Man." [9] General Campbell wrote again to Lord Albemarle on 8th August that "I thought it better to send Oneil to your Lordsp than to London, thinking it not impossible but that something might appear against him, which might entitle Him to the fate of Belew." [10]

Lt de Belieu had landed in Gairloch from the *Bien Trouve*, to search for the Prince. An Irishman, said to have been in the French army, he had changed into highland dress, and had been captured. Unfortunately for him, he was recognised by his captors, who had served in Flanders, as having been a spy in the British camp at the battle of Fontenoy in May 1745. De Belieu was hanged at Fort William.

On 11th August Lord Albemarle, who had taken a statement from O'Neille, wrote to General Campbell that "Capt ONeille is not hanged but sent to Inverness till His Majestys Pleasure is known. He is a handsome, sensible man, & upon his being examined here, has told me much the same thing as he has to you." [11]

Capt Felix O'Neil had charmed his way past Lord Albemarle. O'Neille was sent to Inverness and then to Edinburgh Castle, where he remained until July 1747. He eventually returned to France.

On Wednesday, 13th August *Eltham* was ready to sail. General Campbell wrote to Dunstaffnage that "You will deliver to the bearer, John McLeod, Miss Mcdonald, to be conducted her[e] in his wherry; Having no officer to send, it would be very proper you send one of your Garrison alongst with her." [12]

Flora, with Kate MacDonald her maid, went on board *Eltham*, but contrary winds kept the ship storm bound in Horseshoe Bay. On 15th August General Campbell disembarked from *Furnace*, with Capt George Anderson, his aide de camp, his servants, and soldiers, and was given an eleven gun salute by *Eltham*.

Next day, at Dunstaffnage, Angus MacDonald of Milton made a declaration to General Campbell that he had accompanied Lady Clanranald to Rossinish, where he had met the Young Pretender and O'Neille. He also admitted to having been taken by young

Clanranald to meet the Prince at Arisaig, when the latter had first landed in Scotland and "press'd Him strongly to Join Him in bearing Arms for the Young Pretender which he absolutely refus'd nor ever did bear Arms against the Government." [13] Milton's declaration secured his release, for he was not shipped to London.

On 18th August General Campbell delivered "all our Prisoners of note over to Commodore Smith in Order to their being sent to London."

There were 26 names. Ranald MacDonald of Clanranald headed the list. From South Uist the general had collected Ranald MacDonald of Torlum, Bailie of Benbecula; Ranald MacEachen, brother of Neil; Donald MacLeod of Galtrigill, the Prince's pilot; Charles MacEachen in Peninerin; Lachlan MacMhurrich; Duncan Campbell and Roderick MacDonald, boatmen; Angus MacAulay and John MacDonald "two Boy's servants to the Baylie of Benbicula Evidences against their Master."; John Maclean, Clanranald's cook; Alexander MacDonald of Boisdale; Allan MacDonald and Alexander Forrester, Priests; Ranald MacDonald of Garryfluich. Other prisoners were Francis MacDonald, taken in Ireland; Duncan Mackenzie; John MacDonald, brother of the Bailie of Benbecula; Alexander MacDonald of Garigole; Francis Bower, "a papist Teacher of Children", and Hugh MacDonald.

The priests had been seperated from the others and put on board *Hound*, and Clanranald had been put alone on *Looe*, but the others had stayed on board *Furnace*.

From Skye the general had collected the old Laird of Mackinnon; John Mackinnon of Elgol and Malcolm MacLeod. James Stewart, "a nattural Brother of Ardshiels" had been picked up in Appin. He was later to be hanged for the murder of Colin Campbell of Glenure.

The 26th prisoner was "Miss Flora McDonald of Milton made Prisoner for having carryd off the Pretenders Son, as her Servant in Womans Apparell. Her Declaration was sent to His Royal Highness the Duke but she further says that Her father in law Hugh McDonald gave Her a Pass to protect Her and Her pretended Servant from the Kings Troops and that He wrote a Letter to His lady recommending His Daughter in Laws pretended Servant to Her favour and protection. This person was sent after but made His Escape." [14]

General Campbell added, to Lord Albemarle, that "by the inclosed list of Prisoners I have deliver'd over to Commodore Smith to be sent to England, it appears that Lady Clanronald has not only been very zealous her Self in serving and assisting the young Pretender while in the Long Island, but has also brought Her Husband and Several others into the same Scrape, for which reason I think she ought to be sent to London." [15] The Duke of Cumberland had commended General Campbell on securing Lady Clanranald, and Lord Albemarle agreed that she should be sent to London. General Campbell ordered one of Commodore Smith's ships to collect her, on its way through the Minch.

Furnace sailed from Horseshoe Bay on 21st August. At 7am next day *Eltham* weighed anchor and sailed with *Looe* into the Sound of Mull. On 23rd August *Eltham* was in the Minch and was joined by *Raven*. In the evening the ships were between the Shiants and Eilean Glass, the isle of Scalpay in Harris. Next morning they were joined by *Serpent*.

At 8am on 26th August *Eltham* anchored in Carston Roads, outside Stromness harbour, and below the bulk of Hoy, in the Orkney Isles.

Furnace and *Greyhound* sailed on 31st August, and *Looe* and *Tryton* in early September. *Furnace* reached Leith on 4th September, and sailed south towards the Thames. On 3rd October Capt Fergussone noted that at "10 AM sent the prisoners to Tilbury fort in the Russell Tender." [16]

Eltham received on board 19 evidences against Sir James Stewart, an Orkney Jacobite. Severe gales hit the islands, and it was only at 2am on 14th September that *Eltham*, with *Serpent*, *Hound* and the *Union* cutter, sailed through Scapa Flow, and east through "Hamsound" between the mainland of Orkney and Burray, passing Lamb Holm.

Flora a prisoner at Leith

At 10pm on 15th September *Eltham* anchored in Leith Roads, where Commodore Smith found *Bridgewater*, commanded by Capt Charles Knowler. On 19th September the Commodore's pennant was moved to *Bridgewater*, and two days later the log recorded "sent on board the Bridgewater 23 Evidences & Miss McDonald." [17] On 21st September *Eltham* sailed from Leith and reached the Nore on 6th October. *Bridgewater* remained at Leith.

Leith was a prosperous port two miles north east of the city of Edinburgh. It lay on the south shore of the Firth of Forth as it opened out into the North Sea. From Leith Roads looking southwards the castle was clearly visible, perched on its rock. The old town with its spires and tall houses marched down the High Street towards Holyrood Palace, lost behind Calton Hill. Rising from Holyrood Park, Salisbury Crag and Arthur's Seat dominated the city. At Leith, and beyond in

Edinburgh, smoke coiled into the air, giving the city its nick name "Auld Reekie". Flora had never before seen so many houses nor so much smoke.

Robert Forbes collected several stories about Flora's time at Leith.

"While she was in Road of Leith, from the beginning of September to the 7th of November, she never was allowed to set her foot once on shore, though in other respects the officers were extremely civil and complaisant to her, and took it exceedingly well when any persons came to visit her. Sometimes they were so obliging as to come ashore for good company to attend her, and frequently declared that if they knew any person to come on board out of curiosity and not out of respect for Miss MacDonald, that person should not have access to her.

"Commodore Smith [Commander of the *Eltham*] behaved like a father to her, and tendered her many good advices as to her behaviour in her ticklish situation; and Captain Knowler of the *Bridgewater* used her with the utmost decency and politeness. When company came to visit her she was indulged the privilege by both these humane and well bred gentlemen to call for anything on board as if she had been at her own fireside, and the servants of the cabin were obliged to give her all manner of attendance; and she had liberty to invite any of her friends to dine with her when she pleased.

"Her behaviour in company was so easy, modest, and well adjusted that every visitant was much surprized; for she had never been out of the islands of South Uist and Sky till about a year before the Prince's arrival that she had been in the family of MacDonald of Largie in Argyllshire for the space of ten or eleven months; and during her confinement she had been all along on board a ship of war till she went to London.

"Some that went on board to pay their respects to her, used to take a dance in the cabin, and to press her much to share with them in the diversion. But with all their importunity they could not prevail with her to take a trip. She told them that at present her dancing days were done, and she would not readily entertain a thought of that diversion till she would be assured of the prince's safety, and perhaps not till she should be bless'd with the happiness of seeing him again. Although she was easy and cheerful, yet she had a certain mixture of gravity in all her behaviour which became her situation exceedingly well, and set her off to great advantage.

"She is of low stature, of a fair complexion and well enough shap'd. One could not discern by her conversation that she had spent all her former days in the Highlands; for she talks English (or rather Scots) easily, and not at all through the Earse tone. She has a sweet voice and sings well; and no lady, Edinburgh bred, can acquit herself better at the tea table than what she did when in Leith Road.

"Her wise conduct in one of the most perplexing scenes that can happen in life, her fortitude and good sense, are memorable instances of the strength of a female mind, even in those years that are tender and unexperienced. She is the delight of her friends and the envy of her enemies." [18]

"When Miss MacDonald was on board the *Bridgewater* in Leith Road, accounts had come that the prince was taken prisoner, and one of the officers had brought the news of this report on board. She got an opportunity of talking privately to some who were then visiting her, and said with tears in her eyes, 'Alas, I am afraid that now all is in vain that I have done. The Prince at last is in the hands of his enemies.' Though at that time great fear was entertained about the truth of this account, yet those that were with Miss MacDonald endeavoured all they could to cheer her up, and to dissuade her from believing any such thing. But still fears haunted her mind till the matter was cleared up and the contrary appeared." [18]

On 5th September two French ships *L'Heureux* and *Prince de Conti* sailed into Loch Boisdale. When they reached Loch nan Uamh, no one knew where the Prince was. Eventually he was located, 50 miles east on Ben Alder, with Cluny MacPherson and Cameron of Lochiel. The Prince made his way back across the Great Glen, and arrived at Borrodale on 19th September. The Prince, with a large number of his followers, including Neil MacEachen, went on board the French ships. Soon after midnight, on the morning of 20th September, the ships sailed out into the Minch. Nine days later they sighted the French coast, and the Prince went ashore at Roscoff.

On 23rd September a report, that the Young Pretender had got away, reached Edinburgh. Lord Albemarle asked Commodore Smith if the Navy might intercept the ships, and in a letter to the Duke of Newcastle, concluded that "I am of opinion that they mean to carry off the Pretender's son and give us no further trouble for the present." [19]

At the end of October Catherine Stewart, of the Dalguise family, wrote to her cousin Miss Mercer that "I was seeing Miss MacDonald but the Captain was much in the Cabin with us so I could not get much talking with her she only told me that the Prince was very well when she left him & that at the partin he said he hoped yet to reward her at Saint James I wish to God how soon that may happen." [20]

When Flora was telling the ladies of the sea crossing to Skye "some of them with raptures cried out: 'O Miss, what a happy creature are you who had that dear Prince to lull you asleep, and to take care of you with his hands spread about your head, when you was sleeping! You are surely the happiest woman in the world!'

" 'I could,' says one of them, [Miss Mary Clerk] 'wipe your shoes with pleasure, and think it my honour so to do, when I reflect that you had the honour to have the Prince for your handmaid. We all envy you greatly.'

"Much about this time a lady of rank and dignity, [Lady Mary Cochrane] being on board with Miss MacDonald in the foresaid ship, a brisk gale began to blow and make the sea rough, and not so easy for a small boat to row to Leith. The lady whispered to Miss MacDonald that she would with pleasure stay on board all night that she might have it to say that she had the honour of lying in the same bed with that person who had been so happy as to be guardian to her Prince. Accordingly they did sleep in one bed that night." [18]

Flora bore all this enquiry and adulation with gravity and fortitude. It passed through her mind that helping the Prince had appeared so simple and easy a thing to her, and yet how many of her Edinburgh bred ladies could have coped with long rides across bleak moors, and the crossing of the Minch in an open boat?

In June the Duke of Cumberland had written bitterly that "The Jacobite ladies at Edinburgh went in Procession in new Plaids and White Cockades to visit their Prisoner Friends in Edinburgh castle. Surely these people are more perverse and stiff necked than the Jews." [21]

The harbour at Leith was dominated by the old Citadel, a fortified windmill. In this building lived the redoubtable Magdalene Scott, Lady Bruce, the 76 year old widow of Sir William Bruce of Kinross. Lady Bruce had contributed to the Prince's cause, and now made her home the centre of support for Jacobite prisoners. Her house had been searched for the Prince at the end of September.

Lady Bruce visited Flora frequently. Others who visited and sent gifts included Rachel Houston, who was eventually to marry Robert Forbes.

"Several ladies made valuable presents to Miss MacDonald, viz., gowns, skirts, headsutes, shoes, stockings etc., etc. Commodore Smith made her a present when she was at Leith Road of a handsome sute of riding cloaths, with plain mounting, and some fine linen for riding shirts, as also a gown to her woman (Kate Macdonald) and some linen to be shirts for poor Kate, who could not talk one word of English, being a native of Sky, and who generously offered herself to Miss MacDonald when she could get not one that would venture to go with her." [18]

"One day in the Road of Leith a lady [Mrs Ferguson of Pitfour in

Aberdeenshire] asking Miss if she had any books on board, she said she had only a prayer book, but regretted much the want of a bible, which that lady soon furnished her with in a present in two pretty pocket volumes, handsomely bound. That she might have some innocent and useful employment for her time, care was taken by a lady [Lady Bruce] to send her a thimble, needles, white thread of different sorts, etc., with some linen and cambrick cut and shaped according to the newest fashions. This piece of friendship Miss Flora admired as much as any instance of kindness and regard that had been shown her, because all the time she had been in custody she was quite idle, having no work to do, and thereby time pass'd very dully on." [18]

Lord Albemarle wrote to the Duke of Newcastle that "Miss Flora McDonald sailed this morning on board the Bridgewater under the care of Captain Knowler; her behaviour has been such during her confinement that Commodore Smith and General Campbell begs your Grace, that when she arrives, she may rather be put into the hands of a messinger than into any common prison, this favour the poor girl deserves, her modest behaviour having gained her many friends." [22]

At 8.00am on 7th November *Bridgewater* weighed anchor in Leith Roads, and sailed in company with 14 merchant ships in convoy.

Bridgewater arrived at the Thames on 29th November. The ship saluted *Royal Sovereign* at 4.30pm and anchored at the Nore an hour later. On 30th November Capt Charles Knowler wrote, probably to Commodore Smith, that "Miss Flora MacDonald is arriv'd here with me and as she esteems you her best friend he [sic] has in the world should be much obliged if you'd be pleased to let her know what is to become of her. I have wrote to the Admirality about her but as it may be some time before it may be settled, as their Lordships will first send to the Secretary of State we may possibly go into the Dock before that time and she be sent on board the *Royal Sovereign*, which would not be very agreeable to her. Therefore I should be glad there could be an order got for her being sent up to London as soon as possible. Miss joyns me in Respects." [23]

To the end, Flora's naval guardians had been kind and considerate. Nigel Gresley, a young volunteer, had shown Flora such kindness that she later gave him her portrait painted by Richard Wilson.

Flora a prisoner in London

Bridgewater anchored at Sheerness at noon on 4th December. Capt John Orme of *Royal Sovereign* noted that in the afternoon "received from Bridgewater 35 men and 3 women part evidence and rebell prisoners." [24] Two days later *Bridgewater* sailed into Sheerness and in the morning "delivered to a Kings Messenger Miss Flora McDonald with her attendants and the evidences received from the Bridgewater." [17]

Robert Forbes noted that Flora "was removed to London and out into the custody of Mr Dick, a messenger, in whose hands were likewise Dr Burton, Aeneas MacDonald, Malcolm MacLeod, Clanronald, senior, Boisdale, etc. But Lady Clanronald was not allowed to be in the same messenger's house with her husband." [1]

William Dick had been carrying letters from the Duke of Newcastle to the Duke of Cumberland at Fort Augustus in July, and like other messengers, was allowed to keep prisoners in open arrest in his house, and charge them for the privilege. Mr Dick charged high enough, at six shillings and eight pence, or a third of a pound, per day, but his house was said to be better than some, where prisoners were crowded into leaking garrets. All this, however, was preferable to the confines of Newgate and prisons elsewhere.

As Flora arrived in London, she, and her fellow prisoners, were soon to learn of the death of Sir Alexander MacDonald of Sleat. The event was to start an avalanche which ultimately was to sweep Flora, and her embittered husband, away to America.

Sir Alexander, born in 1711 of a Jacobite family, had supported the Government during the Rising. He had travelled from Skye to Fort Augustus to see the Duke of Cumberland and to prevent his islands from being ravaged. He was grateful that he had not been at Monkstadt when the Prince had landed close by. Sir Alexander was deeply concerned about the fate of Kingsburgh, and had determined to travel to London to see the Duke of Cumberland again. He set out with Kingsburgh's son, Allan, who was seeking a commission in the Dutch service.

On 23rd November Lt Donald MacDonald wrote from Glenelg to Lord Loudoun that "It is with the deepest sorrow I am to acquaint your Ldshp with the Death of Sir Alexander McDonald of McDonald at this place today about 11 a clock forenoon. He came hither on Wednesday last seemingly in good health, and on Thursday was taken ill of a pleurisy — Your Ldshp has lost a firm friend, and we of his clan a kind father. His Death will be regretted by all his acquaintances and by many who did not know him, being a valuable man in private life, and a good Subject to the King."[25]

Four days later, young Kingsburgh reported Sir Alexander's death to Lord President Forbes, and concluded that "your Lordship lost a firm friend and alas we have lost our happiness on earth."[26]

Lady Margaret blamed Kingsburgh for being the cause of so much turmoil, and for the sudden death of her husband. Pregnant again, and now without a husband or chamberlain, and imprisonned in the hateful island, Lady Margaret fanned her resentment for Kingsburgh by doting on her eldest son, the five year old Sir James MacDonald.

The Jacobites never forgave Sir Alexander for not having joined the Prince. Robert Forbes recorded a less kindly epitaph.

"If Heav'n be pleas'd when sinners cease to sin;
If Hell be pleas'd when sinner enter in;
If earth be pleas'd to lose a truckling knave;
Then all are pleas'd — MacDonald's in his grave."[1]

London was the largest city in Europe. The town had already begun to grow into fashionable Mayfair. Berkeley Square and Grosvenor Square were beginning to be built, with streets running down to Piccadilly. St James, Piccadilly, was the most fashionable church to attend. King George II, a widower, was living at St James's Palace with his mistress. The King's eldest son, Frederick, Prince of Wales, was living in Leicester Square. Both men disliked each other heartily.

Allan Ramsay and Richard Wilson were painting portraits. Joseph Highmore's illustrations for *Pamela* and William Hogarth's series of prints entitled 'Marriage a la Mode' sold everywhere. The fashionable went to Covent Garden to hear oratorios and operas by Handel, who had dedicated *Judas Maccabeus* to the Duke of Cumberland, with the march 'See the conquering hero comes'. Everyone went to Drury Lane, where Garrick was managing the theatre. Smollett was writing *Roderick Random* and Fielding *Tom Jones*. Samuel Johnson had begun work on his dictionary, and was so quiet during 1745 and 1746 that it was rumoured that he had been a Jacobite.

The Jacobite Rebellion had been crushed, and the Lords Balmerino and Kilmarnock executed. Lord Derwentwater was executed a few days after Flora's arrival in London. The slippery Lord Lovat was brought to trial, found guilty of treason and executed on 9th April 1747. A week later London celebrated a frenzied first anniversary of the glorious victory at Culloden, with bonfires and fireworks. Purged of all this Scottish hatred, the King and his Whig Government could now get on with the serious task of fighting the French.

The frenzy of anti Jacobitism had begun to subside in London, and to turn against the Duke of Cumberland and his harsh measures. Like Edinburgh, London was full of crypto Jacobites, who began to reappear. One of these was Lady Primrose, the young widow of Hugh Primrose, 3rd Viscount. Lady Primrose lived in a house in Essex Street, between the Strand and the Thames.

Lady Primrose visited Flora at Mr Dick's house, and later Flora was to stay in Essex Street. Flora was allowed to see her friends, and was accompanied by Mr Dick's daughters. Thomas Pennant was later to write that he had met Flora at the house of Sir Watkin William Wynne, whose failure to join the Prince had so disappointed the Jacobites. Aeneas MacDonald, the banker, had proposed a jaunt to Windsor with Flora.

Alexander MacGregor wrote that "All admired the dauntless part she had acted, and her case excited so much interest, that she had the honour of a visit from Frederick, Prince of Wales, father of King George III. His Royal Highness asked her how she had dared to assist a rebel against his father's throne? when she replied, with great simplicity but firmness, that she would have done the same thing for him had she found him in like distress. The Prince was so struck with this reply and her artless manner, that he afterwards interested himself to procure for her every comfort." 27

In an age of pamphlets, it was not long before Flora featured in one published by J.Drummond. The author vouchsafed "Some Particulars of the Life, Family, and Character of Miss Florence McDonald now in Custody of one of his Majesty's Messengers in LONDON on Suspicion of Treasonable Practices against the Government.

"Upon her Father's Death, her Mother left the Country, and came up to *Edinburgh* for the Benefit of her daughter's Education, of whom she was doatingly fond; a Fondness proceeding not only from Parental Affection, but heightened by the Merit of the Object: For Miss, from infancy, discovered a Sagacity, accompanied with a ready Wit and prompt Memory, scarce to be paralleled in more adult Years; and such a Meekness of Temper, Dignity of Sentiment, and Chastity of Behaviour, as engaged the good Wishes of all that saw her, and filled her fond Mother, with hopes of Joy and Satisfaction, which she could not imagine would be intercepted by the Exercise of those very Virtues she so much admired in her Daughter.

"When she had compleated her in all Branches of Female Education, she returned with her to the Country, where Miss now in her sixteenth Year, drew upon her the Eye of a great many young Gentlemen, suitable to her Rank, but she found in herself no Disposition

Flora MacDonald as a shepherdess
from a painting by Thomas Hudson engraved by J Faber
(Courtesy Scottish National Portrait Gallery)

to the Examples of her Mother, who married much about this time.

"Miss, though fond of her Mother, yet after the second Marriage chose to pass the most of her Time at the House of Lady *Clanronald* her Kinswoman, where it is supposed she met with the unhappy Accident which makes her at present the subject of Conversation."

Flora was educated in the Uists, and had never been in Edinburgh. Her mother remarried soon after Flora's father's death. Flora lived with her brothers, half brothers and half sisters, and with her mother and Hugh MacDonald at Milton.

In the Uists, O'Neille, by accident, "met with Miss *McDonald*, and knowing her to be at least compassionate, if not a Friend to the Chevalier's Interest, proposed to her to assist in concealing him till his Escape should be effected. It is said, that *Miss McDonald* first conducted him to the House of the Lady *Clanronald*, where he remained concealed, till the near Approach of the King's Troops made it necessary for him to seek shelter somewhere else; and then equipped him in the Dress of a Waiting Maid, and in that Character conducted him to the Isle of *Skye*. She intended to have carried him to her Mother's House who lived in that Island, but first made an Attempt to gain him Protection from the Lady of *Sir Alexander McDonald of Slate*; this Lady as it is reported, preferred the Interest of her absent Husband, to any Concern she might feel for the Misfortune of this deserted Fugitive, and wisely refused him Admittance into her House. This Lady, according to the Story, was in so much Agitation when Miss *McDonald* made the Discovery to her that she betrayed, by her passionate Exclamations, the Secret to those who were in waiting about her, one of whom, less Scrupulous, and on whose Mind an Estate did not make such Impression, undertook to conceal the Wanderer, and relieved his Wants, which were then very great, by which Means Miss McDonald was deliverd of her Charge." One of those waiting about Lady Margaret was Kingsburgh, who willingly took the Prince to his house.

"Whether this Story of her's be true or false, I cannot take upon me to aver, only a Suspicion of Facts of this Nature is supposed to be the grounds of her present Confinement.

"She is a young Lady about Twenty, a graceful Person, a good Complexion, and regular Features; She has a peculiar Sweetness mixed with Majesty in her Countenance; her Deportment is rather graver than is becoming her Years: Even under her Confinement she betrays nothing of Sullenness or Discontent, in all her Actions, bespeak a Mind full of conscious Innocence, and incapable of being ruffled by the common Accidents of Life."[28] Flora was, in 1747, twenty five years old.

On 4th July 1747, the King declared a general amnesty, and on application most of the Jacobite prisoners in London and Edinburgh were freed. Flora was not set at liberty immediately, but when she was released she went to stay with Lady Primrose in Essex Street. Here her portrait was painted by Richard Wilson, and it was the least flattering. She was shown in a low cut dress with slashed sleeves of red and black tartan, with white bows. Wilson painted her with a pointed chin, rosy cheeks, sharp nose and hazel eyes. In a second, more formal portrait she was shown in a blue dress, with a tartan bow, holding her pass, with a boat in the backgound.

Lady Primrose started a subscription for Flora which eventually raised over £1500, a very large sum of money. Lady Primrose arranged for Flora to travel back to Edinburgh, not in the coach, which took twelve days, but by chaise. Flora was asked to choose a travelling companion and selected Malcolm MacLeod.

Malcolm MacLeod had walked across Skye with the Prince, and had been taken prisoner. On parting with his family in Skye, he had told them "to dry up their tears, for that he hoped to return yet from London in a coach. This merry saying of his prov'd not amiss, for he came from London in a post chaise with Miss Flora MacDonald, passing for one Mr Robertson, and Miss, for his sister; they not chusing to discover themselves upon the road, lest the mob might insult them and use them ill. They arrived in Edinburgh upon Sunday evening, August 2nd, 1747." [1] Malcolm told James Boswell, with a triumphant air, that "I went to London to be hanged, and returned in a post chaise with Miss Flora Macdonald." [29]

CHAPTER 10

Flora in Edinburgh

Upon Saturday, January 23rd, 1748, Captain Donald Roy MacDonald and Miss Flora MacDonald dined with my Lady Bruce in her own house at the Citadel of Leith, when I took the freedom to ask particular questions at Miss MacDonald in presence of the Company about the prince's landing with her in Sky.
— Robert Forbes

Flora left London in a post chaise with Malcolm MacLeod. She spent two days in York with Dr Burton, who had been a fellow prisoner at Mr Dick's house, and arrived in Edinburgh on 2nd August.

In Edinburgh the Jacobite sympathisers had been busy. Robert Forbes was the assistant priest at the Episcopal Church in Leith. On his way to join the Prince he was taken at Stirling, and imprisoned at the castle.

In February 1746 Robert Forbes was moved to Edinburgh castle. It was in meeting fellow prisoners there that he started "a collection of speeches letters journals etc relative to the affairs of Prince Charles Edward Stuart." He called it *The Lyon in Mourning* and was to devote much of his life to it, completing more than 3000 pages. The work was never intended for publication. On 27th May 1747, he was released and went to live in the house of Lady Bruce of Kinross, at Leith.

Robert Forbes's first circumstantial narrative came with "A genuine and full Account of the Battle of Culloden, with what happened the two preceding days, together with the young prince's miraculous escape at, from and after the battle, fought on April 16th, 1746; to his return to the continent of Scotland from the Western Islands on the 6th of the succeeding July. Taken from the mouths of the old Laird of Mackinnon, Mr Malcolm MacLeod, etc., and of Lady Clanronald and Miss Flora MacDonald, by John Walkingshaw of London or Dr John Burton." [1]

The account was to start Forbes on his quest for accuracy and completeness. He never used editorial powers to correct or alter any statement made, but he did try to check all his material.

On 4th July Alexander MacDonald of Kingsburgh petitioned for his release. A week later Kingsburgh and his lady were dining with Lady Bruce at the Citadel of Leith, "when it was proposed to read the above Account or Journal in the hearing of Kingsburgh, that so he might give his observations, or rather corrections upon it." [1]

This was to be the start of an affectionate friendship between Kingsburgh and Forbes. Kingsburgh admitted that "they had never been so much afraid of any person's conduct as that of MacKechan, because he was a goodnatured man and very timorous in his temper. But they frankly owned they had done him a great injustice by entertaining any suspicion about him; for that he had behaved to admiration, and had got abroad with the prince, the great wish of his soul." [1]

On 14th July Kingsburgh and his lady left Edinburgh.

Forbes acquired a copy of Capt Felix O'Neille's journal. On 20th July he made a collection of "Remarks, etc., and particular sayings of some who were concerned in the Prince's preservation." These dealt with O'Neille and Flora; her visitors while a prisoner at Leith Roads, and Lady Kingsburgh's spirited interview with Capt Fergussone.

Flora and Malcolm MacLeod arrived in Edinburgh on 2nd August, but Flora did not to stay with Lady Bruce or with her stepfather's nephew, James MacDonald, a carpenter in Leith. She showed an independence of spirit, which, after her year long imprisonment, was not surprising. Remembering the fawning adulation she had received, when a prisoner on board ship at Leith, the previous summer, Flora hid herself away from Jacobite society.

Flora determined to receive tuition to improve her writing. In September 1747 Mr David Beatt, a Jacobite schoolmaster, wrote that "As I have entered with Miss Flory McDonald, who waited five weeks for my return to Town, and who needs very much to be advanced in her writing, confines me to daily attendance, and must do so till she is brought some length in it, which obliges me to keep the Town close," [2] Despite David Beatt's tuition, and she was a willing pupil, Flora's handwriting and spelling were never good.

Flora's extended stay in Edinburgh, however, cannot have been only to improve her handwriting. Shunning the Jacobite friends who had previously imposed themselves upon her, and uncertain what to do with herself, Flora even avoided returning to her family in Skye. So much had changed in her life and personality that she could not face journeying back to the scenes of her celebrated adventure.

On 7th August, at James MacDonald's house, Forbes met Malcolm MacLeod, and got an account of the Prince's time in Raasay and Skye, and his journey from London with Flora. Later Malcolm suggested that

James MacDonald should arrange a meeting for Forbes with Donald
MacLeod and Flora, and James agreed to do so. The latter, however,
could not persuade Flora to meet Forbes. Indeed it began to seem that
Flora was avoiding him. She kept herself entirely to herself, and made
no splash in Edinburgh or Jacobite society.

On 22nd August Forbes bid farewell to Malcolm MacLeod as he set
off for Skye. "Then I begged him to try Armadale would vouchsafe me
a written account of his part of the management."[1] Armadale,
however, proved to be much too discreet, and wisely said little and
wrote down nothing at all about his central part in the Prince's escape.

On 7th September Forbes wrote to Kingsburgh that "For my own
part I am resolved to leave no stone unturn'd to expiscate facts and
characters, that so *the honest man* may be known and revered, and
those of the opposite stamp may have their due."[1] He had dined with
Donald MacLeod, to whom he gave the letter. Two days later Forbes
met Ned Bourk who gave him an account of the Prince's wanderings.

In October Malcolm MacLeod wrote to Forbes from Raasay of his
safe return, and added that "You'l received from the bearer all that was
to the for of the west coat that the P gave me; because nobody could get
it where I put it till I came here myself. Likewise tow of the buttons
that was in it."[1] This was a piece of Ranald MacAlister's second best
suit, which his wife had given to the Prince at Kingsburgh, and which
the Prince exchanged with Malcolm MacLeod. Forbes pasted the
fragment into the boards of his book, and so began a collection of
memorabilia associated with the Prince.

In November Dr John Burton arrived in Edinburgh, to make
enquiries about the Prince's affairs. A romantic Jacobite, he had been
confined at York castle two years before, and transferred to Mr Dick's
house in London in March 1746, where he remained for a year.

On 19th November Dr Burton met Robert Forbes, and allowed him
to make a copy of Aeneas MacDonald's journal.

Unlike Forbes, however, Dr Burton had no difficulty in arranging a
meeting with Flora, a fellow lodger at Mr Dick's house. Flora had
stayed with Dr Burton at York, and they had become affectionate
friends. Flora dictated a sixteen page account of her adventures. She
credited Capt O'Neille with the plan for the Prince's escape, and was
quite open about her stepfather having given her a passport.

On 23rd November Forbes saw Dr Burton and copied Flora's
journal, but was frustrated by not being able to speak to her. "Happening to mention several questions that were fit to be proposed to Miss
MacDonald, the Doctor desired me to give him them in writing,
for that he would endeavour to procure direct answers to them.

Accordingly, I gave them to him in writing, and he performed what he had promised. Here follows an exact copy of the questions and their answers.

"QUESTION 1st — Ask particularly at Miss MacDonald by what lucky accident it came about that she and Captain O'Neil had a meeting at first to concert measures? Whether or not it was by direction of her stepfather, Armadale, or any other person? For as O'Neil was an entire stranger in the country this is a material question, and must remain a mystery till Miss clears it up.

"ANSWER — When the Prince and his few men were skulking in the Long Isle, O'Neil used to scour about frequently by himself to try what he could learn, and this led him to be several times at Milton before he made the proposal to Miss MacDonald, as they were skulking thereabouts. O'Neil, by being free and easy with Miss and her brother, came soon to learn their history, and that their mother lived in Sky, etc.," [1]

Flora's answer was transparently false. O'Neille never visited Milton, and had never been out on his own scouring about, since he spoke no Gaelic. It was on his return from Harris that he had met Flora at Nunton. The person who had been scouring about was Neil MacEachen.

"2 — Ask particularly if Armadale had any private meeting (in person) with the Prince while skulking. For it is certain that General Campbell complained that Armadale was the person who had misled him when searching for the Young Pretender in the Long Isle."

Flora answered that Armadale had meet the Prince on the shore, when the Prince had first landed in Scotland, but had returned to Skye. [1]

Her second answer was no more convincing than the first. In no other account of the Prince's landing at Borrodale was Armadale mentioned. But Donald MacLeod of Galtrigill had told Forbes, on 20th August, that "They likewise agreed in saying they had good reason to believe that honest Hugh MacDonald of Armadale in Skye (stepfather of Miss MacDonald) had a meeting with the Prince at Rushness in Benbecula, that he got the Prince's pistols in keeping, and that he had them still in his custody. They added further, they were persuaded he would sooner part with his life than these pistols, unless they were to be given to the proper owner; and that he was the grand contriver in laying and executing the scheme for the Prince's escape in women's cloaths from the Long isle to the Isle of Skye. They said they had often heard that Armadale sent a letter by Miss Flora to his wife, wherein he used some such expression as this, 'that he had found out an Irish girl, Bettie Bourk, very fit for being a servant to her, and that among her other good qualifications she had this one, that *well could she spin*, which, he knew, she liked well.'"[1]

It seemed unlikely, however, that Armadale visited the Prince at Rossinish. When the Prince was there, Armadale was marching his men to Loch Boisdale. The Prince's pistols were given by the Prince to Milton, who gave them to his stepfather.

"3 — It is said that Armadale writ a letter, which he sent by Miss MacDonald to her mother, recommending the Irish girl, Bettie Burk, as a good servant, and giving an account of her good qualifications as such. It were to be wished that Miss could recollect the contents of said letter as exactly as possible, in order to give a narrative of the same.

"ANSWER — The substance of the writing which Armadale sent to his wife, was as is already mentioned in Miss MacDonald's own journal."[1]

Flora's irritation and testy answer was not what Forbes had expected. Forbes was not told the wording of the letter until he met Donald Roy MacDonald in January 1748.

The remaining questions concerned the songs which the Prince had sung on the crossing, and the drinking of milk and wine in the boat. Dr Burton added a question about the length of time between the Prince leaving Kingsburgh house and Capt Fergussone's visit there.

Flora's reluctance to speak with Forbes, and her evasive answers, showed an irritable streak in her character. But they were also caused by her wish to protect her stepfather, Hugh MacDonald of Armadale, who was still under suspicion, and Neil MacEachen, for it was widely suspected that the Jacobite clique had been infiltrated by Government agents.

Neil MacEachen had sailed to France with the Prince in September 1746. A year later Neil, now calling himself MacDonald, was in Scotland again. Two intelligence reports from Fort William stated that a MacDonald had been at Fort Augustus in September and in the Braes of Rannoch in October.[3] Neil was in Scotland on a secret mission, and while in Edinburgh he probably met Flora. When Neil returned to France he was commissioned as lieutenant into the Albany Regiment on 12th December. In the summer of 1746, and even before that, Neil MacEachen may already have been a secret agent.

In December Robert Forbes copied out Felix O'Neille's attested journal, which he had signed on 30th August 1747, at Berwick upon Tweed. O'Neille had been on parole there, awaiting his exchange and return to France.

Late in December, Donald Roy MacDonald, his foot now healed, set out to walk to Edinburgh. On 9th January 1748 he was introduced to Forbes by James MacDonald, the carpenter.

On 12th January Forbes began taking down Donald Roy's account, which ran to 65 pages. In it Donald Roy gave the text of Armadale's letter to his wife, and his meeting with the Prince at Portree. He also gave Forbes copies of two Latin poems that he had written about his wounded foot and the aftermath of Culloden, while he had been skulking in his caves in Trotternish.

Donald Roy had no difficulty in finding Flora and she allowed him to call on her. They had not met since they had parted at Armadale, on 10th July 1746. Another visitor was her half brother. Now in the Dutch service, James had already brought the Prince's blue garters to Edinburgh for Flora. He met Forbes, who described him as "an officer amongst the Scots Hollanders, who was going a recruiting to Sky and the Long Isle. He is son to honest Armadale, and thereby brother to Miss Flora MacDonald only by the mother." [1]

Between them, Donald Roy and her half-brother James, persuaded Flora that she should come out of her self imposed seclusion and meet her Jacobite admirers.

James set out for Skye on 22nd January, carrying letters from Forbes to Hugh MacDonald of Baleshare, Malcolm MacLeod and Kingsburgh.

Robert Forbes meets Flora

Rev Robert Forbes wrote that "As truth is my only aim in making this collection, so I gladly embrace every opportunity of correcting any mistake in the accounts I receive, or any error I myself may happen to comit, in the marginal notes.

"Upon Saturday, January 23rd, 1748, Captain Donald Roy MacDonald and Miss Flora MacDonald dined with my Lady Bruce in her own house at the Citadel of Leith, when I took the freedom to ask particular questions at Miss MacDonald in presence of the Company about the prince's landing with her at Sky.

"She told me likewise that Neil MacKechan went so often to the prince upon the shore that at last she became angry with him lest the frequency of his going should be remarked, and thereby become the means of making a discovery. However, she owned that in the event, his going so often proved serviceable, as no observation happened to be made of it.

"Miss MacDonald said that when at Mouggistot she could not help observing Lady Margaret going often out and in as one in great anxiety, while she in the meantime endeavoured all she could to keep up a close chit chat with Lieutenant MacLeod, who put many questions to her, which she answered as she thought fit. She acknowledged she knew nothing at that time of Donald Roy MacDonald being at Mouggistot, as he had not come into the house, or of the conference he had had with Lady Margaret (in the open air) and Kingsburgh about the safety of the Prince.

"Miss MacDonald likewise owned she knew nothing at all (when at Portree with the Prince) that Malcolm MacLeod was thereabouts, or about what course the Prince was to take. Only she had a suspicion that he might be going to Rasay, as Portree is opposite to it. She remarked how the prince fell briskly to his victuals, at Portree, in his shirt, what a great desire he had to have Donald Roy MacDonald along with him, etc., and that his farewell to her was in these words: 'I hope we shall meet in St James's yet, and I will reward you there for what you have done.'" [1]

Encouraged by Donald Roy and her half brother, Flora had at last met Robert Forbes. His enthusiasm and knowledge of the subject won her over, and they became friends. After five months of seclusion, Flora had come to terms with her Jacobite past.

Flora also knew that Neil MacEachen was safely back in France, and mentioned his name freely.

On 12th March Flora met Forbes again, and confirmed the words of the letter written by Armadale to her mother, but added " 'I have sent Neil MacKechan along with my daughter and Bettie Burk to take care of them.' At the same time Miss MacDonald assured me that her brother, MacDonald of Milton, was the person who delivered the Prince's pistols into Armadale's hands." [1]

Flora gave Robert Forbes a piece of the blue garters worn by the Prince. She was later to allow him to try on the Prince's apron, and gave him a part of the apron tape. Forbes also had a piece of the material from Betty Bourke's dress, as well as the scraps of the Prince's waistcoat.

At the end of March, Kingsburgh wrote to Forbes and entrusted the letter to his son Allan. Forbes noted that the original was "delivered to me by Kingsborrow's own son, upon Thursday, April 14th, 1748, when he was favouring me with a visit. At the same time he gave me a pair of pretty Highland garters in a present from his mother." [1]

The previous year Lady Margaret MacDonald had sent Allan to Edinburgh, and implored his brother in law, Ranald MacAlister, to "admonish him to be frugal and careful, which will be an Advice more Seasonable from you than me." [4] Allan perhaps called upon Flora. They may have met before, when Flora's stepfather had taken over the tack of Armadale from Kingsburgh in 1745. And again when Allan had been stationed at Kinlochnadale in the spring of 1746. Allan was not long in Edinburgh, for on 3rd May he was back in Skye.

On 19th April, Flora, herself, with Peggy Callander, one of Robert Forbes' circle of Jacobite ladies, set out from Edinburgh.[1] But though Flora had motivated herself to leave the security of her seclusion in the capital, she still could not bring herself to return to Skye. Instead she travelled to Argyll, where she spent three months, probably with her cousins at Largie.

In May James MacDonald, young Armadale, returned from recruiting in Skye, with a letter and journal from Hugh MacDonald of Baleshare for Robert Forbes.

On 29th June Dr Burton wrote to Forbes that "Just a little before I received yours, I was favour'd with a line from Miss F McD telling me she was just going to visit her friends in the west, and should not return to E till September, when she intended to favour me with her company at York in her way to London; and the longer she makes the visit the more she'll oblidge my wife, myself, and friends. For I would have her see our country a little, and not hurry away so soon.

"Notwithstanding the great puffs in the papers about peace, I can assure you the most thinking part of mankind, both in the South and here, can't but think otherways."[1]

On 5th July Forbes replied to Dr Burton that "I have never heard directly from Miss Flora MacDonald; but I have heard frequently of her. In crossing a ferry to Argyleshire she had almost been drown'd, the boat having struck upon a rock; but (under God) a clever Highlander saved her. Miss reached the Isle of Skye about the beginning of July, and waited upon her mother and the worthy Armadale, I believe she may be in Edinburgh some time this month."[1]

At last, in July 1748, two years after her adventure and hurried exit, Flora returned to Skye. No authentic account survived of Flora's homecoming, but she was made welcome by her family. She had many callers, and made some visits. All about her, Flora saw that her fame and good fortune had left others involved in the Prince's escape in poverty and sickness.

Alexander MacGregor wrote that Sir Alexander MacDonald "In honour of his fair namesake, got up a splendid banquet, to which all the principal families in the island were invited, together with a number of Government officers still sojourning in Skye. The festivities extended over four days, when high and low were entertained in a manner that did credit to the friendly generosity and hospitality of the great *MacDhomhnuill* of the Isles."[5]

This good story was spoiled by the fact that Sir Alexander had died at Glenelg almost two years before.

Flora could not stay in Skye, and so she returned to Edinburgh. In September Dr Burton wrote to Robert Forbes that "we are all heartily sorry for poor Flora's fright, but rejoice much that she is safe." [1] Dr Burton was still working on his booklet, and asked Forbes for additional material.

On 7th October 1748, the treaty of Aix la Chapelle ended eight years of the War of the Austrian Succession. Fort Louisbourg in Cape Breton was restored to the French and Madras, in India, to the British. The right of the Hapsburg heiress Maria Theresa to the Austrian lands was guarenteed, with the right of succession of the House of Hanover in Great Britain. Another condition was that Prince Charles, the Young Pretender, must leave France. In the commercial struggle between Britain and France nothing was settled in the West Indies, Africa and India, so that the treaty was no basis for a lasting peace.

Neil MacEachen, now a French officer, was in Edinburgh where he met Flora. She also met Forbes, and by her, on 5th November, he sent a letter to Dr Burton thanking him for his letter and that he would have answered sooner, "but that I don't chuse to correspond with any one by post, as a practice prevails of opening letters in post offices, and therefore I beg not to receive letters by post.

"Pray let us have the history of your persecutions. It is not in my power to gratifie you in your request for some time before receipt of yours. I was obliged to secret my collection, having been threatened with a search for papers. I have therefore put my collection out of my own custody into the keeping of a friend where I cannot have access to it without some difficulty, and I resolve to keep it so, that so I may defie the Devil and the Dutch. However, I am still collecting in scrapes as fast as ever." [1]

Dr Burton's pamphlet, *Narrative of the Several Passages of the Young Chevalier* was now printed, and he sent a copy to Forbes. It was an accurate and concise account of the Prince's wanderings. When he had learned that Capt Scott had landed in South Uist and General Campbell on Berneray, Dr Burton wrote that the Prince "finds himself surrounded with forces on both the landsides of him, without any sort of vessel wherein to put to sea. In this perplexity, Capt O Neille thought of applying to Miss Flora Macdonald, who he knew was then at Milton, her brother's house, in S Uist, wither she had lately come from the isle of Sky for a visit.

"Though Miss Macdonald is very justly described by an author, who from her own mouth relates her story, yet, as we can boast the same advantage, for that very reason we dare not use the same freedom with a young Lady, whose modesty is equal to her merit, and consequently to her fame. Besides, it is not our design here to paint characters in a pompous shew of words, which are as justly as generally believed to have no meaning, or one that should offend those they are meant to please. Our sole object is genuine narration, and actions will always speak better than words.

"This young Lady he intreated to come to his master's aid. She objected at first to the captain's proposal; but upon his demonstrating the necessity of her immediate going to the P----, who could not come to her, she was prevailed with to set out, taking Neil Macechan with her as a servant."

Dr Burton noted that "Miss finding the boatmen had blabbed every thing, was also fain to acknowledge to Gen. Campbell the whole truth ... The fair prisoner found now another protector in Commodore (now Admiral) Smith; whose ship soon came into Leith road."[6]

On 29th November Prince Charles, while on his way to the Opera, was arrested and detained. He eventually agreed, grudgingly, to leave France and travelled to the Papal lands at Avignon. The Prince's arrest and imprisonment caused a sensation. Prince Charles was the most famous and glamourous man in Europe. The French Government expected an outcry, but the reaction of the French public took it by surprise.

Meanwhile Flora returned to London, where she stayed with Lady Primrose in Essex Street, and visited friends. Flora was more at ease here than in Edinburgh or Skye, but she had come with a purpose. Flora had not sought fame, and always behaved with discrete modesty, but Lady Primrose had organised a subscription from amongst her Jacobite well wishers in London. Flora was shrewd enough to ensure that she did not loose out on her good fortune. Throughout her life Flora was determined to keep what was hers, and managed money prudently.

Allan Ramsay painted a portrait of Flora, and she was transformed. Gone was the shy, diffident look of Wilson's portrait. Flora had matured into a woman, self confident and assured. Ramsay was more flattering than Wilson, and painted Flora with a less pointed face, pink cheeks, a touch of auburn in her hair, and pale gray blue eyes. She wore a blue bodice with wide linen sleeves, and a red tartan shawl pinned at the left shoulder and draped over the right arm. She wore a white Jacobite rose in her hair and two more in a corsage. Ramsay also made a charcoal sketch of Flora, holding a banner, perhaps as the basis for a dramatic painting, which was never executed.

On 17th February 1749, Neil MacEachen, in Paris, wrote to Flora in

London, addressing her as "Dear Florry." He had meant to write before, since their meeting in Edinburgh, and hoped that her visit to London would be successful.

"The gentleman who delivers this is a friend of mine, and I hope this is enough to make you exert yourself among the honest and worthy, to help him dispose of some valuable toys he has on hand.

"I am sure it will give you sensible joy to hear the person you once had the honour to conduct, is in perfect health. Soon may they enjoy any other blessing the world can give. Clanranald has his kindest compliments to you, and hopes next time you'll both be in better spirits than when you last saw him. He and I dined with somebody the day they were took. Good God what a fright we got."[7]

Neil MacEachen, or MacDonald, as he now called himself, had been with the Prince in the glory days after his triumphant return to France in September 1746. Neil and young Clanranald had dined with the Prince just before the latter had been taken on the way to the Opera.

On the day that Neil wrote to Flora from Paris, the Prince, in disguise, rode out of Avignon, and began a period of wandering which was to take him all over Europe. Neil was abandoned like so many others who had given unstintingly of their time and energy.

On 10th June 1749, Dr Burton wrote to Forbes that "I heard of Miss Flora lately. She was very well but thin. She intends for Scotland in this month, and goes to Springkell to Sir William Maxwell's; promises to let me have the pleasure of her company here for ten days."[1]

After a winter in London, Flora travelled to York and then to Carlisle. Springkell, near Kirtlebridge in Dumfriesshire, was seven miles north west of Gretna on the English border. The house had been built in 1734 by Sir William Maxwell, 2nd Bt of Springkell, close to the ancient castle of Kirkconnel. Sir William was a cousin of James Maxwell of Kirkconnel, who had fought with Lord Elcho's Dragoons for the Prince.

Flora spent the winter in Dumfriesshire, and in the spring of 1750, she was back in Edinburgh. On 31st March Flora visited Robert Forbes and gave him the names of those who had crossed to Skye: "Flora MacDonald, Betty Burk, Neil MacDonald MacKechan, John Mac-Donald (cousin german to Glenalladale) at the helm, Duncan Campbell, [blank] Macmerry, and Alexander MacDonald. All the said five attending the prince and Miss MacDonald were people belonging to the Long Isle ... The above John MacDonald at the helm was afterwards drowned in passing from the Long Isle to the continent."[1]

Flora's list, given almost four years after the event, was the least satisfactory, making no mention of the two Rory MacDonald's, one of whom was brother to John. John and Rory were the sons of Lachlan MacDonald of Dremisdale, who was 'cousin german' to Flora herself. They were also cousins of Glenalladale through their mother.

In the summer Flora travelled to Armadale. For almost three years she had been living in lodgings or with acquaintances and admirers. Many of the people with whom she stayed were older couples, like Sir William and Lady Maxwell and Dr and Mrs Burton, who enjoyed Flora's serious nature. Flora had been to Skye only once since her arrest. After three years of wandering, she returned to her mother's home. With her financial affairs in order, Flora had determined at last to settle down, and to find herself a husband.

On 11th July Robert Forbes wrote to Flora that "the agreeable accounts of your safe arrival at Armadale by your letter to Miss Main, afforded me no small pleasure, as I will ever think myself interested in every event of life that happens to Miss Flora MacDonald whether prosperous or adverse; a mixture of which we must pass through in this lower state, which is a chequered scene at best.

"You have already experienced both sides of fortune, and your conduct in each of them has engaged the attention of the public, and has justly entitled you to the esteem of every well thinking person. You have had a recent instance of that blending of sweet and bitter which inseparably attends the transactions of human life.

"I feel somewhat of that mixture of joy and grief which would ensue upon your first meeting with your mother, joy to see one another once more in health and safety, but grief in your mutual condolences for the affecting loss of two hopeful youths ... May God support you both under the trying affliction.

"There are many worthy persons in your corner of the world for whom I entertain a great veneration. Pray be so good as to remember me kindly to them when they happen to come in your way ... Present them my most respectful and best wishes to Armadale and your mother, Rasay and his family and Malcolm MacLeod, Kingsborrow and his family, MacKinnon and his lady, Balshar and Milton, etc., etc., etc., etc. I heartily wish you all things good and happy"[1]

One of the youths was probably James, lieutenant in the Scots Brigade in Holland. He did not appear in any later record.

Flora was in Skye when, on 16th September, Prince Charles landed at Dover and travelled to London. The Prince's plan to come to London was known in general terms by the English Jacobites, but his arrival caught them unawares. The Prince, in disguise, was ushered into Lady Primrose's house in Essex Street, where he found her playing cards. She recognised him at once and dropped her cards in astonishment.

Lady Primrose, however, quickly recovered her composure and began to arranged matters, and fifty Jacobites met in a house in Pall Mall. The Prince made a tour of London, and visited the Tower. In a church in the Strand, not far from Essex Street, the Prince renounced his Catholic faith and was received into the Church of England. The Prince, however, discovered that the Government could not be toppled by a lightning strike. Six days after his arrival, the Prince left London.

During the late summer Flora visited her friends in Skye. She went to Kingsburgh, where she called on Alexander MacDonald and his wife. Flora saw Kingsburgh's daughter, Anne MacAlister. At nearby Skirinish, in September 1749, Anne had given birth to her first daughter. The child was named Flora, after both her grandmothers, but also for Flora MacDonald of Milton, who was the most famous woman in Scotland. On 1st November 1750 Anne gave birth to her sixth child, and fifth son, who was named Allan, for her brother.

Flora saw Allan, young Kingsburgh. Allan was about the same age as Flora. His father had moved to Kingsburgh in 1734, and five years later Allan was in Edinburgh being educated at the expense of Sir Alexander MacDonald. Allan returned to Skye, where he helped his father with running the farms at Kingsburgh and Armadale, and in droving cattle.

In October 1745 Allan received a commission as lieutenant in John MacDonald of Kirkibost's Independent Company. He marched to Inverness in December, and was involved in the 'Rout of Moy' in February 1746, when the Government troops had been humiliated by the Jacobites. With Lord Loudoun, he withdrew to Skye in March, and remained there until after the battle of Culloden. He may have met Flora then, before he went off to Fort Augustus in May, and she crossed to South Uist in early June. Later in the month Allan returned to Skye and crossed to South Uist in search of the Prince, on the day that Flora and the Prince crossed to Trotternish.

When the Independent Companies were disbanded, in September 1746, none of the officers received half pay. Several officers attempted to get into the Dutch service. John MacLeod of Talisker and young James MacDonald, Armadale's son, were successful. Though Allan had applied for a commission, and had accompanied Sir Alexander MacDonald as far as Glenelg, where the latter had died in November 1747, Allan had not been rewarded.

Flora and Allan met at Kingsburgh and a marriage was arranged.

CHAPTER 11

Flora Marries Allan MacDonald

Mrs Flory Macdonald by these present Assigns Trans-
fers and Dispones to the said Allan Macdonald her
husband, his heirs and Assigneys the sum of Seven
hundred pounds sterling money of principall, and the
annualrent and interest thereof now due.
— Marriage contract between Flora MacDonald
and Allan MacDonald

On Tuesday 6th November 1750 Flora married Allan MacDonald, younger of Kingsburgh, at her mother's house at Armadale. The announcement in *Scots Magazine* reminded readers that "This is the young lady who aided the escape of the young Chevalier." [1]

Flora married into the most powerful MacDonald family in Skye. Her father-in-law, Alexander MacDonald of Kingsburgh, was the Chamberlain and Trustee of eight year old Sir James MacDonald of Sleat, Bt. Kingsburgh, with the support of John MacKenzie of Delvine, ran the MacDonald estates. In addition he held the tacks of Kingsburgh and Monkstadt. His daughter Anne was married to Ranald Mac-Alister, who held Skirinish, a few miles south of Kingsburgh, and was factor for Trotternish.

Flora herself came of a good family. Her brother Angus held Milton in South Uist and Balivanich in Benbecula, and was married to Clanranald's eldest daughter. Flora's step father held Armadale in Sleat. Flora had acquired a substantial subscription while she was in London, and was the most famous woman in Scotland.

Dr Johnson later wrote that "A hundred pounds is a portion beyond the hope of any but the Laird's daughter. They do not indeed often give money with their daughters; the question is, How many cows a young lady will bring her husband." [2] Flora brought £700 as her dowry.

Flora and Allan's marriage was founded on a firm legal basis. Flora was twenty eight, and sensed that the years were slipping by. Her early life had trained her to be a dutiful wife; to have children and to run a household. Allan was a strong, attractive man, and he was to be a good husband and father. Flora had no knowledge, then, that Allan's financial affairs were to collapse twice, and that he was to be imprisoned for fighting for the wrong side. At the end of their days Flora and Allan were beset by poverty and sorrow, and yet they lived together through almost forty eventful years. Affection and love had time to grow.

Flora wore a black silk wedding dress, in mourning for her two lost half brothers. According to Alexander MacGregor, Flora wore a dress of Stuart tartan, and the marriage festivities were conducted on a large scale and lasted for almost a week. He stated, however, that Allan was already living at Flodigarry, and that the wedding took place there. A sample of red tartan, but not Stewart, at Fort William, was also said to be part of Flora's wedding dress.

Flora and Allan went to live at Kingsburgh. So hurried had been the marriage that it was only on 3rd December that a contract was drawn up and signed. It was a formidable document, written out on five pages of stamped paper. It formalised agreements made before and at the marriage, and allowed Flora to be independent, with an annual sum of £50 sterling, payable in two instalments at Whitsun and Martinmass, "during all the days of her Lifetime", and also after the decease of her husband.

Considering the size of the dowry that Flora brought to the marriage, it was "agreed in case it should so happen (which God forbid) That the saids Allan and Mrs Flory Macdonalds should either through choice or necessity seperate and not Cohabite Together", then Flora would receive a yearly sum of £40 sterling. Flora had ensured her future, whatever happened to her marriage. In addition, she was to share the benefits of all lands and rents acquired by Allan after their marriage. There were complex provisions for any number of combinations of male and female children.

"FOR WHICH CAUSES on the other part, The said Mrs Flory Macdonald by these present Assigns Transfers and Dispones to the said Allan Macdonald her husband, his heirs and Assigneys the sum of Seven hundred pounds sterling money of principall, and the annualrent and Interest thereof now due."

The whole long document was written out by Dr John Maclean and witnessed by him and Donald MacDonald of Castleton, who had arrested Flora, by Hugh MacDonald of Armadale, her stepfather, and by Alexander MacDonald of Kingsburgh, and signed by "Allan McDonald" and "Flory Macdonald".[4]

Rev Robert Forbes, in Leith, had been informed that Flora and Allan were to be married. He wrote to Malcolm MacLeod asking him to give his best wished to the young couple.

Kingsburgh wrote to Forbes in December that Malcolm had been ill, and had "sent your letter to me in order to be sighted to the new maryed couple, which, you may easily believe, was acceptable to old and young ... the young folk has the gaity of youthood to cheer them." [5]

Forbes replied in January 1751 that "Your handwriting of December 31st proved a real cordial to me, especially as I had some anxiety to have agreeable accounts about you and your concerns.

"The welfare of the happy pair I heartily rejoice at, and shall be glad to have the like information renewed to me as frequently as possible. That match is much to the good liking of all friends and wellwishers, who agree in affirming it to be one of the best judged events of life that could be devised by any sett of honest folks.

"Pray make an offer of my best wishes, in the kindest manner, to my worthy Mrs Flora MacDonald," wrote Robert Forbes, and added, a little annoyed, "and tell her, from me, that I looked for some few lines under her own hand to let me know her marriage day, which I and some others are quite ignorant about.

"Sometime ago I writ to Dr Burton accounts of your son's marriage, upon which he writ me the following words. "I heartily wish my worthy Flora as happy as it is possible to be on this side the grave, and that she may live to see her children's children so too; and also peace upon Israel, which God grant that we may soon see and we be saved. Amen.'

"All friends here join with me in wishing all things good and happy to you and Mrs MacDonald, the young pair, and Mr and Mrs MacAllastar, and in praying that all of you may enjoy a happy and prosperous year with large amends." [5] Forbes signed himself 'Donald Hatebreeks'.

At Kingsburgh, Flora wrote anxiously in April to Messers Innes & Clerk, Merchants, London that "I understand my Lady Primrose had lodged in your hands for my behoof 627 Sterg, and that her Ladyship had in view, to add more." [6]

A month later Mackenzie of Delvine, in Edinburgh, wrote that a further £800 had been lodged by Lady Primrose "of Mrs Flora McDonald's money" with Messers Thomas & Adam Fairholms. The discharged bill was endorsed 10th June 1751. [6] Ranald MacAlister of Skirinish saw Delvine in September and received the sum of £191, and a promissory bond for £567 drawn on Sir Alexander MacDonald, paying interest of 5%. In October Ranald MacAlister was back in Skye, and at Kingsburgh witnessed the discharge for this sum between Mackenzie of Delvine and Mrs Flora and Allan MacDonald, younger of Kingsburgh. [6]

Meanwhile Allan had applied for and had received the tack of Flodigarry. The previous tenant, Martin Martin had formerly got the

"Tack of the seven penny lands of Flodigarry and Isle of Altivik and the six penny lands of Glenhylass, granted to him by Sir Alexander Macdonald for 19 years from Whitsunday 1732."[7] Flodigarry consisted of about 960 acres. The change did not endear the Kingsburgh MacDonalds to the Martins, who held a grudge against the family ever after.

Allan came into possession of Flodigarry at Whitsunday 1751. His term was probably for 16 years. He required money to purchase Martin's stock and his buildings, which belonged to the tacksman, and not to the landlord. Allan paid a rent of at least £25 a year, and an initial grassum, or entry fee, of about four year's rent.

The tack of thirteen penny lands was considerable. Some of the land was held in hand by the tacksman, but most was sublet to tenants, who paid rent to the tacksman. Around the edge of the clustered villages, or townships, were landless men, or cottars, who had a patch of land for growing oats, and who worked the tenants' and tacksmen's fields for minimal wages.

The tacksman did not farm the land himself, though he certainly had cattle, and was involved in the cattle trade. In times of war, however, the tacksman, in return for his low rental, was expected to turn out with 30, 50 or 100 armed men to defend his chief.

The wealth of the country was in hardy black cattle. These were taken to market, and hence were called marts. In a country where coined money was scarce, rents and debts were paid on promissory notes against the sale of cattle. There were local cattle sales in Skye, but then the cattle were driven in droves, at the rate of ten miles a day, to the Tryst at Crieff in October. Here Lowland and English drovers purchased the cattle for cash, and took the cattle on the long journey to England, where they were fattened in East Anglia and sold at Mr Smith's Field in London the following spring.

The managing of droves was a skilled business. Kingsburgh had been Sir Alexander MacDonald's principal drover, and his son Allan came to be called the 'great drover of the isles'.

Into this complex world of bonds, promissory notes, and cattle, Allan and Flora established themselves at Flodigarry. They had the prospect of 16 years in their new home, which Allan began to improve. Allan's family now held four large tacks in Trotternish. Allan's brother-in-law was factor in Trotternish and his father was Chamberlain and Trustee for the young Chief.

Everything was set fair. Only the Martins resented the advancement of the family, and more significantly, Lady Margaret MacDonald, the third of her son's Trustees. Still blaming Kingsburgh for the death of her husband, and now finding his son married to the 'gypsy', Lady Margaret abandoned her prison in Skye, and removed herself to London, where she indulged her eldest son, Sir James, and neglected her younger children, Alexander, and Archibald, who had been born after Sir Alexander's death.

Sir James was a serious and studious boy and was being educated at Eton College, near Windsor, in England. He would not come of age until he was twenty one years old, in December 1762. Until then the Kingsburgh MacDonalds were pre-eminent in Skye, and Allan had made a dazzling match with Flora MacDonald of Milton.

Flodigarry was on the eastern side of Trotternish. The house lay in a hollow, below a bluff, in the broken ground between the tall lava cliffs of Quiraing and the shore. It looked out east across the sea to Rona and Gairloch, on the mainland. To the south were the fertile lands of Staffin. The situation was a spectacular one, but in winter the sun quickly sank behind the Quiraing ridge, and it became gloomy.

On 22nd October 1751, at eleven o'clock, Flora gave birth to her first child, who was named, not for either of his grandfathers, but Charles, in romatic memory of the Prince. Two years later, on 18th February 1754, at eleven o'clock, a daughter was born. She was named Ann, for Ann, Viscountess Primrose, Flora's patron in London. On 21st February 1755, at 12 o'clock, a second son was born and was named Alexander for his paternal grandfather. A year later, on 16th August 1756, at three o'clock in the morning, a third son was born and was named Ranald for his maternal grandfather. On 30th November 1757, at three o'clock in the morning, Flora gave birth to her fifth child, and fourth son, who was named James, for Sir James Mac-Donald, his Chief. Two years later on 30th October 1759, at five o'clock in the afternoon, a fifth son was born, and was named John, for John Mackenzie of Delvine, such a staunch friend to the family.[8] Flora had six children in eight years.

Anne MacAlister at Skirinish, already with six children, was to give birth to eight more children by March 1761.

Flora had to cope with a growing family in a small single storeyed house. The cottage still stands today, enlarged and modernised, the rooms named for Flora's children, behind the house, now an hotel, built by Flora's great-great-grandson.

Flora had servants to help her, but running a household was a difficult business in a remote rural area. There were no shops in Skye. All produce had to be grown locally, but there was beef and mutton, and fish from the sea; milk, butter and cheese; oatmeal for porridge and oatcakes and bere for bread; there was kail as greens, and turnips and potatoes were beginning to be introduced. From the moors there were grouse and stags to be shot.

Red wine had been imported into the Highlands for centuries, and brandy was the spirit drunk by the gentry. There was beer, but whisky was still a very crude alcohol, made from distilled barley. It was drunk by the cottars, in an ever increasing number of drinking houses.

Though cramped and crowded by modern standards, with servants sharing family life, the tacksman's house was well appointed. The floors may have been of compacted earth, but there were good beds with linen sheets; there were table cloths and napkins; silver cutlery and china.

Every house had some books, and it was from these that the children, and particularly the young girls, received their education. Dr Johnson wrote that "In Skye there are two grammar schools, where boarders are taken to be regularly educated . . . Having heard of no boarding school for ladies nearer than *Inverness*, I suppose their education is generally domestick."[2]

Kingsburgh, his son Allan and Flora were all religious people. Allan conducted daily worship in his house and on Sundays the family and servants walked and rode the four miles to Kilmuir church, on the west side of Trotternish.

In 1755 Alexander MacDonald of Kingsburgh effectively demitted office as Chamberlain to Sir James. Kingsburgh was 66, and had run the estate for 38 years. His health had suffered during his imprisonment at Edinburgh Castle, but he was to live for another 17 years.

Few of the rentals on the MacDonald estates have survived for this period, but in 1749 Ranald MacAlister had collected £2,586 for the whole estate. Almost half of this, including the rent in kind — bere meal, butter, cheese and wedders — was from Trotternish, with a little less from Sleat than from North Uist. The estate then bore debts, in bonds, of almost £3,500, which was more than a year's income, at interest of £3½%.

Though Kingsburgh nominally remained Chamberlain, and received a fixed salary, Allan took over as chief factor for the estate. The collecting of rents was the responsibility of the factor as a private contract with the chief. Since much of the rent was computed in cattle, the factor's ability to get a good price for the marts, and to take them to Crieff and get a good price there, meant the difference between being able to settle his account with his chief, and have something over for his pains, or making a loss, which he then owed to the chief. It was a system that worked well as long as the factor applied himself industriously, kept good accounts and cattle prices were rising slowly. It exposed the factor in times when cattle prices fell.

Ten years after Flora's imprisonment in London, Lady Primrose had collected a further £200 from Flora's admirers, and in April 1758 Allan wrote anxiously to MacKenzie of Delvine asking for the money. Allan was also concerned to recover a bill of his for £220 in the hands of Rory MacLeod "as he Seems to be a very Dangerous person to have the Least transactions with and that being too great a Sum for a person of my Lowe Stock to have hovering over his head." [9]

Allan was always anxious about money, and less than eight years after his marriage, he was having financial difficulties.

In March 1759 Flora MacDonald, Lady Kingsburgh, died. Both Flora and Anne MacAlister described how she was buried in the sheets in which the Prince had slept on 29th June 1746. Even though his father was now 70, Allan continued to live at Flodigarry.

Flora's half sister, Annabella had married Alexander MacDonald of Cuidrach, a tack a few miles north of Kingsburgh. Her younger half sister, Flora, had married Archibald MacQueen. The MacQueens were a powerful church family in Skye. Archibald's brothers had been ministers in Sleat and North Uist. His cousin, Rev Archibald, was minister of Snizort, until his death in 1754, and was the father of Rev William, who succeeded him at Snizort, and Rev Donald, minister at Kilmuir. Rev William had the tack of Penduin, between Kingsburgh and Cuidrach, and Rev Donald lived at Kilmuir, and was Allan and Flora's minister.

Hugh and Marion of Armadale had moved to Camuscross, in 1753, and Hugh had become factor for Sleat.

In 1762 Ranald MacAlister died suddenly, and Anne, Kingsburgh's daughter, was left a widow to provide for thirteen surviving orphans.

Sir James MacDonald was educated at Eton and then Oxford where his brilliance was noted. He made a tour of Europe with the Duke of Buccleuch and Adam Smith, who later wrote *Wealth of Nations*.

On 26th December 1762 Sir James came of age, and took over the management of his estates into his own hands. He announced that all the tacks on his lands would be terminated at Whitsunday 1764, and that he would spend the summer of 1763 setting the new tacks himself.

Allan travelled to Edinburgh to see Delvine, to work out a scheme for the rents for the new tacks. Allan immediately became alarmed. For all his father's and his own experience, and his wife's money, Allan had not made a success of his farming or his financial affairs.

In March 1763 Hugh of Camuscross, Flora's stepfather, wrote to MacKenzie of Delvine, that "I have seen Kingsborrow of late who Believes his Son Allan has a subject of fifty thousand marks in his hands and will Doe all manner of Justice to his Creditors. he is to sell of all his Stock to Relieve his debts which most be great if this Subject Will not Relieve him."[9] 50,000 merks Scots was about £2,780 sterling, and represented almost a year's rental on the whole estate.

Sir James arrived in Skye in mid July, with his doting mother, Lady Margaret, and stayed at Camuscross. Sir James, burning with all the enthusiasm of youth, discovered how difficult it was going to be to set the new tacks. Aware that his estates in Skye and North Uist were his only source of income, Sir James proposed to augment, or raise the rents, and to give tacks for only seven years. He wrote a series of frank and heart searching letters to Mackenzie of Delvine in Edinburgh.

"I do not chuse at my time of life to lock up my own hands rashly so as to become entirely incapacitated for my whole life from correcting what I might upon a further experience disapprove of."[9]

On 15th July Allan wrote from Flodigarry to Delvine, sending his last account which "is not right Ballanced . . . Sir James is now in Slate & will not be in Uist this fortnight yet."[9]

On 30th July Sir James was at Monkstadt, where he installed his mother, and met Flodigarry and sent him to Edinburgh. A week later Sir James was visited by Norman MacLeod of MacLeod, and his son John. In the middle of August Sir James crossed to North Uist, where, at the end of the month, he met Clanranald. He returned the compliment at Nunton, and at the end of September Sir James returned to Skye.

On 1st October Sir James wrote from Monkstadt to Delvine that "I am happy that so much of my business is over though I have still a very troublesome piece of Work to come in this part of the Country. I shall say nothing to you about it till it is over —

"I am very glad Allan has paid so much of his debt; I wish he may fulfill the remainder of his promise at next Market."[9]

Sir James had received a visit from MacDonnell of Glengarry, who was in serious financial difficulties. He wrote on 6th October that "You cannot well conceive the perplexity I have been in since I came from Uist. I would not submit to the same anxiety & drudgery again upon any account — I have been plagued with everybody's demands, & have often been forced to the pain of refusal & sometimes perhaps too easily led into compliance. I have endeavoured to do my best, tho' I cannot quiet my own mind. The state of suspence & misery I am in is not to be described.

"Notwithstanding the favour that has been shewed to Allan & the generosity to his father, I find that Kingsborrows family are much disappointed that the whole country is not divided among themselves,

& several people put to beggary on their account.

"That family possesses at present near one third of Trotternish, & if they had the whole they would not be more thankfull — I do not chuse to say more upon this subject, though I could say a great deal, as I shall always behave with delicacy where Kingsborough is concerned — only I must confess that many parts of his conduct will be no rule for mine, & that I must be excused from not complying with many unreasonable expectations of his Children, which perhaps he himself has authorized — I find Allen has picked up bonds against me in this country to the amount of near £1000 — the interest has been already paid for these. It is hard if he does not at least pay me interest for what he owes me, when I could so easily cancell both principall & interest of so much of my debt by seizing these bonds in his hands — It would be still stronger if it should appear that some of my own money has been employed in procuring these very bonds. I leave it to you to state this matter to Allen as you please; but I wish he may at least be made sensible of the gentleness with which he had been treated." [9]

Despite his harsh words, Sir James gave Kingsburgh a yearly pension of £50 sterling, "in return for the long and faithful services done and performed by him to my deceased father, and to myself during my minority, when he was one of my tutors and curators; being resolved, now that the said Alexander MacDonald is advanced in years, to contribute my endeavours for making his old age placid and comfortable." [10]

On 16th October Sir James wrote from Monkstadt that he had had a bitter struggle with Anne MacAlister, at Skirinish, about recovering a piece of ground, and with Kingsburgh's younger son, James, who was demanding a tack held by someone else. A week later Sir James had moved to Portree, where he wrote to Delvine that "The difficulties I have combated in order to settle this affair so as to accommodate the greatest number of the people, to prevent removals which are always burdensome to tenants; & to secure my own rents; cannot be imagined by any one at a distance.

"I see that it is absolutely impossible to prevent an incredible number of the people remaining destitute. But as all of them never were nor ever can be served, I shall comfort myself with thinking that at least as many hold lands now as formerly, besides that some are added to the number." Sir James was enthusiastic about planning a village at Portree with 22 houses and room for further expansion. [9]

On 3rd November Sir James was at Kingsburgh, visiting Alexander MacDonald. That day Lady Margaret, at Monkstadt, wrote a vitriolic letter to Delvine, stating that "allmost Every thing in this Country [is] in confusion, the falling off of King[sburgh]s resolution & Activity is so very remarkable for some years Past ... it is shamefull that those under him and of his own appointment should have been so remiss in their duty, but the plain Truth is, that their Whole thoughts have been Tournd to monopolize as much as they coud." [9]

Lady Margaret had urged her son to challenge Kingsburgh himself about these matters, but Sir James would not. All the mills, except the one nearest Kingsburgh, at Romesdal, were in disrepair or ruin. The farm at Monkstadt was a perfect waste. Some of the houses at Portree had fallen down. Kingsburgh "has not deserv'd by his care Sir James's add[iti]onal Generosity, And Every Body here will be surprisd at it, as it does not yett appear, that he has given himself any sort of Trouble for years past ... he has been in Short Blinded by his Son and the Indolence of Old Age, And his own family's want of discretion," and this had "lost him the Affection of Most People here." [9]

Lady Margaret had highly approved of Sir James taking back a part of Skirinish and refusing a tack for Kingsburgh's son, James. "Sir Js has not Comply'd with this unreasonable demmand which has given great Offence." Lady Margaret had also urged Sir James to write to Delvine about the bonds that had been taken up by Allan. "It is very hard he [Sir James] shoud be paying intrest to Allan, while he is likeway getting ffactors fees for rents he has not yet Recd." [9]

Meanwhile in Edinburgh, Allan attempted to purchase a commission in the Army for his eldest son, Charles. He wrote on 22nd October to Delvine that he would visit him the following week, "As I plainly can see by my Superiors Letter he hath gott Some bad notions in general of our poor family even of them that hath not Deserved it as weel as they that have; and that absolutely throw my envey of getting Kingsborrow, my father getting £50 Stg for Life & the Steelboll Tack of Mugstot and the Containoning Skernish with my sister for her own Suport & thirteen orfants — Now Dr Sir it woud be Charity in you to say some thing for us or for Such of us as have not egregiously offended Sir James McDonald — especially such of us as have numberous weak families." [9]

On his way home, Flodigarry met Sir James and Lady Margaret at Broadford in Skye. It was a frosty meeting, for Sir James allowed Allan the tack of Kingsburgh and Monkstadt, but for only seven years and at rent increased by £10 per year. The rent for Monkstadt was £70 per year. Allan had not been allowed the remaining three years of his father's tack at the old rent. Sir James and his mother went on to Inverness and travelled by Castle Menzies and Abercairney, visiting relations, to Edinburgh and London.

On 18th November Allan was back at Flodigarry, where he wrote to Delvine that "as you are my family patron and best friend I cannot help troubling you when I have anything to say relating to my poor Family.

"I was afraid he [Sir James] had been angry at me throw the ill will And envy that others bear to me & my father; but god is my witness that I woud risk my Life, person, and fortune, if I had any to Service him, and that I never with my will or knowledge wronged him in a Sixpence."

Allan begged to be allowed the three remaining years at Kingsburgh at the old rate, thus saving him £10 a year, "which is a Considerable Sum to a man of my family & Burdine.

"I also once thought he was inclined to lett me have more than Sevin years of Kingsborrow . . . only I would wish to have [more] years of it so as to Ripe [reap] some of the profits of what Improvements my father made there and what I will make my self, for I am Determined to begin immediately to Inclose, plant, and sett quicksets, and to Build all my office houseis with Ston & Lime I mean Barns, Byres and Kiln —"

Allan complained that his successor at Flodigarry, Martin Martin, had refused to buy the house and farm buildings. He suggested that Sir James should purchase the buildings himself, at the valuation of any two tradesmen in Skye. The Martins had resented losing Flodigarry in 1750. On one occasion Allan was said to have had a friendly wrestling match with Martin, but having got the upper hand, caught his spur in a sack and was thrown. Allan's crushing hug was later claimed to be the cause of Martin's death. A cousin of Allan wrote a song about the incident, and some young followers came to blows.

Allan concluded to Delvine that "As it is not in my power to reward you for all your by passd favours to me and my father (who is not at present in sound health and I fear not far from his Last days I believe accassoned by this years fateegs) I pray god reward you here." [9]

Allan and Flora, with their six children and servants, removed from Flodigarry to Kingsburgh at Whitsunday, in May 1764. The tack was the largest on the MacDonald Estates, at over 3,000 acres. Though only fifteen miles from Flodigarry, Kingsburgh was quite different in character. The house was much larger, being built on two floors. The present house at Kingsburgh, although almost a ruin, was the house in which the Prince stayed, and in which Flora and Allan lived. At the time of the Prince's visit there were at least four bedrooms, and a hall or parlour, where the Prince was entertained.

The two storey house stood below a bluff, close to the shore of Loch Snizort, and was surrounded by trees. Opposite lay Treaslane and Aird Bernisdale on the MacLeod shore, green and gentle country. Behind the house to the east, masked by the bluff, marched the ridge line of Trotternish. From the bluff, on a fine day, MacLeod's Tables and the peaks of the Cuillins could be seen.

Flora and Allan were 42 years old, and at the height of their powers. Allan had returned to the home his father had lived in for thirty years, and Flora to the house where she had brought the Prince. There would be room for all the children, and for Allan's father. Allan had a good farm, and was chamberlain of the MacDonald estates. But the return was marred by the antagonism of Sir James and Lady Margaret MacDonald, by financial worries, and a stagnant economy at the end of the Seven Years', or French and Indian, War. From Skye many young men had been recruited by Capt William MacDonald and Lady Margaret's brother for Montgomery's Highlanders, and some had settled in North America.

In the spring of 1764 Sir James MacDonald travelled from London to Paris, and then came north to Skye in the summer. Gloomy about the prospects in the cattle trade, Allan offered to give up the factorship. Allan then owed Sir James about £360. But Sir James refused.[3]

While out with a shooting party in North Uist, Sir James was accidently shot in the leg by his kinsman John MacLeod of Talisker, colonel in the Dutch service. Sir James was rushed to the home of Ewen MacDonald of Vallay. Already a sickly man, Sir James struggled to recover. He returned to London in the autumn, and went to Paris.

Dr Johnson wrote that "the cattle of *Sky* are not so small as is commonly believed. Since they have sent their beeves in great numbers to southern marts, they have probably taken more care of their breed. At stated times the annual growth of cattle is driven to a fair, by a general drover, and with the money, which he returns to the former, the rents are paid.

"The price regularly expected is from two to three pounds a head; there was once one sold for five pounds. They go from the Island very lean, and are not offered to the butcher, till they have been fatted in *English* pastures."[11]

In October Allan travelled to the Tryst at Crieff. He later wrote that in "that very year haveing Twenty eight hundred Cattle bought; and after disposing of them and Ballanceing the Transactions of the Season, there plainely appeared £1354.13s — of a Ballance that my List of Buying includeing the Driving expence exceeded my list of selling."[9]

If Allan had paid £2.10s a head for his cattle in Skye, he would have accumulated bills worth £7,000. When he got to Crieff, if he had only been able to get £2 a head for his cattle, he would have received £5,600, a difference of £1,400. Cattle prices had fallen by about 20%.

The number of cattle Allan had purchased seemed huge, representing at least half of those sold in Skye. But he had probably been purchasing that many cattle for several years, and if, after deducting his expenses, he had made a shilling on each beast sold, then he would have made a profit of about £140, more than enough to pay the rents on both his tacks.

Allan had made a bad judgement, and now he was ruined financially, and was never to recover from the blow. Allan returned to Kingsburgh in despair, and received little sympathy from those from whom he had purchased the cattle. The reign of the MacDonald house of Kingsburgh was almost at an end in Skye.

In the spring of 1765, Allan later wrote that "I was called to Edr to settle accotts and help in the drawing up of a plan for the incomeing Sett; This I faithfully executed with my father and Hugh McDonald's assistance, from my books, my knowledge of the Country and State of the people — going and retouring from Edr at my own expence;

"And after all was deprived of the factory that very year after my misfortune & almost utter ruine when I had a fair chance of makeing up a good part of my Loss; nay there was proclamations at ye Church doors to give me no Cattle on my Credit as non of my Bills woud be takein but to give the Cattle to Charles McSween." [9]

Having offered to demit the factorship when he owed Sir James about £360, and fearing a fall in cattle prices, Allan had been forced to continue, and incurred further huge debts of over £1354. Having travelled to Edinburgh to make financial arrangements, he had then been deprived of the factorship, doubtless at the insistence of Lady Margaret MacDonald. Even worse, he had been denied credit. Allan became bitter and disillusioned.

At last Lady Margaret was avenged of the Kingsburgh family, for all the years of resentment she had harboured against old Kingsburgh, for being the cause of her husband's death; his son, Allan, for having run the MacDonald estate for his own ends, and his daughter in law, the 'gypsy' Flora, for having been a heroine in 1746, when she had been a panicking liar.

Sir James was a sick man, but he was in Edinburgh in the summer of 1765. To Allan's sorrow, and to Sir James's near ruin, Charles MacSween proved to be "a cheating fellow who was introduced to Sir James under the character of a good honest dealer, but that very year trip't of with himself to Antigua haveing his pockets lined with honest mens money, and was bold to Carrie of Slate rents along with ye rest." [9]

In January 1766 Flora was in Edinburgh, and at the end of the month set off for Skye with a letter for Dr John Maclean, now factor in

Trotternish, and a charter for the Mackinnon lands in Skye, purchased by underhand means, by Sir James MacDonald for his brother, Alexander. Sir James was aware of his mother's neglect of his younger brother, and tried to make provision for him. Flora reached Skye on 14th March.

On 6th May, at 8 o'clock in the morning, less than two months later, Flora gave birth to her seventh child, a daughter named Frances, but known as Fanny. After a gap of seven years, at the age of 44, Flora gave birth to her seventh child. Flora was a hardy woman, despite her small stature, and the birth of the girl brought some joy into the household. Allan and Flora were still in serious financial difficulties.

Sir James was very ill. In the winter of 1765/66 he travelled to Italy for his health, and in the summer of 1766 moved to Rome, where on 26th July he died, aged twenty five years. Sir James's death was much lamented in Rome, Paris, London, Edinburgh and Skye. His mother had an over elaborate memorial carved for him in the church at Sleat.

Dr John Maclean wrote that Delvine's letter brought "the sad Accounts of Sir James MacDonald death ... What a Disappointment after the great happiness which we promised our Selves by his return, poor unlucky people we are, & very few of us Sensible of the Loss we have Suffer'd, the youngest of us will never see a person of a warmer heart, better principles or more inclined to do all the good in his power." [9]

The older Sir Alexander MacDonald had been determined to live with his people in Skye. His sudden death in November 1746 had been the first blow to the MacDonald estates. His son, Sir James, visited Skye only twice, after he had reached his majority, but as his heart searching letters showed, he had a strong feeling for the welfare of his people.

Sir James's brother Alexander, now Sir Alexander, was of a quite different disposition. Born at Monkstadt in March 1744, he was educated at Eton and St Andrews University, and had been totally neglected by his mother. In May 1761 he received an ensign's commission in the Coldstream Guards. He did not share his brother's interest in the Gaelic traditions of his people.

Dr John Maclean wrote to MacKenzie of Delvine, from Kingsburgh, that "I hope Sir, all the Bills which I sent payable at ffalkirk have answer'd, as that Tryst turn'd out so very favourable to our Drovers and all from McLeods Country were punctual enough, and Kingsburgh assures me his will, he goes to Edinr himself after Crieff — You have here enclosed a Bill of his for Sixty pounds — I have not been able get any more tho' I am diligent enough." [9]

After the fall in price for black cattle in 1765, the price was now much improved. This came too late to benefit Allan, who had been denied credit. He had been down in Edinburgh, but avoided seeing MacKenzie of Delvine.

From Kingsburgh Allan wrote, in January 1767, to Delvine apologising for having not seen him. "It is true, and I own; that my Conduct hath been foolish in many steps of my by passed Life. But weis [woe is] me the loss is intyrely to myself and family.

"Therefore, it woud be greater Charity in any man who professes friendship for me, my poor wife and seven children to recommend me to the man on whome all my dependence is And fix him so my friend, that the groundless Backbiteings of my evil wishers may not gaine ground on him to my Disadvantage;

"What offence have I given that cannot be forgiven, God is my witness that I went with integrity and ane honest heart about my Dr Deceased master's business, while I managed it for Eleven years, and tho I fell so deeply in his areers, yet I hope you have so much charity for me, as firmly to believe I had no Dishonest plan to heart;

"God — forbid that I should complain of my Dr friend, as the hardships I underwent then were not his doings, yet I cannot forgett my own melancholy State at that time;"

Allan had been criticised for attempting to obtain a commission for his young son; he had offered to resign the factorship; he had been ruined by the fall in cattle prices and then Charles MacSween had gone off to Antigua with the Skye rents.

"Now Dr Sir if I have not intyrely merited your displeasure, will you not put in a favourable word for me to help throw the getting me a lace [lease] of this Tack which would encourage me to go on chearfully with my little improvements, and help the education of my family who are now growing men & women on my hands ... in short was there anything in the world thrown in my way which woud help their own & mothers suport I woud chearfully submitt to any slavery to better them and the doing of it woud be friendly —

"And as I have paid the best part of my Bond I am hopefull with the asistance of God I will have it all clear against August next and August comes twelve month only if Interest is asked of me it will hurt me much, and be a means of stoping me from puting my poor family in a way of doing for themselves —"

Allan was being envied for the £50 given as a pension to his father but "all he pays me yearly by way of Bord wedges which he himself indeed proposed is £14 10s Sterling for himself and servent and should he not pay a farthing he woud be excessive welcom with me." [9]

In June Allan wrote from Kingsburgh to Delvine that he hoped that Sir Alexander would come to Skye, so that he could get to know his people, "among that noumber I make one who my nighboures will attest is as usefull a member of Society as any of themselves and who, and my father before me hath improved our tack and Laid out on Building planting and incloseing &c more than the whole Estate put together."

Allan had sown rye grass and clover; he had brought three varieties of potato, which had now spread throughout the island to displace the "Small Red Scotsh sort." Three years before he had brought in a large flock of sheep and had given rams to the tenants, "by Crossing the Brood with our own very Small Kind hath given the Country a very fine appearance of haveing ane hardy Strong good Brood of Sheep." He had also brought in pigs — "In Short I will Say nothing of my Self but what the Country will attest —"

Allan asked for a lease of three times nineteen, or even forty years, as "I deserve to be Distinguished from the Rest and Considering this and the Service of my old father whom Sir James of Blissed memory both fully rewarded I shoud think it wud be no Dificult Task for my poor familys weel wishers to make me & my wife & berns happy As I Suffered more than any factor that ever was on the Estate when I had the management of afairs and was Turned of the very next year when I had a faire Chance of makeing at Least a part of £1300 I lost the year before —

"I do think that my present situation Should be considered and that as I am Strugling to Give Schooling to my Childering and at the same time endeavoureing by degrees to clear of the lode that wicked year left over my neck Ive to my master and others Say friends Shoud put all Irons in the fire to get me on a Sure footing." [9]

Allan had sunk into a deep depression, and grovelled before John MacKenzie of Delvine, begging him to intercede on behalf of his family. Allan even remembered Sir James, who had been so antagonistic, and had deprived him of the factorship, as 'my dear deceased master,' and of 'Blissed memory.' Allan feared what the new chief might do.

CHAPTER 12

Following Their Friends to America

*Of this family ... there will soon be no remembrance
in this poor miserable Iland, the best of its inhabitants
are making ready to follow their friends to America,
while they have anything to bring there, and among the
rest we are to go, especially as we cannot promise
ourselves but poverty and oppression.*
— Flora MacDonald

Sir Alexander MacDonald did not visit Skye until August 1767. When
he arrived, he discovered that he would make more money from kelp
than from his agricultural tenants. Kelp, made with back breaking
labour from seaweed, was to transform the MacDonald estates, and
make Sir Alexander a rich man.

In October Sir Alexander stayed at Kingsburgh, but Allan had
received no new, or extended lease. Sir Alexander returned to London.

In 1768 Sir Alexander married Elizabeth Bosville, heiress of Thorpe
Hall, in Yorkshire. The newly weds came to Edinburgh, where they
spent the winter. In December Sir Alexander caused much bitterness
amongst his tenants, by removing his business from John MacKenzie of
Delvine, whose family had acted for the MacDonalds for more than
fifty years.

An unsigned letter addressed to Sir Alexander, written a year later,
stated that "After purchasing the conveniences and elegancies of Life
Money is no farther desirable than as it procures its power and
influence. A Highland Chief inherits more power and influence than all
the Dukes and nabobs of England can obtain with all their Gold.

"But a highland chief must preserve the affection of his clan. He
must look upon them as his kinsmen and behave like a father to them.
If he does not, the best and most generous principle may wither and
instead of being a respectful chieftain he may find himself a punny
tyrant. You have the honour of being a *MacDonald* — Don't let us see
you a *Mock* Donald." [2]

At Kingsburgh Allan and Flora were pulling themselves painfully
out of debt. They succeeded in placing their eldest boy. Through the
influence of Lady Margaret MacDonald, whose hatred had relented a
little, Charles became an officer in the East India Company, "My Lady

Dowager Primrose having Rigged him out & paid for his passage." [3]

In 1770 their elder daughter Ann, aged 16, married Alexander MacLeod of Glendale. Born about 1730, he was the illegitimate son of Norman MacLeod of MacLeod. Alexander was educated at his father's expense, and then in 1744 joined the Marines, and retired in 1766, on lieutenant's half pay. His father, with whom he was a favourite, gave Alexander the tacks of Hamara and Husabost in Glendale. In 1767 he was appointed factor on the MacLeod estates, a post he held until his father's death in 1772.

Lt Alexander MacLeod of Glendale, aged about 40, was a wealthy man, and a good catch for Ann. Flora was relieved that her daughter had made a financially advantageous match. But despite the difference in their ages, Alexander and Ann were to be a devoted couple.

At this time old Kingsburgh's daughter, Anne MacAlister, a widow for more than ten years, married Lachlan Mackinnon of Corrie-chatachan. She moved from Skirinish to Corrie in Strath.

There had been a cattle plague in 1769, and prices had plunged the following year. Then the Spring of 1771 came to be called the Black Spring in Skye. Most unusually snow lay on the ground for eight weeks, and many cattle died. Others had to be sold early and those that remained were emaciated. On the MacDonald Estates the seven year leases, set in 1764, were due to run out at Whitsunday 1771. The rents were to be increased sharply.

A group of eight tacksmen in Skye formed an association to petition for a grant of 40,000 acres in North Carolina. The men included James Macdonald Merchant in Portree; Edmund Macqueen, schoolmaster in Portree; rev William MacQueen, minister of Snizort; Hugh Mac-Donald of Camuscross and his son in law, Alexander MacDonald of Cuidrach.

The petition was rejected, because land was only being granted to foreign Protestants, and the government hoped to prevent gentlemen from going to America. But Alexander MacDonald of Cuidrach and Hugh MacDonald of Camuscross, now a widower, decided to emigrate in any case. Late next year Hugh, with his daughter Annabella and husband Alexander, left Skye. Annabella took her four girls with her, but her son Donald was left behind, to join his parents later. Alexander's brothers, James, the inn keeper at Portree, and Kenneth, also joined them later in North Carolina.

In April 1771, old Kingsburgh, unable to write, dictated a letter to MacKenzie of Delvine thanking him for the kindness shown to Flora, when she had been in Edinburgh, and for agreeing to take in and educate her son Johnny. Edmund MacQueen, schoolmaster in Portree, commended the 12 year old boy to Delvine, sending a specimen of his handwriting. "His genius is Tolerably good with application Suitable to his years, I am pretty well Satisfied the progress he has made." [1]

Kingsburgh lamented the passing of Sir Alexander, and his son, Sir James. "Were Either of them in being the Bearer Mr James Macdonald would not be sent to London to freighte Vessels for about 500 Passengers from this Place to America; They have also united their Stocks into one Capital to purchase lands; Since they were forced to take this Step, tis a Pity they had note able friends to assist them in Procuring of a grante." [1]

In Edinburgh Flora had visited the elderly Robert Forbes, since 1762 Bishop of Ross and Caithness, for in May Bishop Forbes wrote that "Two thousand emigrants are preparing for their departure from the isle of Sky to one part of our foreign settlements, perhaps the Island of St John. They are all of the estate of Sir Alexander MacDonald, who may chance to be a proprietor of land without tenants. That they go as a formed colony a parochial preacher and a thorough-bred surgeon are to go along with them. They have already subscribed £2000 sterling for the purpose. Last year 800 went from Argileshire and about 500 from the island of Islay, and others are still making ready to emigrate, which, if not timeously and wisely looked to, may terminate in depopulating Old Caledon! All, *all* this is owing to exorbitant rents for land." [4]

On 15th January 1772, Alexander MacDonald of Kingsburgh died. His son Allan wrote to Delvine that "little before he dyed . . . he desired me to let you know of his death and his last blissing to you for the many kindnesses he received at your hands." [1]

The *Scots Magazine* reported his death, under the date 13th February. "Our readers will remember this gentleman's hospitality to the Young Pretender in 1746, his bold avowal of what he had done, when in a situation that would have intimidated a man of less resolution." [5]

Bishop Robert Forbes noted that "died the hospitable, disinterested and worthy Alexander MacDonald of Kingsborrow, aged 83.

Let all the world say what they can,
He liv'd and died an honest man." [4]

In July Thomas Pennant visited Skye. Everywhere he noted destitution and suffering. "The poor are left to providence's care: they prowl like other animals along the shores to pick up limpets and other shellfish, the casual repasts of hundreds during part of the year in these unhappy islands." [6] So rare was the sight of a field of oats or barley, near Kingsburgh, that Pennant described it as a field "laughing with corn." [6]

Pennant wrote that "after a passage of a mile landed at KINGSBURGH

... immortalized by its mistress the celebrated FLORA MACDONALD, the fair protectress of a fugitive adventurer; who, after some days concealing himself from pursuit, in the disguise of the Lady's maid, here flung off the female habit.

"I had the pleasure of her acquaintance at the first Sir Watkin William Wynne's in the year 1746; but at this time I unfortunately found that she was absent on a visit. Am lodged this night in the same bed that formerly received the unfortunate *Charles Stuart*." [6]

Flora had been away visiting again, but in August Flora was back at Kingsburgh and sent her son Johnny to Edinburgh with a letter for MacKenzie of Delvine. "May the Blessings of the almighty attend you ... which is all the return I am able to make for your many and repeated freindships shown to me and this family; of which there will soon be no remembrance in this poor miserable Iland, the best of its inhabitants are making ready to follow their friends to America, while they have anything to bring there, and among the rest we are to go, especially as we cannot promise ourselves but poverty and oppression.

"Haveing last Spring and this time two years lost almost our whole Stock of Cattle and horses; we lost within these three years, three hundred and twenty seven heads, so that we have hardly what will pay our Creditors which we are to let them have and begin the world again, anewe, in another Corner of it."

Flora added lamely that "Allen was to write you but he is not well with a pain in his Side these ten days past." [1] Allan had begun to find ways of avoiding writing difficult letters.

Allan and Flora's finances were in complete disarray again. The winter had been severe on the black cattle, and the dead beasts were worth between £600 and £700. The prospects at the trysts looked poor. Old Kingsburgh had died, and many of their friends had left. Allan, in a fit of despair that had reduced him to illness, had decided to throw up the tack of Kingsburgh and to emigrate to North Carolina. Flora, despondent at her husband's inability to make farming and cattle pay in Skye, saw no solution but to give up everything; tear herself away from her homeland and "begin the world again, anewe, in another Corner of it."

In March 1773 Allan wrote dejectedly to Delvine that "The only newes in this island is Emegration; I believe the whole will go for America — In 1771 there Shipped and arrived Safe in North Carolina 500 souls. In 1772 there Shiped and arrived Safe in said place 450 souls. This year they have already signed & preparing to go, above 800 souls and all those from Sky & North Uist —

"It is melancholy to see the State of this miserable place; The superior sumoning the tennents to remove for not paying the great reants &c the tennents the Superior for oppresion, for breaking the Conditions of his tacks, and for violent profits — The factor tennents at Law for Iniquitous and wrong Accots and force them out of their lands in the month of May & June without previous warning —

"No respect of persons, as the best are mostly gone, Stealing of Sheep In constantly, and picking and thieving of Corn, gardin Stuffs, and potatos, perpetually Lying, Back byting, and slandery — honesty intyrly fled, villany and Decat, [deceit] suported by down right poverty in this place — most miserable is the State of this once good and great family —

"When this next Emergrasion is gone, only old Aird, and other three old men, will be all, that will be in Slate and troternish of the name of McDonald." Allan was bitterly resentful of his MacDonald world that had crumbled about him, taking all his cherished values with it.

The only good news was that his son Ranald had obtained a commission in the Marines. "This week I send off one of my Boys for Capt Charles Douglas of the St Albans of Glasgow — god reward the good Gentleman he acts the part of a friend to me and my wife." [1]

In July 1773 the Edinburgh *Courant* reported that eight hundred people from the Isle of Skye were to emigrate to North Carolina. "The extravagant rents started by the landlords is the sole cause given for this spirit of emigration which seems only in its infancy." [7]

In the late summer, James Boswell, an Edinburgh advocate, in company with Dr Samuel Johnson, the English lexographer, writer and raconteur, arrived in Skye on a tour of the Hebrides. Both men took an instant dislike to Sir Alexander MacDonald, with whom they stayed at Armadale. Boswell was related to his wife.

"It was in vain to try to inspirit him. Mr Johnson said, 'Sir, we shall make nothing of him. He has no more ideas of a chief than an attorney who has twenty houses in a street and considers how much he can make of them. All is wrong. He has nothing to say to his people when they come to him.'" [8] Boswell and Johnson travelled to Broadford, where they stayed with Mackinnon of Corrie, and his wife, Anne, old Kingsburgh's daughter.

"I observed to Mr Johnson that if Sir Alexander was a fierce barbarian, there might be something grand in observing his ravages; but that so much mischief should be produced by such an insect, really vexed me. At Coirechatachan the universal voice was against him . . . It was said Sir Alexander is very frightened at sea. Said Mr Johnson, '*He's* frightened at sea; and his tenants are frightened when he comes to land.'" [8]

Dr Johnson and Boswell crossed to Raasay, where they were entertained by John MacLeod of Raasay, the young Rona of the 1745 Rising. On the island they met young Norman MacLeod of MacLeod, who had succeeded his grandfather, and Col John MacLeod of Talisker, who had commanded the Independent Companies in Skye in 1746. Dr Johnson was invited to visit Dunvegan Castle and Talisker House.

James Boswell wrote, however, that "we were resolved to pay a visit at Kingsburgh and see the celebrated Miss Flora Macdonald, who is married to the present Kingsburgh."[8] Sir Alexander, created Lord MacDonald in 1776, wrote to Boswell that "at your own behaviour every one felt some degree of resentment when you told me your only errand into Skye was to visit the Pretender's conductress, and that you deemed every moment as lost which was not open in her company."[8]

The travellers crossed back to Skye. "We came into the harbour of Portree, which is a large and good one. There was lying in it a vessel to carry off the emigrants. It was called the *Nestor*. It made a short settlement of the difference between a chief and his clan:

"Raasay and I and the rest went on board of her. She was a very pretty vessel, we were told the largest in the Clyde, being of 800 ton. Harrison, the Captain, showed us her. The cabin was commodious and even elegant. There was a little library, finely bound ... The accommodation for the emigrants was very good. A long ward I may call it, with a row of beds on each side, every one of which was the same size every way, and fit to contain four people.

"We landed at Portree ... We found here a very good half finished inn, kept by James Macdonald, who is going to America." James MacDonald was Cuidrach's brother. He had been the leading petitioner for land in 1771, and was to emigrate to North Carolina. From Portree Dr Johnson and James Boswell rode to Kingsburgh House.

"It was fine to see Mr Johnson light from his horse at Kingsburgh's who received us most courteously, and after shaking hands supported Mr Johnson into the house. He was quite the figure of a gallant Highlander — 'the graceful mien and manly looks.' He had his tartan plaid thrown about him, a large blue bonnet with a knot of black ribbon like a cockade, a brown short coat of a kind of duffle, a tartan vest with gold buttons and gold buttonholes, a bluish filibeg, and tartan hose. He had jet black hair tied behind and with screwed ringlets on each side, and was a large stately man, with a steady sensible countenance."

The filibeg, in Gaelic feile beag, or little wrap, was an unsewn kilt of about four yards of tartan pleated and belted around the waist.

"There was a comfortable parlour with a good fire, and a dram of admirable Holland's gin went round. By and by supper came, when there appeared his spouse, the celebrated Miss Flora. She was a little woman, of a mild and genteel appearance, mighty soft and well bred. To see Mr Samuel Johnson salute Miss Flora Macdonald was a wonderful romantic scene to me.

"We had as genteel a supper as one could wish to see, in particular an excellent roast turkey, porter to drink at table, and after supper claret and punch. But what I admired was the perfect ease with which everything went on.

"Miss Flora (for so I shall call her) told me she heard upon the mainland, as she was returning to Skye about a fortnight before this, that Mr Boswell was coming to Skye, and one Mr Johnson, a young English buck, with him. He was highly entertained with this event."

Dr Johnson "was rather quiescent tonight and went early to bed. I was in a cordial humour, and promoted a cheerful glass. The punch was superexcellent, and we drank three bowls of it.

"My heart was sore to recollect that Kingsburgh had fallen sorely back in his affairs, was under a load of debt, and intended to go to America. However, nothing but what was good was present, and I pleased myself in thinking that so fine a fellow would be well everywhere. I slept in the same room with Mr Johnson. Each had a neat clean bed in an upper chamber.

"Monday 13 September. Last night's jovial bout disturbed me somewhat, but not long. The room where we lay was a room indeed. Each bed had tartan curtains, and Mr Johnson's was the very bed in which the Prince lay. To see Mr Samuel Johnson lying in Prince Charles's bed, in the Isle of Skye, in the house of Miss Flora Macdonald, struck me with such a group of ideas as it is not easy for words to describe as the mind perceives them. He smiled, and said, "I have had no ambitious thoughts in it." The room was decorated with a great variety of maps and prints. Among others was Hogarth's print of Wilkes grinning with a cap of liberty beside him.

"At breakfast he said he would have given a good deal rather than not have lain in the bed. I said he was the lucky man; and to be sure it had been contrived between Mrs Macdonald and him. She said, 'You know young *bucks* are always favourites of the ladies.'

"He spoke of the Prince being there, and said to Mrs Macdonald, '*Who* was with him? We were told in England, there was one Miss Flora Macdonald with him.' Said she, 'They were very right.'

"She then very obligingly told him out of her own mouth, how she had agreed to carry the prince with her out of Lewis when it was known he was there; the country was full of troops and the coast surrounded with ships. He passed as her maid, an Irish girl, Betty Bourke. They set off in a small boat. The people on shore fired after them to bring them to. But they went forward. They landed in Skye. She got a horse and her maid walked beside her, which it seemed is common in this part of the world, but Betty looked somewhat awkward in the women's clothes. They came to Monkstadt. She dined at the table with Lady Margaret Macdonald, where was an officer who commanded a party watching for the Prince, at whom she often laughed a good deal afterwards as having deceived him; and her maid was I do not remember where.

"Mr Johnson said all this should be written down. She said Bishop Forbes at Leith had it." [8]

James Boswell compiled a long account of the Prince's wanderings, for his *Journal*. He wrote that "Flora MacDonald waited on Lady Margaret, and acquainted her of the enterprise in which she was engaged. Her ladyship, whose active benevolence was ever seconded by superior talents, shewed a perfect presence of mind, and readiness of invention, and at once settled that Prince Charles should be conducted to old Raasay, who was himself concealed with some select friends." [8]

This description bore no resemblance to the panicking indecision which Lady Margaret displayed in June 1746. But then, though Boswell might criticise her son, a mere baronet, he would not speak ill of an earl's daughter, especially the daughter of an earl whom he knew in Ayrshire.

Boswell also wrote that Anne Mackinnon of Corrie, old Kingsburgh's daughter, stated that "Lady Margaret was quite adored in Sky. That when she travelled through the island, the people ran in crowds before her, and took the stones off the road, lest her horse should stumble and she be hurt." [8] Anne, then the widowed Mrs MacAllister, was the woman who had caused Sir James, and his mother, so much grief by not wishing to part with the tack of Skirinish in 1763.

Lady Margaret may, indeed, have been loved in Skye, not only for her rank, but also as the champion of the party opposed to the Kingsburgh MacDonalds, whom so many people disliked. No one was reported to have cleared stones away from Flora's horse.

Dr Johnson's account of his visit to Kingsburgh was brief. He wrote that at Portree "we dined at a publick house, I believe the only inn of the island, and having mounted our horses, travelled in the manner already described, till we came to *Kingsborough.*

"We were entertained with the usual hospitality by Mr *Macdonald* and his lady *Flora Macdonald,* a name that will be mentioned in history, and if courage and fidelity be virtues, mentioned with honour. She is a woman of middle stature, soft features, gentle manners, and elegant presence."[9]

Allan and Flora put on brave faces, masking their difficulties with a show of plenty, but their secure and privileged world had crumbled into ruin about them.

Dr Johnson was a perceptive man and commented that "The Chiefs, divested of their prerogatives, necessarily turned their thoughts to the improvement of their revenues, and expected more rent, as they have less homage. The tenant ... does not immediately see why his industry is to be taxed more heavily than before. He refuses to pay the demand, and is ejected; the ground is then let to a stranger, who perhaps brings a larger stock, but who, taking the land at its full price, treats with the Laird upon equal terms, and considers him not as a Chief, but as a trafficker in land. Thus the estate perhaps is improved, but the clan is broken ... It seems to be the general opinion, that the rents have been raised with too much eagerness.

"There seems now, whatever be the cause, to be through a great part of the Highlands a general discontent. That adherence, which was lately professed by every man to the chief of his name, has now little prevalence; and he that cannot live as he desires at home, listens to the tale of fortunate islands, and happy regions, where every man may have land of his own, and eat the product of his labour without a superior.

"Those who have obtained grants of American lands, have, as is well known, invited settlers from all quarters of the globe; and among other places, where oppression might produce a wish for new habitations, their emissaries would not fail to try their persuasions in the Isles of Scotland, where at the time when the clans were newly disunited from the Chiefs, and exasperated by unprecedented exactions, it is no wonder that they prevailed."[9]

Dr Johnson concluded that "There was perhaps never any change of national manners so quick, so great, and so general as that which has operated in the Highlands, by the late conquest, and the subsequent laws. We came thither too late to see what we expected, a people of peculiar appearance, and a system of antiquated life. The clans retain little now of their original character, their ferocity of temper is softened, their military ardour extinguished, their dignity of independence is depressed, their contempt for government subdued, and their reverence for their chiefs abated. Of what they had before the late conquest of their country, there remain only their language and their poverty. Their language is attacked on every side. Schools are erected, in which *English* only is taught.

"That their poverty is abated, cannot be mentioned among the unpleasing consequences of subjugation." [9]

Dr Samuel Johnson and James Boswell continued their tour to Dunvegan, and back to Sleat, where Boswell wrote that "We had again a good dinner, and in the evening a great dance. We made out five country squares without sitting down; and then we performed with much activity a dance which I suppose the emigration from Skye has occasioned. They call it 'America'.

"A brisk reel is played. The first couple begin, and each sets to one — then each to another — then they set to the next couple, the second and third couples are setting; and so it goes on till all are set a-going, setting and wheeling round each other, while each is making the tour of all in the dance. It shows how emigration catches till all are set afloat." [8]

Allan and Flora had been caught by emigration, and were about to be set afloat. They started winding up their affairs in Skye. Flora's daughter Ann, married to Alexander MacLeod with two sons, Norman and Allan, named for their grandfathers, was also preparing to leave Skye with her parents.

Flora was determined to provide for her other children. Her youngest child, Fanny, just eight years old, Flora was content to leave behind in Skye. She was sent to live with the MacLeods of Raasay.

Flora made a desperate bid to place her second son Alexander, by writing to the Duke of Atholl. Allan knew the duke a little, but would not bring himself to ask a favour. Exasperated with her husband's weakness, Flora had the courage to write. The duke was the son of Lord George Murray, the Jacobite general. To show off Alexander's hand-writing, Flora dictated a letter, which her son wrote.

"Necessity often forces both sexes to go through many transactions contrary to their inclinations. Such is the present one as nothing but real necessity could force me to give your Grace this trouble, & open my miserable state to your Lordship's view with the hope of getting some comfort through your wonted goodness of heart to many who have been in less tribulation of mind then I am at present.

"The case is as follows — my husband by various losses & the education of our children (having no other legacy to leave them) fell through the little means we had, so as not to be able to keep this possession, especially as the rents are so prodigiously augmented; therefore of course must contrary to our inclination follow the rest of our friends who have gone this three years passed to America; but before I go would wish to have one or two boys I have still unprovided for in some shape or other off my hands.

"The oldest of the two called Alexander is bordering on nineteen years of age, hath a pretty good handwriting, as this letter may attest, went through the most of the classicks & the common rules of Arithmetick, so that he is fit for whatever providence and the recommendation of well wishers may throw in his way; your Grace's doing something for him would be the giving of real relief to my perplexed mind before I leave (with reluctance) my native land & a real piece of charity.

"Had I this boy off my hands before I leave the Kingdom I could almost leave it with pleasure, even tho' I have a Boy and a lassie still depending on the protection of kind providence.

"This freedom I am hope full your Grace will forgive as nothing but the care of my family could prevail with me to use such.

"Mr Macdonald though he once had the honour of a little of your Grace's acquaintance could not be prevailed upon to put pen to paper therefore I with the assistance of what remained of the old resolution, went through this bold task. And with the prayers of a poor distressed woman (once known to the world) for the prosperity of your family." [5]

Annoyed with Allan, Flora could not resist blaming her husband, by his losses, for falling through the little means they had. But she was deeply distressed at leaving Skye, and at having failed to provide better opportunities for her children. In her moment of grief she harkened back to happier days, when Flora MacDonald had been known as the saviour of Bonnie Prince Charlie, and when she had been the most famous woman in Scotland. Flora's letter produced no preferment.

Allan and Flora moved out of Kingsburgh at Whitsunday, in May 1774. It was a melancholy task, packing up almost twenty fours years of married life. The last ten years in the old house had been bitter, filled with worry and financial failure. Allan sold his horses and his stock of cattle, the cattle that had meant so much to him, and yet which had failed him so often. He sold his buildings, which he had improved at such cost. The purchaser was William MacLeod of Ose, the incoming tenant at Kingsburgh.

Having cleared their creditors, Allan and Flora were left with a sum of about £800. This was little more than the dowry of £700 which Flora had brought with her at their marriage. All the rest had gone — the value of the stock and buildings at Flodigarry and Kingsburgh, and the rest of Flora's money. They packed up their personal belongings, books, plate and furniture, which later they valued at £500.

Alexander MacLeod of Glendale made a list of his own goods. The inventory of "Beds & curtains, Bed clothes & Table & Bed line," amounted to £228. There were 27 pairs of blankets and 20 pairs of sheets; 11 bed covers, the best in fine satin; four sets of bed curtains, the best in crimson, with matching window curtains; four feather beds. There were 41 table cloths, and a dozen fine damask towels; 12 dozen fine dornick towels and 6 dozen "Towels that were some time in use."

The inventory of silver amounted to £87. There was one case with a dozen knives, forks and spoons, and a second with a dozen green, ivory handled knives and forks, silver mounted with a dozen spoons. In addition there were bowls, table spoons, cruets, salt cellars, sugar boxes, and a wine funnel.

Alexander MacLeod made a complete inventory of his 324 books, which he valued at £56. His taste was eclectic. There was history, poetry, novels, including *Robinson Crusoe*, *Abelard and Eloise* and *Don Quixote*, farming and theology. There were two copies of Johnson's dictionary. The most valuable works were Plutarch's *Lives*, Livy's *Roman History*, Lloyd's *Bibliotheca Biographia, History of the Arabians,* Hale's *Husbandry*, Davidson's *Horace*, and Milton's *Poetical Works*.

Alexander MacLeod listed "Household Furniture, Tables, Chairs, Chests, Drawers, looking Glasses &c, with China, earthen & Stoneware, Glasses & Kitchen furniture" valued at £157. Alexander's "own Wearing Apparel & Linen" was valued at £80, and Ann's at £120.[10]

Allan and Flora cross to North Carolina

Allan later testified "That he is a Native of North Britain, and in the autumn of the year 1774, embarked from there for the Province of North Carolina, in America."[12]

Flora, in 1789, stated sadly that "Mrs Flora McDonald followed her husband to North Carolina where a great many of the Clan were obliged to go, not being able to pay the rents demanded of them."[13] Flora probably did not follow after Allan, on a later boat, but the use of the word indicated that she went dutifully, and reluctantly.

James Banks, a North Carolina attorney, wrote in 1857 that "In 1774, Flora McDonald and her husband sailed from Campbelltown, Kintire, for Wilmington, North Carolina, on board the good ship 'Baliol'. One of their fellow passengers, Bethune, died only about five years ago."[11]

There was no record of any *Baliol* arriving at Brunswick or Wilmington in 1774.

Alexander Campbell of Ballole, in Islay, sailed to North Carolina at the end of the year, and arrived in February 1775. When, in the 1850s, James Banks asked Bethune about the ship on which Flora had sailed, the latter, remembering events of 75 years before, may have stated that it was a ship chartered by Ballole. Banks perhaps interpreted the Gaelic pronunciation 'bally ole' as *Baliol*, and thought that it was the name of the ship. Ballole himself, however, did not sail on the same ship as Flora and Allan.

The port of entry book for Brunswick, North Carolina, though mutilated, was complete for the period from July 1773 to July 1775.[14] In November 1773 two ships had arrived at Brunswick from the Isle of Skye, carrying 244 and 228 "Scotch Passengers". The first was *Margaret of Clyde*, which James Boswell had seen in Loch Bracadale on 22nd September, "a kind of melancholy sight."[8] Bonded out of Greenock on 12th August, the captain was Robert Speir, and the owner John Buchanan. The second ship was *Nestor*, which James Boswell had visited in Portree bay on 12th September. The skipper was John Harrison.

In February 1774 *Ulysses*, commanded by Capt James Chalmers and owned by Walter Ritchie, arrived from Cork in Ireland with a mixed cargo. Walter Ritchie, and his associate James Gammell, from Greenock on the river Clyde, sent nine ships to Brunswick in 1774 and 1775, with cargoes of linen, silk, leather, soap, iron and wine. *Ulysses* made three journeys, returning to Brunswick on 18th October 1774, and later on 25th June 1775.

93 emigrants came on board *Ulysses* at Greenock in August 1774, and a further 18 elsewhere, perhaps at Campbeltown. Allan and Flora, with two children, and Alexander and Ann MacLeod, with two children, and ten servants might have made up this party. In North Carolina Allan and Flora had at least eight servants, and Alexander and Ann MacLeod had at least twelve servants. These twenty or more servants, indentured for five year's service, probably came with them from Scotland.

While *Ulysses* was at Greenock, another ship was preparing to sail to North Carolina. *Cato* had been built at Montego Bay in 1774 for James Tusker. The ship was certified at Greenock on 3rd August and bonded at the same port a day later with a cargo of ballast. The captain, John Denystone, sailed to the Isle of Skye, where, in September, he collected "312 highland Passengers." *Cato*, after a long passage of some ten weeks, reached Brunswick on 1st December 1774.

While *Ulysses* and *Cato* were preparing to sail at Greenock, a third ship, *Diana*, was also being made ready. *Diana* was a much older vessel, built at Montego Bay in 1765. The owner was Robert Sinclair and Co, and the captain Dugald Ruthven. *Diana* was certified at Greenock on 19th August and bonded a day later with a mixed cargo. In Kintyre the ship picked up 34 Highland passengers, and arrived at Brunswick on 10th December. Kingsburgh's party of eight, with servants, could have made up this group of 34.

It was probably on board *Cato* with a great many other heart-broken folk from Skye, that Allan and Flora sailed to North Carolina, in September 1774. They were accompanied by their sons Alexander and James, and by their daughter Ann, her husband, Alexander MacLeod of Glendale, and their two young children.

In 1849 Catherine Crowe wrote that "One of the most remarkable instances of warning that has come to my knowledge, is that of Mr M, of Kingsburgh. This gentleman, being on a voyage to America, dreamt one night, that a little old man came into his cabin and said 'Get up! Your life is in danger!'. Upon which, Mr M awoke; but considering it to be only a dream, he soon composed himself to sleep again. The dream however, if such it were, recurred, and the old man urged him still more strongly to get up directly; but he still persuaded himself it was only a dream; and after listening a few minutes, and hearing nothing to alarm him, he turned round and addressed himself once more to sleep. But now the old man appeared again, and angrily bade him rise instantly, and take his gun and ammunition with him, for he had not a moment to lose. The injunction was now so distinct that Mr M felt he could no longer resist it; so he hastily dressed himself, took his gun and ascended to the deck, where he scarcely arrived, when the ship struck on a rock, which he and several others contrived to reach. The place however, was uninhabited, and but for his gun, they would never have been able to provide themselves with food till a vessel arrived to their relief." [15]

Was Mr M, of Kingsburgh, Allan MacDonald? Had Kingsburgh, after all, crossed to America before Flora and had he been saved from ship wreck by a dream?

CHAPTER 13

Flora and Allan in North Carolina

*My Large Plantation, containing four hundred seventy
five acres of which seventy were cleared and in cultivation, with three good Orchards of Peach and Apple and
other Fruits; a Dwelling house, with Barn, Keeping
House, Kitchen, Stable and Crib for holding Indian
Corn; a Grist Mill in a good Run of Water, by permission of Assembly, the yearly income of which
keeped the whole family in bread.*
— Allan MacDonald of Kingsburgh.

In the autumn of 1774, Allan and Flora sailed from Scotland to North
Carolina. With their children, son-in-law and grandchildren, they took
the cabin accommodation on the ship. James Boswell had written that
Nestor "was a very pretty vessel ... The cabin was commodious and
even elegant. There was a little library, finely bound." [1]

A few months after Flora's voyage, Janet Schaw made the same
journey. Brought up in Edinburgh, she sailed with her elder brother
Alexander, to the West Indies, and her young Rutherfurd cousins to
North Carolina. Janet, a sharp observer, kept a lively journal. [2]

Janet shared a narrow stateroom, six foot long and five foot wide,
with Fanny Rutherfurd, while her maid slept on the floor between the
bunks. Alexander Schaw, with Fanny's two younger brothers and his
Austrian manservant, slept in the cabin.

Boswell added that "the accommodation for the emigrants was very
good. A long ward I may call it, with a row of beds on each side, every
one of which was the same size every way, and fit to contain four
people." [1] What Boswell did not point out was that the beds were only
six foot square, and that the upper bunk was less than two feet above
the lower bunk, and only two feet below the deck. Janet Schaw wrote
that the emigrants on her ship "were fully as sensible of the motion of
the Vessel as we were, and sickness works more ways than one, so that
the smell which came from the hole, where they had been confined, was
sufficient to raise a plague aboard." [2]

In a storm, Janet's ship was severely mauled, and the masts had to be
cut away. All the provisions brought on board by the Schaws were

137

washed overboard, and Janet discovered that their regular rations had been left behind. She "had the mortification to find that the whole ships provision for a voyage cross the Tropick, consisted of a few barrels of what is called neck-beef, or cast beef, a few more of New England pork (on a third voyage cross the Atlantic, and the hot Climates), Oat meal, stinking herrings, and to own the truth, most excellent Potatoes. Had our stock escaped we had never known the poverty of the Ship, as we had more than sufficient for us all.

"Lobscore is one of the most savory dishes I ever eat. It is composed of Salt beef hung by a string over the side of the ship, till tender and tolerably fresh, then cut in nice little pieces, and with potatoes, onions and pepper, is stewed for some time with the addition of a portion of water. This is my favourite dish; but scratch platter, chouder, stir-about, and some others have all their own merits.

"But alas our Voyage is hardly half over; and yet I ought not to complain, when I see the poor Emigrants, to whom our living is luxury.

"They have only for a grown person per week, one pound of neck-beef, or spoilt pork, two pounds oatmeal, with a small quantity of bisket, not only mouldy, but absolutely crumbled down with damp, wet and rottenness. The half is only allowed a child, so that if they had not potatoes, it is impossible they could live out the voyage. They have no drink, but a very small proportion of brackish water." [2]

Janet arrived safely at Antigua and then sailed to St Christophers, or St Kitts, where her brother Alexander was to take up an appointment. He obtained leave to travel to North Carolina with his sister and her young wards.

After six or eight weeks at sea, passengers were thankful when the North Carolina coast came into view. But Janet wrote that "At last America is in my view; a dreary Waste of white barren sand, and melancholy, nodding pines. In the course of many miles, no cheerful cottage has blest my eyes. All seems dreary, savage and desert; and was it for this that such sums of money, such streams of British blood have been lavished away? Oh, thou dear land, how dearly hast thou purchased this habitation for bears and wolves. Dearly has it been purchased, and at a price far dearer still will it be kept. My heart dies within me, while I view it." [2]

When Allan and Flora sailed into Cape Fear river, their hearts may have died within them too. Used to wide and distant vistas of sea, islands and mountains stretching away for forty or fifty miles, Flora and her family now saw nothing but white barren sand, and melancholy, nodding pines.

The ship sailed up river to Fort Johnston, a crudely made defence of lime and crushed oyster shells. Anchored off shore was HMS *Cruizer*, a sorry hulk of a ship, covered with barnacles. From the fort the ship continued up river to Brunswick, the official port of entry into North Carolina. Brunswick was a poor place, with two streets and fifty houses. Richard Quince was the principal merchant. Janet Schaw wrote that "He is deeply engaged in the new system of politicks, in which they are all more or less, tho' Mr Dry, the collector of the customs, is the most zealous and talks treason by the hour." [2]

Allan and Flora landed at Brunswick, but, unlike Janet Schaw, did not have the comfort of an easy ride to a relation's house, close at hand, when they went to Wilmington. This town, 13 miles up river from Brunswick, but on the east shore, had a better harbour and was less exposed to storms, and raids from daring pirates. It had a population of about 250 people. Closer to the back country, and its natural supplies, Wilmington prospered as Brunswick declined.

Like Janet Schaw, Allan and Flora were made aware of the political situation at once. In May 1774 General Thomas Gage had arrived in Boston, and had closed the port in retaliation for the 'Tea Party' of the previous December. At the end of August 1774 a provincial congress had met at New Bern, North Carolina, in open defiance of the royal governor, Josiah Martin, and had elected three representatives to attend the Continental Congress, which met in Philadephia in September.

The first Continental Congress, while reasserting its loyalty to the King, advised the colonies to form militia units; local committees of safety, and to adopt a non-import non-export agreement.

Allan and Flora naturally took the side of the King and the British Government. Allan and his son-in-law Alexander MacLeod had served King George, and had prospered during the Whig supremacy of the 18th century. Allan had no argument with Government in London, but with his chief, Sir Alexander MacDonald, who lived in Edinburgh, and who sought to extract high rents from his estates. In Skye Allan would have considered himself to be a Whig, supporting the Government, and yet in North Carolina he found himself labelled a Tory.

There was no contemporary account of Flora's life in North Carolina, but a number of stories, collected 70 or 80 years after the events, have been woven into a romantic tapestry by American writers.

Eighty years after her arrival, James Banks, an attorney in Fayetteville, gave a talk and then published a booklet, *The Life and Character of Flora MacDonald*. Much of the historical detail concerning the adventures of Flora in Scotland was incorrect, and Banks stated that in 1750 she was "married to Alexander McDonald of Kingsboro', son of

Kingsboro' who had aided in the Prince's escape."[3] Banks confused Allan with his cousin Alexander of Cuidrach. Cuidrach had married Flora's half sister Annabella, and had emigrated to North Carolina earlier. The error flawed Banks' account of Flora's time in America.

Banks wrote that "In 1774, Flora McDonald and her husband sailed from Campbelltown, Kintire, for Wilmington, North Carolina, on board the good ship 'Baliol'."[3] There was no record of *Baliol* arriving at Brunswick in 1774.

Banks continued that "The fame of her earlier years had preceded her to the Western World, and upon her arrival in Wilmington a ball was given in her honor, which she graced with her presence, and took pleasure in the degree of attention paid to her eldest daughter, Anne, who was just blushing into womanhood, and bore a striking resemblance to her mother when at the same age.

"In 1775, her daughter Anne married Alexander McLeod of Glendale, Moore county, who subsequently distinguished himself in the European Wars, and rose to the rank of Major General in the British Service. This daughter died some years ago at Stein, Scotland."[3]

Ann had married Alexander MacLeod in 1770, and was the mother of two children. Ann was pregnant with a third child. They did not meet in North Carolina. Alexander did not fight in the European Wars and did not become a major general, though Ann did die at Stein!

Despite James Banks' fanfare, it was unlikely that Flora's fame had preceded her. She had left Scotland to get away from all that. Married for 24 years, Flora was known as Allan of Kingsburgh's wife, not the saviour of Prince Charles. It was unlikely that they attended a ball at Wilmington. The Committee of Safety was against such entertainment, and later banned balls. There was no contemporary notice of Flora's arrival at Cape Fear and no echo of Flora's passing through Wilmington in Janet Schaw's journal. Later Janet was in the same house in Wilmington as Allan, but did not know that he was Flora's husband.

There was a good road from Wilmington up country to Cross Creek. Allan and Flora may have travelled by horse and cart, but they were more likely to have gone by river. The wide expanse of the northwest Cape Fear river was a natural highway. It took a week for flat boats to be rowed ninety miles up stream to Campbelltown.

Cross Creek and Campbelltown, in Cumberland county, were twin towns, two miles apart. Cross Creek was pleasantly situated on a little bluff, cut by a creek, at the start of the sandhills which marched away to the west. The town was a busy trading centre with mills, shops, dwelling houses, and a pharmacy, bustling with people and wagons from the back country. There were about 200 inhabitants.

Campbelltown was set on the swampy ground down by the river. It boasted only the courthouse, and a few dwellings. In 1778 the two towns were to be united as Campbelltown, and in 1783 renamed Fayetteville, the first town so to honour the Marquis de Lafayette.

Highland emigrants had first come to Upper Cape Fear in 1739, when a group of 350 persons, from Jura and Kintyre in Argyll, arrived in the area. The group was led a Campbell, three MacNeils, and a MacAlester. In 1740 they were granted over 14,000 acres.

In 1829 an early history of North Carolina claimed that pardoned Jacobites settled in the province, after the collapse of the 1745 Rising. Since then, a dozen historians have followed suit, but Duane Meyer has shown conclusively that the 'exile theory' had no foundation in fact. He concluded that the notion that "the North Carolina settlement of Highlanders on the upper Cape Fear was enlarged by the coming of numbers of pardoned Jacobites in 1746 and 1747 is an interpretation that is, on the basis of present evidence, subject to grave doubt. The large group of pardoned rebels who were transported to America came as indentured servants, not as settlers.

"A survey of land grants to people with Highland names who lived in the Cape Fear counties does not reveal an increase immediately after the rebellion of 1745."[5]

Highlanders had began to arrive on Upper Cape Fear, in numbers, in the 1750s and 1760s, bringing indentured servants with them. In the early 1770s numbers rose steadily, jumping to a dramatic peak in 1774. There were 10,000 Highlanders in the area, but this formed only half the population, the rest being Lowland Scots, English, Irish, Welsh, German and a few French.

The Province's wealth was in the endless pine forests, from which pitch, tar and turpentine were extracted and shingles and wood cut for naval supplies. These were transported to the West Indies, for building ships, and to Britain. Much of this, however, was tedious work, undertaken only by slaves. The plantation owners near the coast had slaves, but there were fewer inland, though many of the Highland gentlemen brought indentured servants with them. But all was not well with the economy, and it was proving difficult to export naval supplies.

Almost all the Highland gentlemen came to Upper Cape Fear on the recommendation of relatives and friends, seeking land to own and farm for themselves. The earlier emigrants had taken up land grants, but those arriving later found it increasingly hard to do so, and purchased existing plantations, which had begun to be cleared.

The Highlanders raised black cattle, as they had done in Scotland, though the wooded countryside was less suited to this, than to raising pigs. After the struggle and toil of wet and windy Hebridean winters, the settlers found that they could grow Indian corn; that they could raise pigs; that they could fish the rivers and creeks; that there were deer, wild turkey, pheasant, quail, ducks, wild geese and wild pigeons to be shot, without fear of poaching. In the woods there were wild grapes, strawberries, blackberries, apples, mulberries, cherries and persimmons that required only to be picked.

The Highland gentlemen were their own masters, owing rent to no landlord, and only a small charge to the Government. They had indentured servants and acquired others to farm their lands. Some purchased slaves. The land grew crops abundantly, and many believed that they had arrived in the Promised Land.

On her arrival at Cross Creek, Flora "received a truly Highland welcome from her old neighbors and kinsfolk, who had preceded her but a few years," wrote James Banks. "The strains of the Pibroch and the martial airs of her native land greeted her on her approach to the capital of the Scotch settlement. In that village she remained some time, visiting and receiving visits from friends, whilst her husband went to the western part of Cumberland, in quest of land." It was most unlikely that Flora was greeted by pipers on her arrival at Cross Creek.

"On visiting Mrs Rutherford, afterwards Mrs McAuslin, who lived at that time in a house known as Stuart place, north of the Presbyterian church, she saw a painting which represented 'Anne of Jura' assisting in the Prince's escape. "Turn the face of that picture to the wa'", said she, in her clear soft accent, "never let it see the light again; it belies the truth of history, Anne of Jura was na' there, and did na' help the bonnie Prince."[3] There was no historical person named 'Anne of Jura', or Anne of anywhere, who helped the Prince.

Rev William Foote, writing in 1846, had noted that "Allan and Flora, with their family and some friends, landed in North Carolina and took their abode for a short time at Cross Creek, now Fayetteville. The place of her residence was destroyed by the great fire that swept off a large part of the town one Sabbath in the summer of 182-. [1831]"[6]

By 1909, everyone wanted Flora to have stayed with them in Cross Creek. J.P.Maclean wrote that "four different spots were pointed out as being the site of her residence."[7]

"In 1849, there was living in Fayetteville, North Carolina, an old Scottish lady, 87 years of age. She remembered well the famous Flora ... She described Mrs Macdonald, who was then about 50 years of age, as not very tall, but very handsome and dignified, with a fair complexion, sparkling blue eyes, the finest teeth, with hair slightly streaked with white, and nearly covered with a fine lace cap.

" 'Her voice was sweet as music, and Oh!,' exclaimed the lady, 'how the poor and the church missed her when she went home after experiencing much trouble here. She was often at my mother's house, when she first came, and I almost worshipped her, because of her beauty and goodness.' " [8] In 1747 Richard Wilson had painted Flora with hazel eyes. In 1750 Allan Ramsay had coloured her eyes pale blue.

It was unlikely that Allan and Flora received a tumultuous welcome in Cross Creek, or stayed long, since Flora's half sister, Annabella, married to Alexander MacDonald of Cuidrach, lived twenty miles west at Mount Pleasant.

J.P.Maclean wrote that "A large number of MacDonalds, principally from Skye and Raasay, and kinsmen of Kingsburgh, had settled north-west of Cross Creek, a distance of twenty miles, about a hill six hundred feet in height, now called Cameron's Hill, but then known as Mount Pleasant. Here Kingsburgh purchased a large tract of land, the record of the deed is still preserved in the court house at Fayetteville. Hard by are the sources of Barbaque Creek, and not many miles down the stream stood the old kirk, where the clansmen worshipped, and where Flora inscribed her name on the roll of membership." [7]

Allan never bought land at Mount Pleasant. It was his cousin Cuidrach who had purchased Mount Pleasant in July 1772, from Duncan Buie. [9]

Cuidrach, with his wife and daughters, had emigrated some years earlier with Annabella's father Hugh MacDonald of Camuscross, and formerly of Armadale. Cuidrach had brought with him about £1100 and purchased 200 acres on the south side of a hill. "The plantation had been first settled about 20 years before. There was a Dwelling house and other necessary Buildings on it and about 30 acres then cleared — to that he added about 12 or 15 acres more, planted some Peach and some Apple trees and made a small addition to the Dwelling house.

"He had 78 head of Black cattle, 100 hogs, 9 horses, on his plantation ... He had a large copper still." [9]

The house at Mount Pleasant was made of squared logs, covered with wooden siding, with a brick chimney at each end. The kitchen and servants' quarters, also built of logs, were separate. The site of the old cleared fields at Mount Pleasant could still be seen in 1990, but now a housing development has been bull dozed over the hillside. Half a mile south of the house there was a spring, from which the household drew its water. There was a local tradition that Flora walked down to the spring below the house.

After a long sea voyage, and a journey of 100 miles from the coast, Allan and Flora relished the comfort of Mount Pleasant, surrounded by familiar furniture, pictures, books and tableware from Cuidrach, and the company of Alexander and Annabella and their children. Their eldest child, and only son, Donald, joined the family at Christmas 1774, and may have travelled from Skye with Allan and Flora.

So much else was alien to Flora. Alexander Schaw wrote that "The roads run constantly thro' woods, which tho' they are generally pretty open, yet objects at any considerable distance are intercepted from the eye, by the trees crowding into the line of direction as the distance increases."[2] Used to vistas of sea, mountains and sky stretching away for forty or fifty miles, Flora now found herself enclosed by tall pines on all sides, and unable to see further than the next tree. It was a country where one creek and valley looked like any other, and a person could be lost within a mile of their home.

The Presbyterian church at Barbecue, six miles down the creek, had been formed in 1768 by Rev James Campbell, but the minister in 1774 was John MacLeod. He had emigrated from Balmore in Skye in 1772. Rev Foote wrote of Flora that "While residing at this place, Mrs Smith, now living in Robeson County ... remembers seeing her, at the Barbecue church, a dignified and handsome woman, to whom all paid great respect."[6] The foundations of the first church are marked by a cairn behind the present building.

James Banks added that "years ago I heard Malcolm McKay, who had been in early life a Cornet in the British Army, remark, that he had seen the Queen of England and many of her attendants, but for grace and dignity Flora McDonald excelled all the women he ever beheld: that it was worth a day's ride to see her graceful manner of sitting, or rising from a chair — that there was a perfection of ease and grace in that simple act, that could be felt but not described."[3]

Flora and Allan were surrounded by relations and friends. Flora's stepfather, Hugh, had settled in Anson County, with land on Mountain Creek and Cheeks Creek. Flora's other half-sister, Flora, had married Archibald MacQueen, and they had emigrated with their children in about 1772.

Alexander MacDonald of Cuidrach and Mount Pleasant had also purchased 200 acres in Anson County, on Mountain Creek, from Luke Robinson, and a further "200 acres were a gift from his Father-in-Law who was something in Claimants Debt — no improvements made by himself on the 200 except what was made by his Brother-in-Law,

[Archibald] MacQueen who he gave leave to settle on them''[9]. Flora and Archibald's son James became a teacher in Anson County, and later married one of his pupils, Anne Macrae.[10]

Donald Roy MacDonald, who had dined with Flora in Portree on 30th June 1746, had also emigrated to North Carolina. In 1773 he purchased from Jacob McLendon 200 acres on both sides of Mc-Lendon's Creek, and a further 150 acres adjoining, and another 150 acres on Suck Creek. Donald died in 1774.

Donald Roy's sister, Katherine, had married Donald Campbell, who had sheltered the Prince on the Isle of Scalpay. The Campbells were in their seventies, but had been persuaded to emigrate, in 1773, by their son John, with his sisters Barbara, Isobel, Christian and Margaret.

In 1774 John Campbell purchased 150 acres from Edward Cox at the head of McLendon's Creek, and five miles from Donald Mac-Donald. Barbara Campbell's husband, Alexander MacLeod of Pabbay and St Kilda, purchased 200 acres from Thomas Elliott, a mile below the Campbell tract. On this land, in partnership with his brother-in-law, Alexander MacLeod built a dam and grist mill.

Isobel Campbell had married Alexander, junior, younger brother of Barbara's Alexander. Isobel and Alexander lived on Mountain Creek. Christian Campbell's husband, Angus Bethune, had died, but she emigrated with her son, Rev John Bethune. About 1774 Rev John Bethune was said to have organised the church at Carmel. Margaret Campbell and her husband Duncan Campbell settled on Cheeks Creek.

Alexander MacLeod of Pabbay had another brother, Capt Donald, in Boston. Alexander's cousin, Rev John MacLeod, was the minister at Longstreet, Barbecue and Bluff churches.

Allan and Flora's daughter, Ann, was married to Alexander Mac-Leod of Glendale. Alexander was a cousin of Alexander Morrison of Skinidin, whose father had been doctor on the MacLeod Estates. In 1771 Alexander Morrison, with 300 of his neighbours, emigrated to North Carolina. He settled at Crosshill, on McLendon's Creek, where he had 300 acres. He practised as a doctor and had a store. He had land on nearby Richland Creek and Suck Creek. There was land on Cheeks Creek.

Glendale purchased land on Mountain Creek, but decided to live not far from his cousin Alexander Morrison at Crosshill.

Alexander and Ann MacLeod leased a tract from Kenneth Black, on MacDeeds, now Wads Creek, and lived in a house on the south side of the water. They called the plantation Glendale, and though the MacLeods lived there for only a few years, it retained its name, 'Glindal

Place', well into the 19th century. The site of the house is now close to Victory Baptist Church.

Kingsburgh would happily have lingered in the comfort of Mount Pleasant, but Flora sent him out to find their own plantation. He claimed, in January 1784, that he had "in the Autumn of the year 1774, embarked from there [Scotland] for the Province of North Carolina, in America, and soon after his arrival there he purchased two several Plantations" containing "four hundred and seventy-five acres of which fifty acres were cleared and in cultivation, and the two houses on them", valued at £400, and "a Grist Mill on a good run of Water, and in excellent condition," valued at £150.

"The value of my Large Plantation, containing four hundred seventy-five acres of which seventy were cleared and in cultivation, with three good Orchards of Peach and Apple and other Fruits, the Grants extant," was £300. "The value of Dwelling House, with barn, Keeping House, Kitchen, Stable and Crib for holding Indian Corn," was £80. The value of "a Grist Mill in a good Run of Water, by permission of Assembly, the yearly income of which keeped the whole family in Bread," was £120. "The value of my Little Plantation of fifty acres, of which thirty were cleared land and in cultivation, with a good orchard of Peaches, Apples, and other fruits, including a farm House, Barn and Crib," was £110.[9]

There were no surviving records of Kingsburgh's purchases of his two plantations in Anson County, but in 1857 James Banks wrote that "Early in January 1776 Kingsboro' MacDonald purchased a tract of land from Caleb Touchstone, on the borders of Richmond and Montgomery counties, and named the place Killiegray."[3]

J.P.Maclean added that "Having been persuaded by Colonel Mac-Queen, Allen disposed of his estate and removed farther west, and, in January, 1776, purchased of Caleb Touchstone a tract of land numbering 550 acres ... on Mountain Creek ... Allen named the estate Killiegray, which contained a dwelling and out houses, which were more pretentious than was then customary among Highland settlers."[7]

Kingsburgh made his purchase a year before January 1776. Banks was the first to mention Caleb Touchstone as the seller, and that Kingsburgh named the plantation Killiegray. But Rassie Wicker, that indefatigable historian of Moore County, showed that the place called Killiegray, containing only 205 acres, was occupied by Isaac Armstrong from 1772 until 1823. In 1824 the land was conveyed to Norman MacLeod. The name Killiegray, a MacLeod island in the Sound of Harris, dated only from that time. Allan, a MacDonald from Skye, would not have called his plantation after a MacLeod island in Harris, but he did name it Kingsburgh, the title by which he was known in Scotland and America.

Rassie Wicker showed that Caleb Touchstone, in 1774, owned a tract of 475 acres and two tracts of 50 acres each on Cheeks Creek, five miles from Killiegray. It was these tracts of 475 acres and 50 acres on Cheeks Creek that Allan purchased early in 1775. A letter from Governor Martin confirmed that Allan lived on Cheeks Creek.[11]

Cheeks Creek, a good run of water, cut through the hills of Anson, now Montgomery, county west of Candor, to join Little River near the Town Creek Indian Mound. Caleb Touchstone had built a house north east of what is now Pekin, looking out over the creek and a broad meadow. The ground was much more broken than at Mount Pleasant, with views up and down the winding river.

The exact site of Touchstone's house is not now known. In the 1950s, the Parsons claimed that the house was 3 miles up a road, now called Loving Hill Road, on the east side across the creek. The Halls, a mile back towards Pekin, claimed that theirs was the site of the house. It was near here, on the west side of the road, that in 1960 a stone was erected to commemorate Flora and Allan.

Rassie Wicker, however, calculated that Touchstone's 475 acre lot spanned the paved road between Pekin and Harrisville, close to where the North Carolina Historical Marker commemorated Flora. He thought that the house itself was exactly a mile up Loving Hill Road, on the east side, on the old Baldwin plantation, close to where, in 1952, Fannie Armitage had a shack, with an old millstone for a step. The millstone was taken away, but though the shack has gone, a stone back door step still remains. Close by was a spring, since closed, and the outrun for a mill on the creek below.

Allan and Flora found a dwelling house and kitchen. The house was named Kingsburgh, different though it was from the one they had known in Skye. With their own furniture and pictures it would soon feel like home. There was space for the servants. There was a keeping house and barn, and a stable for the horses. Allan had about ten horses.

There were seventy acres of cultivated land, though tilling it around the gnarled roots of the cleared trees was difficult. Indian corn was a new crop to Allan, but all the emigrants soon discovered that it was the principal grain of the country. There were three good orchards of peach, apple and other fruit, something that Flora had never had in Skye. Allan had about fifty cattle, which roamed the woods.

Allan had run a mill at Romesdal in Skye, and there was a mill on the creek. When neighbours came to have their grain ground, there was the miller's portion that kept the family in bread. A second plantation of 50 acres on the creek had its own farm house, barn and crib.

The Promised Land was not quite perfect, for the emigrants discovered that the summers could be unbearably hot. There were mosquitoes, and tiny 'chiggers', that were the match of any Skye midge, in the itching of their bite. There were snakes and bears in the woods, and the trees were always attempting to reclaim the cultivated ground.

Even so, Allan and the boys, Sandie and Jamie, went out shooting wild turkeys, and Flora visited her relations and friends from Skye. After all the trauma and stress of leaving Scotland, and shaking off their debts, and the wearisome journey across the Atlantic, Allan and Flora believed that they had made the correct decisions to "begin the world again, anewe, in another Corner of it."

James Banks wrote that at Killiegray "two of Flora's children died, and the present owner, McLelland, keeps a spot fenced in, sacred to the memory of Flora's offspring." [3] Allan and Flora had seven children. Four children did not come to North Carolina, but Alexander, James and Ann, married to Glendale, did accompany their parents. The departure of these children was recorded and none of them died in America.

Two of Flora's children did not die in North Carolina.

Whatever traditions James Banks may have collected at Killiegray, in the 1850s, did not relate to Flora. Affidavits taken in the early 1900s only confirmed that those interviewed had read, or heard of, James Banks' account of the two dead children. All the events that followed, though sincerely undertaken, were misplaced. [12]

CHAPTER 14

The Highland Gentlemen Remain Loyal

When the American Rebellion brock out, and Congress
forcing her husband to joyne them, being a leading
man among the highlanders, and seeing he would be
obliged to joyne either party, he went in disguise to
Fort Johnston on the mouth of the River Capefear, and
there settled the plan of riseing the highlanders in arms,
with Governor Martin. — Flora MacDonald

In North Carolina the Governor was Josiah Martin, an impulsive young man, bursting with self confidence, but sometimes lacking judgement. He attempted to maintain Royal authority, despite receiving minimal support from the Ministry in London. Throughout the winter of 1774-75, however, the Committees of Safety began to rule the province.

In March 1775, Governor Martin issued a proclamation calling for loyalty to King George III. He wrote to Gen Gage, in Boston, confident that he could raise 3,000 Loyalists and Highlanders, and asking for arms and ammunition. He also wrote to the Earl of Dartmouth, Secretary of State for the Colonies, offering to raise a regiment of Highlanders and asking for his lieutenant colonel's commission to be restored.

In April Governor Martin made a second proclamation and summoned a meeting of the Assembly, the legitimate colonial legislature, and forbade the meeting of the Provincial Congress. The Assembly met at New Bern, under the charge of John Harvey, the Speaker, but on its own initiative transformed itself into the illegal Congress, with John Harvey as Moderator. Governor Martin was furious, and dissolved the Assembly after only four days. The Congress re-elected three members to the Continental Congress, and approved the non-importation agreement. Signing the agreement came to be the 'test' for loyalty to the American cause.

By dissolving the legitimate Assembly, Governor Martin effectively lost control of government in the Province. He wrote bitterly to Lord Dartmouth that Royal authority had been humiliated.

Janet Schaw exclaimed "Good God! what are the people at home about, to suffer their friends to be thus abused. Two regiments just now

149

would reduce this province, but think what you will, in a little time, four times four will not be sufficient." [1]

Alexander MacAlester, one of the early settlers on Upper Cape Fear, wrote to his brother Hector, in Scotland, that "The Colones is much alarmed one account of sume acts of parliment that was past last year. We did Expecte this new parliment would repeile those pernisious acts which will bring America to meare slavery. If they should be put in Execution all the Colones is unanimusly agreed not to receive them one any terms. They are fully Determined to fight to the last before they will give up ther most valuable privledg which is ther liberty." [2]

On 19th April 1775 the skirmishes at Concord and Lexington proved to be the first shots to be heard around the world. News of the fighting reached North Carolina on 3rd May, and on 20th the people of Mecklenburg County made their 'Resolves', which according to Governor Martin surpassed "all the horrid and treasonable publications that the inflammatory spirits of this Continent have yet produced." [3]

On 24th May the Governor's palace at New Bern was attacked, and the Governor fled to Fort Johnston. He arrived there on 2nd June, and went on board *Cruizer*. On 16th June Governor Martin made a third proclamation, but the Committees of Safety were now in full control of the Province. The Governor's pledge to protect his dutiful and faithful subjects was almost impractical. Nine days later the Governor convened the Royal Council, but only five men appeared. The Council agreed that the Governor should issue Militia Commissions, especially in those counties which were well affected.

On 17th June a battle was fought at Bunker Hill outside Boston, though news of it was not to reach North Carolina for some weeks. Congress, in Philadelphia, appointed Col George Washington to command the Continental Army.

Alexander Morrison of Crosshill later wrote that "with regret, seeing the approaching troubles in America, at the request & solicitation of a majority of the inhabitants of Cumberland county, served as one of the members of the committee of said county, His design was to moderate the violence of the party then forming, but finding redress of grievance converted into Rebellion, your Memorialist, and indeed two thirds of the committee, espoused the Royal cause." [4]

Allan MacDonald of Kingsburgh later wrote that "Your Memorialist, whose principles were always steady to King and Country (having served as Lieutenant of an Independent Company of Highlanders all the time of the rebellion in 1745 and 1746 ...) with the assistance of a few more, appointed a meeting of the leading Highlanders." [4]

Those leading Highlanders included Flora's step father, Hugh, colonel of the Anson Militia; her brother-in-law, Cuidrach; her son-in-law, Glendale; Alexander Morrison; the Campbells of Scalpay and the MacLeods of Pabbay. All were steady for King and Country. Some remembered the harsh measures taken against the rebels after the last Jacobite Rising. Some were officers on half pay. All believed that monarchy was a form of government ordained by God, and considered that republicanism was horrid and unnatural. And the Highlanders had a burning desire not to be separated from Scotland, which they loved dearly.

Alexander Schaw saw that two groups of Highlanders existed. He was later to write to Lord Dartmouth that "There is now a numerous body of the sons and grandsons of the first Scotch highland settlers, besides the later emigrants, who retain that enthusiastic love for the country from which they are descended, which indeed scarce a highlander ever loses, that they will support its dignity at every risk." [1] The The later emigrants in the west of Cumberland and in Anson were newly arrived in the province. Some, like Alexander Morrison, had served on local committees, and had resigned. Most were out of touch with events in the east of the province. The later emigrants were acquainted with, and some related to, the first Highland settlers in North Carolina, who held land along Cape Fear river, at Cross Creek and to the north. The latter, men like Alexander MacAlester, were engaged in the work of committees. The two groups were drifting apart. Alexander MacAlester, with his relations, did not form part of Kingsburgh's meeting.

With hindsight, many Americans were surprised, and disappointed, that Allan and Flora remained loyal to King George. J.P.Maclean, writing in 1909, stated that "the disaster would not have overtaken the family had Kingsburgh refrained from precipitating himself into the conflict needlessly and recklessly. His age and past experience should have influenced his course, and bade him remain a silent spectator of the conflict. With blind fatuity he took the wrong side in the struggle, and even then, by the exercise of patience he might have overcome the effects of his folly." [5]

This statement misunderstood Kingsburgh's character. Allan was used to authority and the *status quo*. He now found himself having to join one side or the other. His past experience had taught him to remain loyal to the King. In June 1775 it was not clear that the thirteen Provinces would secede, and it was unthinkable that Britain's great war machine could be defeated. But Allan, unlike Janet Schaw, was not aware that authority and power were draining away from the Governor.

Elizabeth Vining, writing in 1967, stated that "It is always puzzling — and even shocking — to Americans that people who suffered under the Hanoverians, who had endured the atrocities after Culloden, should not, once they were free in a new country, eagerly seize the opportunity to fight for that freedom, against their old oppressors. Many, of course, did, but for the most part the Highlanders in North Carolina — and indeed in other parts of America — were Loyalist." [6]

This statement was based on the "exile theory", that shipload after shipload of discontented and oppressed Jacobites had flocked to the Upper Cape Fear in 1746 and 1747. There never had been such an influx of Highlanders, and there was no group of wronged Jacobites in North Carolina. Jacobitism was dead in Britain, and did not feature in American politics. The majority of the Highlanders, who emigrated to North Carolina in the 1760s and 1770s, had not suffered under the Hanoverians. Some of them, indeed, like Kingsburgh, had rounded up and disarmed those who had rebelled.

The later emigrants were not escaping from the yoke of government in London, but from ever increasing rents demanded by absentee chiefs. The forced separation in body from Scotland, made the spiritual bond all the stronger. The freedom that the Highlanders were to fight for was to live in America and to be Scots.

The first Highland settlers, though still nurturing an enthusiastic love for Scotland, did not resent Scottish chiefs and landlords, but Parliament in London, in which they perceived that they were not represented. Many of the first settlers joined the American side.

Of the meeting of the Highlanders, Kingsburgh wrote that "it was determined your Memorialist should wait on Josiah Martin, Esq., Governor, and inform him that the Highlanders were ready and willing to obey his orders and command." [4]

Flora later wrote that "When the American Rebellion brock out, and Congress forcing her husband to joyne them, being a leading man among the highlanders, and seeing he would be obliged to joyne either party, he went in disguise to Fort Johnston on the mouth of the River Capefear, and there settled the plan of riseing the Highlanders in arms, with Governor Martin." [7] Kingsburgh, with one or two others, set off from Anson and Cumberland counties, towards the end of June.

On 30th June Governor Martin began a letter to Lord Dartmouth complaining that he had received no official news of the battle of Bunker Hill, but what he had seen in the newspapers. He wrote that the Highland emigrants were immoveably attached to the King, and that he had been assured that 3000 effective men could be mustered.

"Ten Thousand Stand of Arms at least with proper Ammunition

may be disposed in hands that would make a good use of them . . ., and good store of Ammunition, some pairs of Colours, Drums, etc, and such a supply of money as might be necessary for the support of such a force." [3]

On 2nd July, Janet Schaw went to Wilmington. "Good heavens!" she wrote, "what a scene this town is; Surely you folks at home have adopted the old maxim of King Charles: 'Make friends of your foes, leave friends to shift for themselves.'

"We came down in the morning in time for the review . . . They at last however assembled on the plain field, and I must really laugh while I recollect their figure: 2000 men in their shirts and trousers, preceded by a very ill beat drum and a fiddler, who was also in his shirt with a long sword and a cue at his hair, who played with all his might. They made indeed a most unmartial appearance. But the worst figure there can shoot from behind a bush and kill even a General Wolfe." [1]

At dinner Janet Schaw had a brush with Robert Howe, colonel in the American militia. Then she went into town and discovered that most of the leading men were being held prisoner, in the middle of the street, for not taking the 'test'. " 'This, Ladies,' " said one of the prisoners, "turning to me, who was now joined by several Ladies, 'is what they call their Test, but by what authority this Gentleman forces it on us, we are yet to learn.' 'There is my Authority,' [said an officer] pointing to the Soldiers with the most insolent air, 'dispute it, if you can.'

"Oh Britannia what are you doing, while your true obedient sons are thus insulted by their unlawful brethren; are they also forgot by their natural parents."

Janet Schaw went to a friend's house "whose husband was indeed at home, but secretly shut up with some ambassadors from the back settlements on their way to the Govr to offer their service, provided he could let them have arms and ammunition, but above all such commissions as might empower them to raise men by proper authority. This I was presently told tho' in the midst of enemies, but the Loyal party are all as one family." [1]

Janet Schaw was not told, or did not care to repeat, the names of the ambassadors, but one of them was Kingsburgh. Allan wrote that he went to the coast, "tho' with some danger, two partys being sent out from Wilmington to intercept him on his way to Fort Johnson, on the mouth of the river Cape Fear, where the Governor then was." [4]

Kingsburgh came on board *Cruizer* on 3rd July, with a letter from Glendale, and met Governor Martin and Alexander Schaw, Janet's brother, for the first time. The Governor was greatly impressed. Next day Governor Martin wrote to Glendale that he was parting with Kingsburgh reluctantly. He applauded the gentlemen who had kept the Highlanders loyal, and he promised to represent their merits to the King. He agreed that the Highlanders should not declare themselves until it was necessary to call them into action. He also thanked Glendale for information about Farquhar Campbell, who, though holding a Government post, appeared to be siding with the Americans.

"The part you have taken, Sir, upon the present occasion, does you the highest honour, and cannot fail to recommend you in the most effectual manner, to His Majesty's favour.

"I concur in your opinion of your service being more useful here than anywhere else, & have concerted a plan with Mr Macdonald (for which I beg to refer you to him) of making use of your influence here, as well for your own advantage as that of our Royal Masters." [3]

Governor Martin finished his letter to Lord Dartmouth by once again offering to raise a battalion of 1,000 Highlanders, and by asking for the restoration of his rank as lieutenant colonel.

"If I am so happy to meet with His Majesty's approbation of this proposal, I would most humbly beg leave to recommend Mr Allan McDonald of Kingsborough to be Major, and Capt Alexd McLeod of the Marine now on half pay to be first Captain, who besides being men of worth, and good character, have most extensive influence over the Highlanders here, great part of which are their own name and familys."

There were several other gentlemen, including "lieutenant Alexr McLean late of the [114th] Regiment now on half pay, whom I should be happy to see appointed Captains in such a Battalion, being persuaded they would heartily promote and do credit to His Majesty's Service."

Governor Martin concluded that "I daily see indignantly, the Sacred Majesty of my Royal Master insulted, the Rights of His Crown denied and violated, His Government set at naught, and trampled upon, his servants of highest dignity reviled, traduced, abused, the Rights of His Subjects destroyed by the most arbitrary usurpations, and the whole Constitution unhinged and prostrate, and I live ingloriously only to deplore it." [3]

For all his disguise, and the loyalist party being as one family, the Committee of Safety at Wilmington quickly learned that Kingsburgh had been in town. On 3rd July, the day on which he met Governor Martin, the Committee wrote to "Allen McDonald of Cumberland County to know from himself respecting the reports that circulate of his having an intention to raise Troops to support the arbitrary measures of the ministry against the Americans in this colony, and whether he had not made an offer of his services to Governor Martin for that purpose." [3]

Kingsburgh returned safely to Cheeks Creek. He later claimed £28 for "14 days from home to settle plan of rising Highlanders with Gov. Martin." [4]

Allan had spoken for all the Highland gentlemen of his acquaintance, when he decided to support the Royal Governor, and the inalienable rights of the King. It had not been a difficult decision for him to take, for he had always supported Royal authority. And the Governor's offer of a commission held out the pleasing prospect of half pay for the rest of his life, once the present troubles were over.

Governor Martin, in a second letter to Lord Dartmouth, wrote that "I have engaged Mr Alexr Schaw whom I have now the honour to introduce to your Lordship to charge himself with this letter . . . [He] is qualified by his intelligence, his candour and his accurate observation, during some months that he has resided in this Colony, to give your lordship every information that you can desire to its present condition and circumstance." [3]

Alexander Schaw was to be the first strand that bound up the fate of the Loyalists in North Carolina.

Governor Martin also took the opportunity to write to his brother Samuel Martin in London, of "my proposition of raising a Battalion of Highlanders in this Country out of the emigrants from the Scottish hills settled here who are excellent Materials for Soldiers and I have a certainty of doing it with very little trouble or charge by my influence among them." [8]

Capt Tollemache and *Scorpion* had arrived off Cape Fear on 5th July, and sailed on 8th July with Alexander Schaw. The ship reached Boston on 29th July. Schaw crossed the Atlantic to England, but did not reach London until the end of October. Copies of Governor Martin's letters, send by a different route, had reached England in September.

Governor Martin had been appointed agent for Lord Granville's huge estates in North Carolina. The Governor was anxious about his secretary, John Burnside, from whom he had been separated. Burnside was at Halifax and was about to leave the country. The Governor wrote to Burnside that "Finding that Ld Granvilles Papers may be deposited in the greatest security with my friend Mr McDonald of Kingsborough living upon Cheeks Creek in Anson County, I am resolved to place them under his Guardianship, provided you shall find they may be removed thither in Security.

"Suppose you should give out if the Papers & Baggage cannot be sent away Secretly that I intend spending the Summer at Salisbury — and that they are sent there for my accommodation & to enable me to make necessary arrangements at the same time in Ld Granvilles Affairs." The Governor concluded that "I firmly trust that You will give me opportunity to see you in Cumberland if not here in the Course of the Summer." [8]

Governor Martin and John Burnside were not to meet, nor did either of them visit Cheeks Creek. Lord Granville's papers never got to Kingsburgh. This letter, written by Governor Martin, proved conclusively that Allan and Flora lived on Cheeks Creek, in Anson County.

Samuel Williams, from Cumberland county, "came down about the 7th of July with a Petition to Governor Martin then at Fort Johnston from many persons in his County and on his return staid but one night at home, but he had a letter to Mr McDonald which he carried to Kingsborough." [3] This letter confirmed that Allan's house on Cheeks Creek was called Kingsburgh.

Later in July the Governor removed himself from the Fort, tossing the guns over the walls, to *Cruizer* still moored in the Sound. The Americans marched on the fort and burnt it, and ordered that the Governor be arrested if he went ashore. The Governor became a virtual prisoner of the Committee of Safety, which forbade anyone to write to or converse with him, and allowed him only minimal provisions.

On 21st July, Governor Martin wrote to James Cotton, lieutenant colonel of the Anson militia, urging him and his friends to unite against sedition, and "at a proper season you may depend I shall render myself among you, and in the meantime let nothing discourage you." The Governor sent his compliments to Hugh MacDonald, colonel of the Anson Militia. [3] James Cotton was to be summoned before the Anson Committee of Safety, and had his lands pillaged before he escaped to Governor Martin on *Cruizer*. [3]

At about the same time, in the middle of July, two Highland gentlemen arrived at Edenton, the most northerly port in North Carolina, and were arrested. These men — one of whom would die for his country — were the second strand that was to tie up the fate of the Loyalists.

In London, in April 1775, Lt Col Allan Maclean, commandant of the disbanded 114th Regiment, proposed to raise a regiment from amongst the Highland emigrants in New York and North Carolina. Lt Col Gorham had also proposed to raise a regiment of rangers. Lord Dartmouth approved both plans, and wrote to General Gage inviting him to "take the proper Steps for carrying those plans into Execution; but you will observe that whatever Commissions are given by you for that purpose, must be in your own Name, without conveying to the Officers any Claim to Rank in the Army (except when embodied) or to half pay."[3]

On 12 June 1775 Gen Gage issued orders for raising a corps of 20 companies or two battalions to be called the Royal Highland Emigrants, with himself as colonel. Allan Maclean was to be lieutenant colonel commandant, John Small, major, commanding the 2nd battalion, and Donald MacDonald to be second major. One battalion was to be recruited initially, and when it was completed, a second.[9]

Gen Gage sent two officers from this regiment to recruit in North Carolina. They were Major Donald MacDonald, said to be a relation of Kingsburgh's, and to have fought at Culloden and Bunker Hill, and Capt Donald MacLeod, brother of Alexander MacLeod of Pabbay. The officers arrived at Edenton, where they were arrested but released on claiming that they were on their way to Upper Cape Fear to visit friends. They avoided Wilmington and travelled directly to Cumberland County, and went to the house of Alexander MacLeod at Glendale.

Major Donald MacDonald later testified that he "was sent to North Carolina to raise three companies for the Royal Highland Regiment of Emigrants, being the proportion of that Regiment left with me, as a Field Officer, to complete. I had power to nominate and appoint Officers to said Companies, & Lieut Alexdr MacLeod was appointed by me Captain."[4]

Major MacDonald, without consulting Governor Martin, for whom he had a letter from Lt Col Maclean, offered Kingsburgh and Glendale commissions as captains in the Royal Highland Emigrants. The offer created a problem for them, for they had already been promised higher rank by Governor Martin, though his regiment had not yet been approved. Kingsburgh and Glendale agreed to accept Major MacDonald's commissions, provided that the Governor's regiment was not raised.

Glendale had been running and paying for an intelligence system amongst the Loyalists. In August he sent Dr MacLeod, of Cross Creek, express to the Governor. The information from Major MacDonald did not please Governor Martin, for it contained a letter from Col Maclean informing him that Maclean had been given permission to raise two battalions of Highland Emigrants.

In the summer of 1775, there were two MacDonald family reunions. At Glendale, Ann MacLeod gave birth to her third child, a daughter. The girl was named Flora after her maternal grandmother.

Cuidrach's son, Donald, was given a plantation of 500 acres on

Mountain Creek, by his grandfather Hugh MacDonald. Young Donald was well liked. Kingsburgh had known Donald from childhood, and was a witness to the Deed of Conveyance.

Still on board *Cruizer*, Governor Martin made a fourth Proclamation on 8th August. It was discovered and sent to Wilmington, where it was burnt publicly, and came to be called the Fiery Proclamation.

On 21st August the third Provincial Congress met at Hillsborough. Cumberland county representatives included Alexander MacAlester and his brother-in-law, Farquhar Campbell, and Thomas Rutherfurd, who was married to Alexander's cousin. The Congress agreed to organise two regular battalions for the Continental Army; six military districts, each to raise ten companies of Minute Men, for service in the Province, and Militia units for local defence. James Moore was appointed colonel of the 1st North Carolina Regiment, and Robert Howe colonel of the 2nd.

Janet Schaw wrote that Robert Howe "does not appear to me half so dangerous as another candidate, a Coll: Moor, whom I am compelled at once to dread and esteem ... He acts from a steady tho' mistaken principle, and I am certain has no view or design, but what he thinks right and for the good of his country ... If this man commands, be assured, he will find his enemies work. His name is James Moor; should you ever hear him mentioned, think of the character I gave him." [1]

Congress ordered Anson to raise two companies, and Cumberland to raise one company of Minute Men; Thomas Rutherfurd was appointed colonel; Alexander MacAlester, lieutenant colonel, and Alexander MacDonald, second major. This was Cuidrach, of Mount Pleasant, who wrote that he "was offered a Majority by the Assembly of North Carolina which his Principles would not suffer him to accept." [4]

On 12th September Governor Martin wrote to Lord Dartmouth that the spirits of the Loyalists were drooping; that they despaired of receiving support and feared for the safety of their lands and persons, because they had indignantly refused to yielded to the "overbearing onset of revolt rather than side with it ... Thus, My Lord, the authority the edicts and ordinances of Congress, Conventions and Committees are established supreme and omnipotent by general acquiescence or forced submission, and lawful Government is completely annihilated." [3]

In September Congress appointed a committee to confer with the recently arrived Highland gentlemen to explain to them "the nature of our Unhappy Controversy with Great Britain and to advise and urge them to unite with the other Inhabitants of America in defense of those rights which they derive from God and the Constitution." [3]

One of the committee was Alexander MacAlester, who used all his connections and influence to good effect. Earlier in the summer Lachlan McIntosh, from Georgia, had come to North Carolina to persuade the Highlanders to join the Americans.

Governor Martin wrote bitterly that he had heard "with infinitely greater surprise and concern that the Scotch Highlanders on whom I had such firm reliance have declared themselves for neutrality, which I am informed is to be attributed to the influence of a certain Mr Farquhard Campbell an ignorant man who has been settled from his childhood in this Country, is an old Member of the Assembly and has imbibed all the American popular principles and prejudices." [3]

All the Governor's initiatives had been wrested from him, and seven months had passed since he had written to Gen Gage for arms and ammunition. Governor Martin, confined by the Committee of Safety on board *Cruizer*, felt abandoned by the Ministry in London and the Army in Boston.

In Upper Cape Fear Major MacDonald and Capt Donald MacLeod, with Kingsburgh and Glendale, had been discreetly recruiting for the Royal Highland Emigrants, and had found men for their three companies. The influence of Alexander MacAlester and Farquhar Campbell upon the Highlanders had been exaggerated, for Glendale brought news to the Governor that the Highland gentlemen were still loyal to the King.

Major MacDonald later wrote that "I directed the said Capt MacLeod, on the 18th October, 1775, to proceed to Boston with my report to the Commander in Chief. He, calling at Cape Fear, Governor Martin would not allow him to proceed further, but ordered him to return to the back country." [4]

Governor Martin later wrote to Lord Dartmouth that "the Scotch Highlanders here are generally and almost without exception staunch to Government, and on the same authority I am persuaded to believe that loyal subjects yet abound and infinitely out number the seditious throughout all the very populous Western Counties of this Province.

Glendale "found his way down to me at this place about three weeks ago and I learn from him that he as well as his father in law, Mr Allan McDonald, proposed by me for Major of the intended Corps moved by my encouragements have each raised a company of Highlanders.

"I shall now only presume to add that the taking away these gentlemen from this Province will in a great measure if not totally dissolve the union of the Highlanders in it now held together by their influence, that those people in their absence may fall under the guidance of some persons not attached like them to Government."

Farquhard Campbell's conduct "has proceeded as much from jealousy of the Superior consequences of this Gentleman and his Father in law with the Highlanders here as from any other motive. This schism is to be lamented from whatever cause arising, but I have no doubt that I shall be able to reconcile the interests of the parties whenever I have power to act and can meet them together." The rift between the first Highland settlers and the later emigrants was revealed. Alexander MacAlester and Farquhar Campbell were opposed to Allan Mac-Donald and Alexander MacLeod.

Governor Martin concluded that "the spirit of opposition begins to droop and decline here and that some of the foremost promoters of sedition waver and seem ready to withdraw themselves from the combinations they have taken so much pains to form." [3]

The Governor, still believing that he would raise his own regiment of Highlanders, deliberately obstructed the plans of Gen Gage, Col Maclean and Major MacDonald, in preventing Glendale from travelling to Boston.

On 21st October, 172 Highland emigrants from Scotland arrived on board *George*. The Governor gave them vacant Crown lands, on taking an oath that they would remain loyal.

Janet Schaw had survived until October. Robert Schaw succeeding in smuggling his sister, and the Rutherfurd children, down river to *Cruizer*. "You suppose I have fled from the tarpot," wrote Janet Schaw. "In truth I am not sure what might have happened, had I stayed much longer, for the ill humour was come to a very great height." [1]

Janet Schaw engaged *George* to take her party back to Britain. They slept on board, while it was preparing to sail, but spent the days on board *Cruizer*. Alexander Schaw had met Kingsburgh before he had sailed to Boston. Now Janet Schaw met Glendale before she departed. *George* sailed on 10th November for Glasgow, by Libson in Portugal.

The copies of Governor Martin's letters, sent off by a different route on 7th July, reached Lord Dartmouth in London in September. Lord Dartmouth replied to Governor Martin on 15th September, that "you are too sanguine in your expectations of being able, if properly supported in the manner you suggest to induce a large party of the Inhabitants of North Carolina, to take up arms in Support of Government, but as you speak with so much confidence upon the subject it has been thought proper to order 10,000 Stand of Arms and 6 Light Field Pieces, to be immediately sent to the Commander in Chief.

"I am persuaded you will find that the Power and Authority of your Commission as Governor are fully sufficient for that purpose without restoring you to the Military Rank you thought fit to sell."

Governor Martin's bold scheme for consolidating Royal authority in North Carolina as a bridgehead for retaking the southern provinces had been rejected. The Governor's enthusiastic bid to raise his own Highland Regiment had failed.

Meanwhile Alexander MacAlester wrote to his brother, in Scotland, that "Capt Alexr Mclean from Ila ... finding the Ladies in North Carolina more agreable than the Ladis at home he though proper to make Sute to our Cusin Misst Duboiss." [2] In July Alexander Maclean married Margaret DuBois. In August the Committee of Safety in Wilmington stated that if Capt Maclean, "who has shown himself inimical to the Liberties of America ... does not come into this Committee to make a Recantation of his sentiments in Regard to America within 30 days from this date ... he be ordered to depart the Province." [3] Alexander Maclean claimed that he "never conformed to the Measures of the American Govt in any degree." [8] He survived at Wilmington, but he was to become the third strand that bound up the fate of the Loyalists. Soon after the fateful events he wrote a long account.

On 17th November Alexander Maclean was engaged as a secret emissary and received a letter from the Governor, "Upon the receipt of which Letter Capt McLean went to the different Counties to the respective Gentlemen mentioned, and made them all take an Oath of Secrecy as directed, after which they all had a Meeting & concluded Unanimously they could bring in at least 3000 Men to his Excellency with 1500 stand of Arms." [4]

Soon after Alexander Maclean went into the back country, Governor Martin moved on board HMS *Scorpion*. The ship had arrived off Cape Fear in November, in company with another ship full of Scottish emigrants. On 26th *Scorpion* sailed from Cape Fear, with the Governor on board, for Charleston. Here he met Lord William Campbell, Governor of South Carolina, who revitalised Martin's sagging spirits. Contrary weather prevented *Scorpion* from sailing north, and the ship did not reach Cape Fear until 24th December.

Governor Martin later wrote that "The Progress of Rebellion here, the concurring good disposition of a body of people of the County of Brunswick in this neighbourhood with the friends of Government in the back Country and the notable exertions of the King's loyal subjects at the same time in the upper part of South Carolina had determined me ... to avail myself immediately of the strength of his Majesty's faithful subjects in this province, such as it might be, rather than hazard their total subjugation to the power of rebellion, by waiting for succour of which I saw no prospects." [3]

A few days after his return to Cape Fear, in late December, the Governor was invited by Loyalists in Brunswick county to come "to their relief by the most confident assurances that they would engage in a month's time to join me with Two or Three thousand men.

Full of confidence, and unaware that Governor Dunmore had been defeated in Virginia, and that the Loyalists had been routed in a skirmish in South Carolina, Governor Martin "resolved to unite the strength of the numerous Highlanders and other well affected people of the interior Counties to the force these people promised to collect in the lower Counties . . . The day appointed for the whole to join me was the 1st of February."

The Governor feared that Alexander Maclean had been arrested. He found another emissary, from among the Brunswick people, and sent him out with the Governor's bold plan to raise the Loyalists.

CHAPTER 15

The Loyalist Attempt in North Carolina

*I authorize and empower you, and each and every one
of you, to erect the King's standard, and to raise, levy,
muster, and array in arms, all His Majesty's loyal and
faithful subjects.* — Governor Josiah Martin

By early January 1776, Governor Martin had undertaken to unite the
Loyalists in North Carolina. On 3rd January HMS *Syren* arrived at
Cape Fear with letters for Governor Martin dated September, October
and November 1775. Lord Dartmouth announced that "the King had
thought fit to order a Body of His Majesty's Forces ... to Cape Fear
River." [1]

In October 1775, Alexander Schaw had arrived in London, and had
delivered Governor Martin's July despatches, with proposals that an
army be sent to liberate North Carolina. He arrived a month after Lord
Dartmouth had received copies of these letters. Schaw made his report
and conveyed both his and the Governor's enthusiasm to such an extent
that first Lord Dartmouth, and then his fellow Ministers, and finally
the King himself, changed their minds.

Lord Dartmouth wrote to Governor Martin that the "King has
thought fit to order that a Body of His Majesty's Forces, consisting of
seven Regiments, should prepare to embark at Cork about first of
December in order to proceed with two companies of Artillery and a
proper number of Battalion Guns, Howitzers, etc., to Cape Fear
River."

Governor Martin was instructed to raise a provincial corps, with the
rank of colonel and the disposition of commissions. "I have only to
add, that any corps of provincials that may be formed upon this
occasion, must be raised by your authority, and commanded by you as
Provincial Colonel, with the same pay as a Colonel upon the British
Establishment, but without any Rank in the Army or claim to half pay,
which for reasons already given cannot be allowed." [1]

Governor Martin was to provide pilots for Cape Fear river and
carriages and horses for the use of the army.

In November, Lord Dartmouth had written again sternly to Governor Martin that the enterprise was founded on his assurance that, on

the appearance of a Government force, the Loyalists would show themselves, and crush the rebellion. If this assurance was unfounded, or once the Loyalists had collected, they did not find themselves strong enough, "the Expedition will be of little avail, and all that will be left to the King's General to do, will be to place the Army under his Command in some secure situation until the season of the year will admit of their going with safety to join General Howe."

Lord Dartmouth concluded that the Governor should prepare to receive the force, by instructing the Loyalists to raise and embody as many men as possible. They would be supplied with arms, and the pay of regulars, and must be ready to march down to the coast, on news of the force's landing, bringing horses and wagons with them.

They "should also be instructed to assure the Men so raised, that they will not be obliged to serve out of the Province, without their Consent, not any longer than the present troubles continue. And it may not be improper to engage for a remission of all arrears of Quit rents and for grants of Land to such as shall enter into this Service, in proportion to their Rank and Merit, with an exemption from the payment of any Quit Rents for twenty years from the date of the Grants." [1]

The following day, Lord Dartmouth wrote to Gen William Howe, who had replaced Gen Thomas Gage, as commander-in-chief in America.

The expedition had been due to sail on 1st December 1775, but on 23rd December, Lord George Germain, who had succeeded Lord Dartmouth as Secretary for the Colonies, wrote to Governor Martin that the expedition would be commanded by Lord Cornwallis, on Admiral Sir Peter Parker's fleet. But the fleet was delayed.

On 3rd January 1776, Governor Josiah Martin received Lord Dartmouth's despatches. The Governor wrote, "What was not to be done? I had anticipated the orders they contained to embody the people of the Country, I could not recall the steps I had taken, I had reason to apprehend the rebels were in possession of my secret, which made them acquainted with the names of the principal persons on whose influence, or rather good acceptance with the people, all my hopes of drawing forth the aid of the back Counties depended." [1]

While the Governor was considering what to do, Alexander Maclean returned, confirming the Governor's fears that the Brunswick emissary had been a traitor. Maclean brought assurances that two or three thousand men could be raised, about half of them well armed.

Believing that the British fleet had sailed on 1st December, 1775, more than a month earlier, and with his own preparations for military action in hand, Governor Martin had no hesitation in calling out the Loyalists and Highlanders.

"Pursuant to this resolution My Lord, I furnished Mr Maclean, my unwearied persevering Agent, with powers to proper persons to raise and embody men, and instructions to them being in sufficient force to press down to Brunswick by the 15th day of February or as soon after as might be possible." [1]

On 10th January 1776, Governor Martin wrote a final proclamation, calling all loyal subjects to the King's standard.

"Whereas a most daring horrid and unnatural Rebellion has been incited in this Province against His Majesty's Government, by the base and insidious artifices of certain traitorous, wicked and designing men ... I do hereby exhort, require and command in the King's name, all his Majesty's faithful Subjects on their duty and allegiance, forthwith to repair to the Royal Standard, ... at the same time pronouncing all such persons as will not join the Royal banner, Rebels and Traitors; their lives and properties to be forfeited.

"GOD SAVE THE KING." [1]

Governor Martin told Lord Dartmouth of the encouraging news from the back country which had "determined me before the receipt of your Lordship's late dispatches to avail myself immediately of the strength of his Majesty's faithful subjects in this Province such as might be, rather than hazard their total subjugation to the power of rebellion by waiting for succour of which I saw no prospects."

He would make every preparation, knowing that it would be "highly improper to hazard any check or *contretems* by drawing together the King's loyal subjects prematurely and taking the field with them unprovided of almost every necessary for carrying on War."

Allowing the fleet ten weeks to cross the Atlantic, Governor Martin computed that the fleet would arrive at Cape Fear on 15th February.

"The information I have from time to time given your Lordship of the state of this Province have been founded on facts and ... I can lay my hand upon my heart and with confidence declare I have ever most guardedly avoided falling into any deception myself or misleading your Lordship by any representations of mine." [1]

Lord Dartmouth had instructed the Governor that "any corps of Provincials that may be formed upon the occasion, must be raised by your authority, and commanded by you as Provincial Colonel." [1]

Governor Martin set about mobilising his loyal supporters. Though he had achieved his ambition of being given command of a provincial corps, he did not have the courage to travel west to raise the force himself. He doubtless made valid excuses that he must await the arrival of the British fleet, expected so soon off Cape Fear. Besides, he feared that he would be arrested by the Americans.

Governor Martin wrote, on 10th January 1776, to Allan Mac-Donald of Kingsburgh, at the head of the list, Major Donald McDonald, Alexander MacLeod of Glendale, Capt Donald McLeod, Alexander Maclean, Allan Stewart, William Campbell, Alexander McDonald of Cuidrach and Neal McArthur, in Cumberland and Anson counties, and to 17 others in Chatham, Guilford, Orange, Rowan, Surry and Bute counties, that "I, reposing especial trust and confidence in your loyalty, courage, prudence and fidelity, do by virtue of the powers and authorities in me vested by His Majesty, hereby commission, authorize and empower you ... to erect the King's standard, and to raise, levy, muster, and array in arms, all His Majesty's loyal and faithful subjects within your respective Counties, or in any part or parts of this province."

"And I hereby give and grant to you power and authority to form the forces you shall so raise, into companies of fifty men each, and to appoint one captain, one Lieutenant, and one Ensign, to every company so formed, whose appointment, as well as this commission, shall be good, valid and effectual, during my pleasure ... [and] give to each and every one of you, all power and authority to resist and oppose all Rebels and traitors against His Majesty and his Government by force of arms, and to apprehend, seize and detain them, their accomplices and abettors;

"And you are hereby required immediately and with all possible secrecy, to concert a place of general rendez-vous thence to march in a body to Brunswick by such route as you judge proper, so ordering your movements that you may reach that town on the 15th February next ensuing ... taking all possible care that women and children are unmolested; that no cruelty whatever be committed to sully the arms and honour of Britons and freemen." [1]

Governor Martin wrote that "Thus provided, Mr Maclean again set out for the back Country having my papers in such concealment and in another trusty hand, as it was impossible the rebels should suspect; he passed on to Cross Creek, where the failure of my former Emissary to see the persons to whom he was directed, established his treachery out of doubt." [1]

Alexander Maclean was also suspected of treachery, for, on 15th January, the Committee of Safety in Wilmington ordered him to post a bond of £500 for his good behaviour. Before the Committee could collect its bond, Alexander Maclean had left for Cross Creek.

With Governor Martin's despatches well concealed, and a trusty companion, Alexander Maclean set off. "He immediately went to Cross Creek where he consulted with Mr William Campbell, Mr Neil McArthur & Capt Donald McLeod, it was concluded by them that circular Letters should be sent to all the people concerned to have a meeting the 5 day of Feby at a Friend's house and determine our future Proceedings." [2]

The friend's house was Crosshill, the home of Alexander Morrison. A mile west of present day Carthage, in the fork of the Bensalem Church Road, the house stood in a ruinous state, until it was burnt in the 1950s.

The King had ordered Royal Governors to submit to major generals and brigadier generals in military matters, but despite this, Governor Martin, on his own authority, gave Donald MacDonald a brigadier's commission as "Commander of His Majesty's Forces, for the time being, in North Carolina," and appointed him "as Commissioner . . . for raising a Corps of Provincials in North Carolina." [3]

Governor Martin already had in place a number of Militia officers, to whom the Governor could give commissions and pay from funding under the Militia Act. Hugh MacDonald, Flora's stepfather, was colonel, and James Cotton, surveyor in Anson county, was lieutenant colonel of the Anson militia. Thomas Rutherfurd was lieutenant colonel of the Cumberland militia. Rutherfurd was in a delicate position, for he had also been appointed colonel of the Cumberland militia by the Provincial Congress.

Governor Martin now had powers to embody a provincial corps. The Loyalist gentlemen had always insisted that the Governor should empower them to act legally. The Governor's letter was addressed to 26 men, who acted as his commissioners, or council, delegated to select and appoint officers. This corps was to be paid for from general Army funds, and Governor Martin's accounts for it survived. Being a thrifty man, however, he paid none of his provincial officers above the rank of captain, and most of these were to discover that they had received only half-pay. [3]

"His Excellency Brigadier-General Donald McDonald, Commander of His Majesty's Forces, for the time being, in North Carolina," issued a manifesto, based upon the Governor's proclamation calling all loyal subjects "to repair to His majesty's Royal Standard, erected at Cross Creek . . . Those, therefore, who have been under the unhappy necessity of, submitting to the mandates of Congress and committees — those law-less, usurped, and arbitrary tribunals — will have an opportunity (by joining the King's Army), to restore peace and tranquility to this distracted land." The Manifesto was signed in Donald MacDonald's name by Kenneth MacDonald, Cuidrach's brother, and aide de camp.

Allan MacDonald of Kingsburgh wrote that "Having fixed the place of the rising of the Highlanders; different meetings were held with the Regulators, Country Born and Highlanders, when it was determined to rise in arms and join the Governor." [2]

On 5th February, at Crosshill, only four of the Loyalists called Regulators appeared at the meeting, with all the Highland commissioners. The Highlanders argued that the men should not gather until 1st March. The Regulators claimed that instead of 3,000 men they could muster 5,000, and that 500 had already been brought together. They insisted on taking up arms immediately, and as they were to provide most men, the Highlanders agreed. Capt Donald MacLeod, as the most experienced officer present, went off with the Regulators, to bring back the men to Cross Creek, the place of general rendez-vous.

Governor Martin later wrote that "the Loyalists were in high spirits and very fast collecting, that they assured themselves of being six thousand strong, well furnished with waggons and horses, that they intended to post one thousand at Cross Creek, and with the rest I might rely on their being in possession of Wilmington (the principal Town on this River and within reach of the King's ships) by the 20th or 25th of February at farthest." [1]

Brig MacDonald issued a second manifesto, based upon the governor's orders.

The Loyalist gentlemen began recruiting men. Major, now acting Brig MacDonald, with Capt Donald MacLeod, Kingsburgh and Glendale, had already recruited men for the Royal Highland Emigrants. Glendale later wrote that he, "thus animated with sincere Loyalty towards his Sovereign & strongly attached to the Honour & Interest of the British Nation, was happy to find the good effects of his influence on the minds of his Countrymen, to be remarkably conspicuous when the Royal Standard was erected by Govr Martin in North Carolina; where he raised in four days, a Provincial Batalion concisting of four hundred and fifty Highland Emigrants." [2]

Flora recruits the Highlanders

Rev Foote wrote that Flora "is said to have used her influence over her clansmen and neighbours to join the standard." [4] Rev Caruthers noted that Flora "had been exerting her influence all along to get them enlisted in the cause, and she was not to become weary of any enterprise in which she had once fairly embraced."[5] But James Banks made no mention of Flora recruiting for her husband.

Flora herself later wrote that "When the American Rebellion brock out," her husband "settled the plan of riseing the Highlanders in arms, with Governor Martin. This he and others did, to the number of 1600, having no arms but 600 old bad firelocks, and about 40 broad swords the gentlemen had."[6]

All her life Flora had been resolute, but the years of hardship and anxiety in Skye had also made her bitter. Under an exterior, noted for its dignity and calm, burned a desire not to lose everything again. Flora had helped the Prince in his escape to Skye, because she had happened to be there. She now took an active part in ensuring that Royal authority was not overthrown in North Carolina. The change from demur young womanhood to determined middle age had been gradual, but her passion now burst out with surprising force.

Recruiting soldiers was not women's work, though the Duchess of Gordon was, a few years later, a famous exception. But Flora threw herself into the task of recruiting men, with determined energy.

In 1909 J.P.Maclean could not resist elaborating on the stories collected earlier, and wrote that "The dreams of Flora MacDonald of peace, happiness, and prosperity were doomed to a rude awakening. Before she was well settled in her new home the storm of the American Revolution burst upon her in all its fury. That she was partially responsible for the final disaster that accomplished the complete financial ruin of the family is beyond question; for she was an active participant in arousing the Highlanders to resistance. Without any hesitation she used her powerful influence in forcing the insurrection.

"The sound of the pibroch was now heard in the pine forests of America summoning the clansmen to arms. Nightly balls were inaugurated that the people might assemble and be properly enthused. The war spirit of Flora MacDonald was stirred within her. Night after night she attended these gatherings; addressed the men in their native Gaelic, and urged them to enter the king's army. During the day, on horseback, with her husband, she went from house to house and used her persuasive powers to excite the slow, the indifferent, and doubtful to action. To her personal appeals the success of the gathering was largely due."[7]

At no time during the escape of Prince Charles in 1746 had Flora shown any warlike spirit. Indeed she had been frightened by the gun fired at her small boat in 1746. But all that had changed. If J.P.Maclean's account was to be believed, then she immersed herself whole-heartedly in the male world of war.

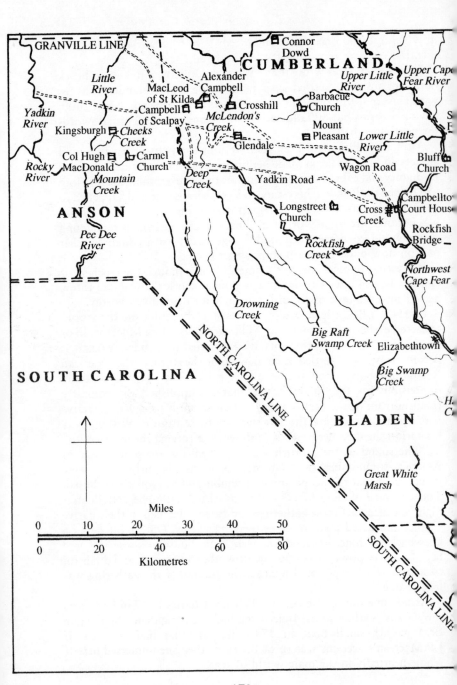

GRANVILLE LINE

CUMBERLAND

Connor
Dowd

Little
River

Alexander
Campbell

MacLeod
of St Kilda

Campbell
of Scalpay

Crosshill

McLendon's
Creek

Upper Little
River

Upper Cape
Fear River

Barbacue
Church

Yadkin
River

Kingsburgh

Cheeks
Creek

Mount
Pleasant

Glendale

Lower Little
River

Bluff
Church

Rocky
River

Col Hugh
MacDonald

Carmel
Church

Mountain
Creek

Deep
Creek

Yadkin Road

Wagon Road

Campbellto
Court House

ANSON

Pee Dee
River

Longstreet
Church

Cross
Creek

Rockfish
Bridge

Rockfish
Creek

Northwest
Cape Fear

SOUTH CAROLINA

Drowning
Creek

Big Raft
Swamp Creek

Elizabethtown

NORTH CAROLINA LINE

Big Swamp
Creek

BLADEN

H
C

Great White
Marsh

↑

SOUTH CAROLINA LINE

Miles

0   10   20   30   40   50

0   20   40   60   80

Kilometres

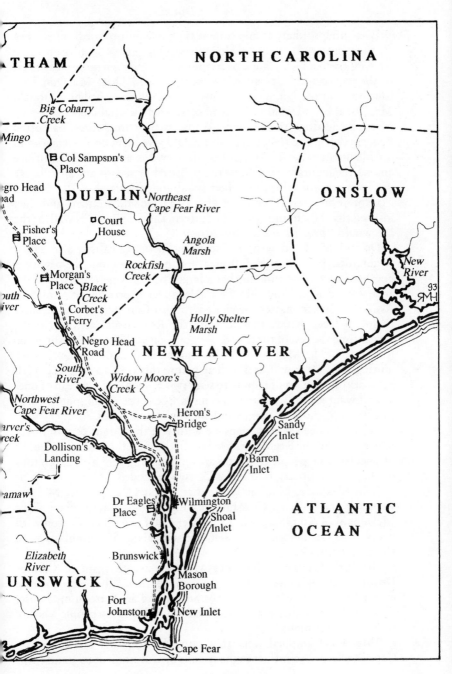

171

Recruiting soldiers at any time was an uncomfortable business. For all their protestations of loyalty to the King, many of the gentlemen were motivated by the hope of commissions, and even more pleasingly, by the prospect of half-pay, when the war ended. Hugh MacDonald, a fourteen year old lad, who lived near Crosshill, described how Donald MacDonald and Donald MacLeod persuaded the Highlanders "to step forward and draw their broad swords, as their forefathers had often done, in defence of their king, who would give them double wages and double honours ... These gentlemen, notwithstanding their influence among the ignorant Scotch, were instigated by selfish and speculative motives; not only they, but their subaltern officers also."

Capt John Martin recruited Hugh MacDonald's father, and then insisted that Hugh, though only fourteen, should join up as well, as the lad would *"procure me a commission"*.[5]

Donald MacLeod went off to bring in the Loyalists, also called Regulators. He collected 500 men, but had to humour them with a hogshead of rum. A rumour that a large body of Americans was in the area, caused panic and they fled. Alexander Morrison, of Crosshill, Assistant Quartermaster General, wrote to Connor Dowd, the merchant on Deep River, that, despite the Regulators' actions, in the "meantime the rest of the friends are going on withe more Steadiness & Resolution. The Men from Anson Cumberland & other Countys are uniting fast, there will be 500 here before this time to morrow [10th February] so that youll require to send two Wagons here instead of one. Theyll want all the Leather you can spare & if you could spare George to cut it out most of them coud sue their own Shoes.

"Capt McLean will perhaps be with you this Night & will direct matters & tho the Regulators are faln in the mire there is yet no Doubt of Success. The people of Anson are on their way here have taken four of the opposite party two killed & two wounded."[3]

Capt Alexander Maclean wrote that "Messrs Campbell & McLean went off the 10th to Crosshill in Cumberland county where Capt McDonald of Kingsborough, Capt Alexr McLeod, Colo Cotton with many other Gentlemen were assembled with about 500 Highlanders & Country born."[2]

On 10th February Alexander Morrison wrote again to Connor Dowd ordering more rations, and added that "they are quitting everywhere, Collonels Murdock & Sutherland are Seize in my house. Wade & Spenser are expected to be safe with the Anson people who are to be here this night."[3]

"Mr Wm Campbell went that same day to Cross Creek," wrote Capt Maclean, "to influence the friends of Government to stand firm,

Colo Rutherford assured him that he would stand by him & others of his Loyal friends to the last, which promise he faithfully performed by coming to the field with near five hundred Highlanders." [2]

Col Thomas Rutherfurd was most unpopular with the Americans. He had been appointed colonel of the Cumberland militia. At the last moment Rutherfurd changed sides, but his lieutenant colonel, Alexander MacAlester, despite being a cousin of Thomas's wife, did all he could to prevent the militia from joining the Loyalists. Col Rutherfurd had some difficulty in persuading his men to follow him.

"Upon the 12 day of Feby," wrote Capt Alexander Maclean, "all the Men encamped at Crosshill Marched for Cross Creek under the command of Capt McDonald, Capt McLeod & Colo Cotton." [21]

It was on 12th February that there were many partings. Capt Alexander MacLeod parted with his wife Ann at Glendale. Ann was to celebrate her 22nd birthday six days later, and was pregnant for the fourth time. John Campbell parted with his aged parents at McLendon's Creek. The Pabbay MacLeods parted with their families.

According to a story collected by Rev Foote, Flora "bid adieu to her husband and relations, in arms, near her residence in the lower part of Anson county." [4] A curious letter supported Rev Foote's tradition. An old lady, in the 1850s, was said to have produced a letter, dated 1st February, written to her sister. "Dear Maggie, Allan leaves tomorrow to join Donald's standard at Cross Creek, and I shall be alone with my three bairns. Canna you come and stay with me a while? There are troublesome times ahead I ween. God will keep the right. I hope a' oor ain are in the right, prays your good friend — Flory McDonald." [2]

The letter, if it was genuine, presented several anomalies. The date was four days before the first Crosshill meeting, and nine days before the Highlanders decided to march to Cross Creek. Flora, in writing to a young woman, would not have named her husband as Allan, nor the military commander as Donald. Flora did not have three bairns at Cheeks Creek. Alexander joined his father; Ann was at Glendale and only James remained behind. The vernacular used in the last two sentences was not found in any of Flora's other letters.

Flora might have been at Glendale, where Ann MacLeod had three bairns, and was expecting a fourth. But other evidence indicated that Flora did not part with her family at Kingsburgh on Cheeks Creek or at Glendale on McDeeds Creek.

Donald MacLeod and Alexander Maclean were sent off to bring in the Regulators. They met Dr Pyle with 40 men and a further 90 appeared. This was a sorry number for the 5,000 men promised.

"They joined the camp at Cross Creek the 14th," wrote Capt

Maclean, "it is well known that the leaders amongst them deceived the people by assuring them that his Excellency Govr Martin was to meet at Cross Creek with a thousand regulars, which they found not to be the case.

"The 15th an order was issued to all the Captains to make a return of the Strength of their Companys when the Army was found to consist of 1400 Men with only 520 Stand of Arms." [2] Governor Martin reported that with 700 or 800 Country People the army amounted "in the whole to about fourteen hundred men." [3]

Later Alexander Maclean wrote that "I also was principally instrumental in raising sixteen hundred men who did go on actual service." [1] Alexander Macrae wrote that in "February in consequence of an order from Governor Martin there was an Assembly to see how many Men be raised to go down and join Governor Martin who was then expecting General Clinton. About 2200 Men assembled." [1]

One surviving extract from Brig MacDonald's order book gave Hugh MacDonald, at the top of the list; Alexander Maclean, appointed Major of Brigade. Majors: MacDonald of Kingsburgh; MacLeod of Glendale; MacLeod of St.Kilda; Donald MacLeod, to command the Regulators. Dr Murdoch MacLeod, appointed Surgeon to the Army. Alexander Stewart, Quarter master General. Lt.Duncan MacNeil, Adjutant General. Lt.Kenneth McDonald aide de camp. Alexander Morrison, Assistant Quarter master General. John Mackay, Captain of Pioneers. Alexander Maclean, Commissary General.

"All the guards particularly instructed to let no suspected person pass without being first brought to the commanding officer.

"Cotton to give similar orders to the corps under his command. Every Captain to set down the orders in a book. —— [the parole] repeated 3 times. Adj't Fraser to receive and deliver Orders and show Orderly Book to officers. Pot for every fifty men be provided. Mr. Campbell provide Guardroom in Cross Creek. Liberty pole, alarm post night or day.

"4 Divisions, viz: Cumberland Militia, Anson Highlanders, Regulators, and Cotton's — Cotton command his own Corps." [5]

At Cross Creek Col James Cotton commanded a unit of country people based upon the Anson Militia, numbering about 500 men in 15 companies. The Cumberland militia was commanded by Col Rutherfurd. Despite Alexander Maclean's optimism, the militia was under strength. Neil MacArthur, Cross Creek, and John Legate, Bladen, with their companies were added to strengthen the Cumberland Militia to about 500 men, in 15 companies.

Brig MacDonald had appointed four majors. One of these was

Donald MacLeod, who was given command of the Regulators, who numbered 130, and perhaps as many as 160 men.

The Anson Highlanders were Governor Martin's provincial corps. The corps came to be named the North Carolina Highlanders. It consisted of two battalions commanded by Col Hugh MacDonald. Kingsburgh, Glendale and Alexander MacLeod of Pabbay and St Kilda, were appointed majors.

The 1st battalion was commanded by Col Hugh MacDonald, probably with Kingsburgh as major, with a dozen companies. Glendale commanded the 2nd battalion, with Pabbay as major, and twelve companies. Each company should have had 50 men, but averaged 32 men per company. If Glendale's battalion numbered 450 men, then Hugh MacDonald's battalion may have numbered only 350 men.

Four companies of engineers and a company of pioneers may have mustered 150 men, and there were quartermaster storemen and wagoners.

One eyed Col Hugh MacDonald, once reckoned to be the greatest swordsman in the Isles, resigned his command at Cross Creek, for he was in his seventies, but he still remained with the army as a volunteer. Command of the Anson battalion of the North Carolina Highlanders passed to Kingsburgh, who was promoted lieutenant colonel. Donald MacLeod, commanding the Regulators, was also promoted lieutenant colonel. Brig. MacDonald had a command structure with four colonels and a major commanding units.

The provincial battalions were woefully short of arms. Capt Alexander Maclean wrote that "an Order was passed to embody a Number of light horse to scour the Country & bring in all the arms they could find belonging to the rebels, in three days time the Camp remained at Cross Creek about 130 stand of arms were brought in, during which time there was taken from the Committee of Cumberland between 10000 & 12000 wt of Powder, which the Merchants of Cross Creek had lodged in their hands to prevent its falling into the hands of disaffected people."[2]

Glendale paid £85 to "Sundries for 30 Guns given to the Highlanders & colours for them" and £6 for swords and pistols. The colours were made by Donald MacDougald, tailor in Cross Creek.[2] Glendale advanced money to both Kingsburgh and Cuidrach to help with recruiting.

Kingsburgh paid £31.10s "To the value of 9 Stands of Arms purchased from Messrs Marshall and George Milln, both Merchants, of Cross Creek @ £3.10.0 each." He paid £9.9s "To a Silver mounted Riffle bought of Mr George Milln" and £7 "To Caleb Tulishstone's

Rifle." Kingsburgh had left Cheeks Creek with five horses, including two batt horses for carrying baggage, valued at £85. "My own Family Arms, including my three indentured Servants' Arms", he valued at £42. Kingsburgh also paid £7.10s "To Cask of Rum bo't of Mr Gillis at Cross Creek for the use of the Highlanders on the Expedition," and almost £19 "To blankets, Shoes and Shirts purchased and given to the Common Highlanders." [2]

The Highlanders at Cross Creek had no uniforms and looked a sorry sight. Janet Schaw would have thought no more of them than she had of the Wilmington militia. The common Highlanders wore country clothes, shirts, coats, buckskin breeches, stockings, and shoes they sewed themselves, and whatever they could find to keep themselves warm.

The officers were dressed in whatever they had, or could get. The half-pay officers had their old uniforms. Some of the Highland gentlemen may have had tartan — a feile-mor, or belted plaid; a feile-beag, or little kilt, and trews, convenient for riding. There may have been time in Cross Creek for the tailor, Donald MacDougald, to make up some uniform coats and crimson sashes for the officers.

The provincial battalions had drummers and pipers, and one of the lieutenants was Donald MacCrummen, until a few years before, here-ditary piper to the Laird of MacLeod at Dunvegan in Skye. Though, as an officer, MacCrummen would not have played the pipes for the army.

Kenneth MacDonald, Cuidrach's brother, was aide de camp, and James Hepburn was secretary to Brig MacDonald. There were doctors and chaplains. Each battalion had an adjutant, and a quartermaster to find lodgings and provide tents, and a commissary, to provide food and clothing. Aaron Vardy was Wagon Master General. Malcolm Maclean was the army's recruiting agent. [1]

Samuel Johnston, however, was contemptuous of the Loyalist army, and stated that, with the exception of their leaders, there was not one person amongst them who owned property to the extent of £100, and William Purviance described the army, officers as well as privates, as Highland banditti.

C.Steadman, Commissary General to Lord Cornwallis's army in the Carolinas in 1780 and 1781 published a history of the war, in 1794, and stated that there was dissention in the Loyalist army.

Rev Caruthers wrote that "they found it no easy matter to organize and arrange the companies, regiments and precedence of rank so as to give general satisfaction and secure a cordial and harmonious co-operation.

"The officers and others who had lately come into the country, were called 'new comers,' and sometimes 'new Scotch:' and were now viewed with jealousy by the others. At least, I infer this much from the brief hints given in McBride's papers; and it was by no means unnatural ... for some were so highly offended at what they considered the injustice done them, or in despair of seeing discipline and efficiency in the army, that they left them and soon after joined the Whigs." [5]

This speculative account was copied and embroidered by J.P. Maclean.

Brig MacDonald's army was officered by a brigadier, four colonels, four majors, at least 70 captains and as many lieutenants and ensigns and a dozen more officers, in all about 240 officers to command 2,200 men. There doubtless was some jealousy amongst those officers who had not been preferred as majors or colonels, but the Governor had been generous in offering a captain's commission for 50 men. There was plenty of opportunity to obtain commissions, and most of the companies were not recruited up to strength. Though short of arms, the Loyalist army was well organised and supplied.

CHAPTER 16

Moore's Creek

Between the hours of 5 and 6 o'clock on yesterday morning the Tories led by McLeod, passed the widow Moore's Creek Bridge, on which the boards were taken off. They were highlanders and advanced with intrepidity to attack Col Caswell who was intrenched on an advantageous ground. They began the fire which was not returned till they were within a short distance of our breastwork when a pretty warm action ensued. McLeod was among the first to fall he was a brave soldier and would have done honour to a good cause.
— Col James Moore.

Rev Henry Foote wrote that at Cross Creek, "one tradition says, Flora McDonald addressed her countrymen and clansmen and near kindred, in words of prophetic import; while another, and probably the correct tradition, says that she bid adieu to her husband and relations, in arms, near her residence in the lower part of Anson County and was not seen in the camp at Cross Creek." [1]

Though Flora, in her own account, made no mention of going down to Cross Creek, other evidence suggested that she did.

Rev Foote added that at Cross Creek some 1,500 men were brought together. "With these were assembled Kingsburg McDonald, the husband of Flora, with their kindred and neighbors, animated by the spirit of this matron, who now, on her former principles, defended George III, as readily as she had aided the unfortunate Charles Edward about thirty years before. Tradition says she accompanied her husband and neighbors to Crosswicks [Cross Creek] and communicated her own enthusiasm to the assembled Scotch. From this fact it has been supposed by some, that she followed the army in its march to join Governor Martin at the mouth of Cape Fear. Mrs Smith, however, [who remembered Flora at Barbecue church] expressly asserts that she did not follow the army; but returned to her residence in Anson, when the army first moved up Rockfish, as it did in a short time, in preparation to march down the river." [1]

Rev Caruthers collected an account that "among others, it seems the far-famed Flora McDonald, who, from her historic fame and her personal accomplishments, was a host in herself, was there and did all she could to infuse into the men a portion of her own loyal and heroic spirit. She had been exerting her influence all along to get them enlisted in the cause, and she was not to become weary of any enterprise in which she had once fairly embraced." [2]

With a husband, son and son-in-law in the army, Rev Caruthers, who liked to moralise, added that "a woman who could make such sacrifices and do it with so much cheerfulness, must have had a heroic spirit and a loyal heart. By thus cheerfully and heroically giving up all her dearest friends, she enforced the eloquence of her tongue by the influence of such a powerful example; and in every way showed as much fidelity and zeal, as much devoted and self-sacrificing spirit for the interests of King George, as she had done for the unfortunate Pretender more than thirty years before in her own country." [2]

An old lady in Fayetteville, in 1849, wrote of Flora that "Her voice was sweet music." The old lady was the sister of 'Maggie', to whom Florry MacDonald had written a letter. This letter stated that Florry had remained at home. The old lady then contradicted the letter, by stating of Flora, that at Cross Creek, "I remember seeing her riding the line on a large, white horse, and encouraging her country-men to be faithful to the King." [3]

J.P.Maclean, commissioned to write a biography in 1909, expanded the story and wrote that "Amidst the dissension and discouragements, Flora MacDonald arose equal to the emergency, and threw the weight of her character, influence, and oratory into the scale. On the public square, near the royal standard, in Gaelic, she made a powerful address, with all her power, exhibiting her genius she dwelt at length upon the loyalty of the Scotch, their bravery, and the sacrifices her people had made. She urged them to duty, and was successful in exciting all to a high military pitch. When she concluded, the piper asked her what tune he should play. Like a flash she replied 'Give them leather breeches', which was probably suggested by the Scots wearing buckskin breeches, rolled up at the bottoms." [4]

There was no contemporary record of Flora addressing the troops, though Brig MacDonald later made a stirring speech. Flora had not been noted before by anyone as an orator, but now her passionate desire not to lose everything launched words out of her mouth.

The piobaireachd 'Give them leather breeches', was the well known tune 'The Carles with the Breeks'. This was a Campbell tune, played when they defeated the Sinclairs, who wore trews, or breeks, in 1680. In 1692 the tune was played by Campbell of Glenlyon's piper before the Massacre of the MacDonalds at Glencoe. On this occasion the piper, a MacGregor, used it as a warning to the MacDonalds, for the words to the tune were 'Women of the Glen, Awake.' Flora would never have called for a Campbell tune, with such tragic memories, to be played on such a stirring occasion. It raises doubts about Maclean's story.

J.P.Maclean added that "On February 18th, the Highland army took up its line of march for Wilmington, and as the regiments filed out of Cross Creek, Flora MacDonald reviewed them from under an oak tree, still standing on Cool Spring Street. Then mounting her snow white charger, she rode up and down the marching columns, and animated them in the most cheerful manner. She had staked much on the army ... The soldiers were in high glee, and as they passed along, with drums beating, pipes playing, and flags flying, they sang their old Scotch songs and rehearsed the stories of their native land."[4]

J.P.Maclean's snow white charger was derived from the old Scottish lady, but Flora's reviewing of the tropps, and riding up and down the lines, if it occured, showed an aggressive side to Flora's nature, that had never been revealed before. She had come to hate the cause of the American patriots with a particular ferocity, and swept up in the emotions of parting, she was driven to such action.

James Banks, who lived in Fayetteville, stated that "When the royal banner was unfurled at Cross Creek in 1776, the loyalist army marched towards Brunswick, under the command of Brigadier General Donald McDonald, an officer sent by General Gage, who ranked Kingsboro', Flora's husband. She, with the true devotion of a wife, followed her husband, and encamped one night on the brow of Haymount, near the site of the United States Arsenal. In the morning when the army took up its line of march, midst banners streaming in the breeze and martial music floating on the air, Flora embraced her husband, and tears dimmed her eyes as she breathed a fervent prayer for his safe and speedy return to her new home at Killiegray. In company with Malcolm McKay, then sixteen years of age, she retreated her steps towards home, and spent the first night with McKay's mother at Longstreet."[5]

J.P.Maclean copied and could not resist improving the story by adding that Flora "embraced her husband, her eyes dimmed with tears, she uttered a fervent prayer for his safety and speedy return to Killiegray; she mounted her snow white horse, rode along the columns of the army, encouraging the men, then retraced her steps, and was soon in Cross Creek, accompanied by Malcolm MacKay, aged sixteen. The first night she spent with Mrs MacKay, Malcolm's mother, near Longstreet. From there she went to Killiegray in Anson County."[4]

Flora had faced emotional partings before, when she had refused to allow Capt Felix O'Neille to join her in the boat, which had carried the Prince over the sea to Skye. Then Flora had felt herself dismissed by the Prince when they had parted in Portree. Bitterly, she had parted with her home in Skye.

As a daughter, wife and mother, Flora was filled with dread at seeing her stepfather, husband, son and son-in-law all going off so proudly and cheerfully to war. Amongst the enthusiasm of the gathered Highlanders, it was imperative that she should believe that they would succeed in marching to Fort Johnston, to join up with the British army, and that Royal authority would be restored. But many of the gentlemen were aware that the American tide was running against them. Flora knew that, should the venture fail, she, and the other women left behind with their families, would be exposed to any marauding Americans, or even to neighbours seeking to settle old scores.

As the Loyalists were gathering in Cross Creek, the Americans began to react to the situation. On 9th February the Committee of Safety at Wilmington ordered Col James Moore to march the 1st North Carolina Regiment towards Cross Creek. He reached Rockfish bridge, seven miles from Cross Creek, by 15th February. He dug entrenchments, and waited for Col Lillington and others, who arrived on 19th February, making up his numbers to about 1100 men. Col Moore thought that the Tories numbered about 1400 or 1500 men. On 10th February the Committee of Safety at New Bern ordered Col Richard Caswell to join Col Moore.[6]

From all over the province more than 90 companies were ordered to converge on the Loyalists.[7]

Brig MacDonald's little army marched out of Cross Creek on 18th February, the day Flora's son, Lt Alexander, celebrated his 21st birthday. Next day Brig MacDonald wrote to "the Commanding Officer at Rockfish", stating that "in case you do not, by twelve o'clock tomorrow, join the Royal standard, I must consider you as enemies, and take the necessary steps for the support of legal authority."[6] Col Moore, awaiting reinforcements, replied courteously, stalling for a day.

The Loyalists prepared themselves to attack, with a result that 200 of Col Cotton's men ran off with their arms. Farquhar Campbell, who had so annoyed Governor Martin by siding with the Americans, came to Brig MacDonald, and advised him to avoid Col Moore's forces; to cross Cape Fear river, and to march down the north side, along the Negro Head road, to the coast.

Prompted by Farquhar Campbell, Brig MacDonald decided not to attack Col Moore, so as to avoiding an engagement. The brigadier hoped to outflank and outmarch Col Moore, but by crossing Cape Fear river, he faced his army with having to cross the northeast Cape Fear to reach Wilmington, and the mouth of Cape Fear to reach Fort Johnston. Col Moore, on the other hand, had placed himself in a vulnerable position, with Rockfish Creek behind him. The Loyalists, despite the defection of Col Cotton's men, outnumbered the Americans, and were ready to fight. Brig MacDonald made a tactical error in not attacking Col Moore's position, whose untried men might well have run away, and left the road to Brunswick and Fort Johnston open.

On 20th February Col Moore wrote again to Brig MacDonald, reminding him of the obligation that he had made to the committee at Edenton, and rejecting his terms and giving him a day in which to submit to the Continental Congress. Brig MacDonald replied tartly that he "observed your declared sentiments of revolt, hostility, and rebellion to the King, and to what I understand to be the constitution of this country.

"As a soldier in his Majesty's service, I must inform you, if you are yet to learn, that it is my duty to conquer, if I cannot reclaim, all those who may be hardy enough to take up arms against the best of master, as of Kings." [6]

Brig MacDonald then addressed his men, in a stirring speech, about the glorious cause they were engaged in. He derided the rascals who had deserted, and stated that if any others were "so fainthearted as not to serve with that resolution of conquering or dying, this was the time for such to declare themselves." There was a general shout, but 20 more of Col Cotton's men laid down their arms and "declared their Courage was not warproof." [6]

With desertions, the Loyalist army now numbered about 1800 men.

The Loyalists marched back to Campbelltown and crossed the river that day, and all through the night. Glendale was ordered forward with 100 men to secure the bridge, 12 miles north east, at South river. The next obstacle to be crossed was Black river, 35 miles away, at Corbet's Ferry.

Col Moore was surprised by Brig MacDonald's move, and sent an express to Col Caswell ordering him to secure Corbet's ferry on Black river, and failing that, to drop back to Moore's Creek bridge. Cross Creek was secured and he set off for Elizabethtown. To the east in Duplin county, the bridges were partly destroyed and men were sent out from Wilmington to Herons Bridge, on the Northeast, and to place a boom across the Northwest river.

"The insurgents," wrote William Purviance, "consist principally, officers as well as privates, of highland banditti, most of whom have been treated in a friendly manner in this town, and many of them charitably relieved with the immediate necessaries of life. There are not 200 of the old Regulators among them, and the whole do not make more, at the most, than 900, being carefully numbered as they marched to Campbletown."[6]

On 21st February the Loyalist army marched to South river bridge, near modern Autryville, and struggled to get the wagons across. Young Hugh MacDonald, who had been forced to enlist with his father, was made to drive one of the wagons, but could not manage the work.

On 22nd the army cut its way south east towards Fisher's place, now Roseboro, on the Negro Head road. The troops marched 15 miles or more. On 23rd the army marched 20 miles, by Morgan's place, now Garland, to get within 4 miles of Corbet's ferry. Command of the horse was given to Col Donald MacLeod, who scouted two miles ahead all day.

At 12 noon Col MacLeod sent word that "the Enemy was within 4 miles of us, upon which the Commanding Officer ordered a halt & desired the Principal Officers to Array their Men in Battle order & all the broadswords in the Army was given to 80 able bodied highlanders who turned out Volunteers, and put themselves under the Command of Capt Jno Campbell [of Scalpay] with orders to March in the centre of the Army."

The Loyalists marched forward, and took two prisoners, from whom they learned that Col Caswell had crossed Corbet's ferry two days before. Col MacLeod went to the river where he found a negro who showed him where a flat boat had been sunk, four miles upstream. The boat was raised, and 1,500 of Thomas Corbet's new rails were used to build a bridge. Corbet also claimed that three axes and an adze were taken, and that his apple, peach and plum trees were cut down and some potatoes stolen.[7] Next day the Loyalist army crossed the river, leaving a party, with pipers, opposite Col Caswell's camp to entertain him. Once across the river Col MacLeod pushed forward and took two bullock waggons and twenty prisoners, including two officers. Kingsburgh was sent out with a force to ambush a party that night.

"Monday 26th marched Ten Miles," wrote Capt Maclean, "and the army & their Baggage crossed Black River, marched forward & joined the detached parties about eight o'Clock in the morning when it was unanimously agreed that Casswell should be attackd immediately, the army being in motion for that Purpose intelligence was brought that Casswell had marched at 8 oClock the night before & had taken possession of the Bridge upon Widow Moore's Creek."[8]

Brig MacDonald's army had turned the flank of Col Caswell's men, only to discover that the Americans had retired to the next crossing.

"That evening Mr Hepburn was sent to the Enemy's Camp with offers of Reconciliation upon their returning to their duty & laying down their Arms."[8]

Brig MacDonald's reconciliation, written out by James Hepburn, stated that the shedding of blood could be avoided by "a timely submission on your part to the laws and Constitution of your Country —

"I at the same time must inform you, that unless those terms are Complied with, I must consider you as traitors to the Constitution, and take the necessary Steps to conquer and subdue you — I reffer particularly to the bearer of this letter, to whom I expect youll show every civility."[9]

Alexander Maclean wrote that James Hepburn upon his "return to Camp informed us that Casswell had taken up his Ground 6 miles from us upon our side of the Bridge upon Widow Moores Creek & that he thought it was very practicable to attack them."[8]

Col Moore had crossed Cape Fear river at Elizabethtown, but had had to wait for provisions. He had then learned that the Loyalists had crossed Black river, so he decided to slip down the river by boat to Dollison's landing, about 60 miles away, and then to march to Moore's Creek bridge. He ordered Caswell to fall back to the same place. He reached Dollison's landing, but could not march forward. He sent an express to Col Caswell and discovered that "Colonel *Lillington*, who had the day before taken his stand at the bridge, was that afternoon reinforced by Colonel *Caswell*, and that they had raised a small breastwork, and destroyed a part of the bridge."[10]

Capt Maclean, who was present at the meeting, stated that, on 26th February, "a council of War being immediately called it was unanimously agreed that the Enemys Camp should be directly attacked."[4]

Brig MacDonald later claimed that he had not been in favour of attacking Col Caswell, since he believed that he was outnumbered, and that only half of his men had arms. C.Steadman, who was in North Carolina in 1780-81, wrote that "great division in the councils of the loyalists" led to the Loyalists defeat.[11] John Smyth, a Scottish doctor, and Thomas Jones, a Royal judge in New York Province, each stated, in their accounts of the war, that there had been dissention.

The weather was wet and cold, and the creeks and rivers were full of water, and presented considerable obstacles. Brig MacDonald, who was in his late sixties, succumbed to the weather and to the fatigue of the march. A sick man, he retired to bed.

Command of the Loyalist army passed to Donald MacLeod, captain of the Royal Highland Emigrants, and lieutenant colonel commanding the few remaining Regulators.

Rev Caruthers noted that Brig MacDonald's illness was the cause of the calamity which befell the Loyalists, for the brigadier had always avoided the risk of battle in his attempt to reach the Governor, and the expected army. Rev Caruthers then speculated about the progress of the council meeting, in contesting the right of way, or taking another route. The older and more experienced officers, according to Caruthers, "were strongly opposed to the measure, and contended that the difficulty and danger of forcing their way in the face of an enemy two thirds their own number, so strongly posted, defended by their entrenchments, mounted with two pieces of artillery, and protected in front by a stream that was impassable except on a narrow bridge, which could be raked all the time by their guns, were too great to attempt, under any circumstances, even with regular troops, much less by militia," when the difficulty could be avoided by marching round to the north.

"But these counsels, so manifestly the dictates of wisdom, and so well supported by the know facts in the case, were opposed by others, especially the young, the self conceited and hot headed, who only sneered at the idea of shunning their enemies, and gave some distant hints of cowardice. They carried their point; and it was determined to make the attack next morning."[2]

Rev Caruthers gave no source for his speculative account. He also used the benefit of hindsight to highlight the apparent hopelessness of the venture. But he misunderstood the Highlanders' decision, for the Council of War agreed unanimously to attack the enemy's camp, which, it believed from Hepburn's report, was on the *west* side of the creek, where the Americans were extremely exposed with the creek *behind* them, which could be crossed only by a narrow bridge.

J.P. Maclean copied Rev Caruthers, without stating his source, and concluded "'Well,' exclaimed MacLeod, as he closed the council, 'at dawn tomorrow we will prove who is coward.'"[4]

Capt Alexander Maclean in his account, written a few weeks after the battle, was attempting to make the best of events, and perhaps exaggerated the unanimity of the Council's decision. Brig MacDonald, who may not have been present, wished to distance himself from the decision, after the defeat. But whether there was dissention in the council, or not, there was no doubt that the Highlanders took up the attack eagerly, believing that the Americans were placed in an exposed position with the creek behind them, which could only be crossed by a narrow bridge.

"The Army was immediately ordered under Arms," wrote Capt Maclean, "and about one oclock Tuesday morning the 27th we march'd Six miles with 800 men, in the front of our Encampment was a very bad swamp, which took us a good deal of time to pass so that it was within an hour of Daylight before we could get to their Camp." [8]

That the Loyalist army had been reduced to 800 men, was suggested by Col Purviance, and was confirmed by Governor Martin, who wrote that it was "daily diminished by the defection of the Country people as danger and difficulty increased upon them, and that at the time of the check was reduced to the Highlanders and about one hundred of the Country People, making in all about seven hundred men." [6]

"Upon our entering the Ground of their Encampment," wrote Capt Maclean, "we found their fires beginning to turn weak & concluded that the Enemy were marched, our Army entered their Camp in three Columns but upon finding that they had left their ground, orders were directly given to reduce the Columns and form the Line of Battle within the verge of the wood (it not yet being day) and the Army should retire a little from the rear in order to have the Wood to cover us from the sight of the Enemy." [8]

C.Steadman wrote that "the insecurity of their position did not escape the vigilance of Caswell; for as soon as night came on, he lighted up all the fires, which he left burning, in order to deceive the loyalists, retreated over Moore's Creek, took the planks off the bridge, and greased the sleepers, which are only passable by one man at a time, and placed his men fifty yards from the banks of the Creek, behind trees, and such little intrenchments as in the course of the night they were able to throw up.

"The loyalists, on the other hand, flushed with the accounts that their flag of truce brought them, determined to attack the rebels in their camp the next morning; and accordingly Colonel McLeod, who commanded the attack, seeing the fires in the rebel camp burning, and nobody there, concluded that the rebels had evacuated it through fear." [11]

This was the critical moment in the battle. Col Donald MacLeod conferred with his officers and decided to surprise the Americans. In the frosty light of dawn the Highlanders moved into position.

In the gloom Capt Maclean had found himself at the bridge, and when challenged replied in Gaelic. On receiving no answer, he opened fire.

"The word of Rallement being King George and Broad Swords,"

wrote Capt Maclean, "upon hearing a shot on the plain in our front betwixt us & the bridge the whole army made a Halt & soon thereafter a firing began at the end of the Bridge it still being dark, the Signal for an attack was given, which was Three cheers the Drum to beat the Pipes to play."

"Upon the firing turning more general in that place Capt Donald McLeod & Capt Jno Campbell repaired to the Bridge and endeavg to cross they were both killed & most of the men that followed them."[8]

Col Richard Caswell wrote, two days after the battle, that "our army was about one thousand strong, consisting of the *Newberne* Battalion of Minute-men, the Militia from *Craven*, *Johnston*, *Dobbs* and *Wade*, and a detachment of the *Wilmington* Battalion of Minute-men, which we found encamped at *Moore's Creek* the night before the battle, under the command of Colonel *Lillington*. The Tories, by common report, were three thousand:

"Captain *McLeod*, who seemed to be the principal commander, with Captain *John Campbel*, are among the slain.

"The number of killed or mortally wounded, from the best accounts I was able to collect, was about thirty; most of them were shot on passing the bridge. Several had fallen into the water, some of whom, I am pretty certain, had not risen yesterday evening when I left the camp. Such prisoners as we have made, say they were at least fifty of their men missing.

"The Tories were totally put to rout, and will certainly disperse. Colonel *Moore* arrived at our camp a few hours after the engagement was over."[10]

Col Moore wrote that "between the hours of 5 and 6 o'clock on yesterday morning the Tories led by McLeod, passed the widow Moore's Creek Bridge, on which the boards were taken off. They were highlanders and advanced with intrepidity to attack Col Caswell who was intrenched on an advantageous ground. They began the fire which was not returned till they were within a short distance of our breastwork when a pretty warm action ensued: between twenty and thirty of the Tories were killed, and I suppose a considerable number wounded. No more than four, however, have fallen into my hands — one is since dead. McLeod was among the first to fall — he was a brave soldier and would have done honour to a good cause."[12]

Lt Col Donald MacLeod had proved to be no coward, and his sword survived the battle. It was returned to his family and taken back to Skye, where it was given to the MacLeod chief, and is now on display at Dunvegan castle.

Later Col Moore added that "next morning, at break of day, an alarm gun was fired; immediately after which, scarce allowing our people a moment to prepare, the Tory Army, with Captain *McCloud* at their head, made their attack on Colonel *Caswell* and Colonel *Lillington*; and finding a small intrenchment next the bridge, on our side, empty, concluded that our people had abandoned their post, and in the most furious manner advanced within thirty paces of our breastwork and artillery, where they met a very proper reception. Captain *McCloud* and Captain *Campbell* fell within a few paces of the breastwork, the former of whom received upwards of twenty balls through his body; and in a very few minutes their whole army was put to flight." [10]

C.Steadman confirmed that Col MacLeod, with about 20 men, got over the bridge, but then stated that they were killed or wounded coming up the bank, only Col Rutherfurd and Capt Fraser escaping unhurt. "The loyalists, dismayed at seeing a leader fall in whom they had so much confidence, after firing off some of their firelocks (which were levelled too high to do any execution), broke and dispersed, every one taking the nearest way he could through the woods to his home." [11]

A month after the battle, the *New York Packet* reported that "the insurgents retreated with the greatest precipitation, leaving behind them some of their wagons &c They cut their horses out of the wagons, and mounted three upon a horse. Many of them fell into the creek and were drowned. Tom Rutherford ran like a lusty fellow: — both he and Felix Keen were in arms against the Carolinas, and they by this time are prisoners, as is Lieutenant Colonel Cotton, who ran at the first fire. The battle lasted three minutes." [13]

Rev Caruthers collected a stirring tale of Col MacLeod marching shoulder to shoulder with Capt Campbell across the greased sleepers, only to be shot on stepping onto the bank. He fell, having been hit by 24 bullets, "calling upon his soldiers to fight on; for America should not be free." [2] Caruthers added that all those who were able ran back as fast as they could. But both Col Caswell, who was there, and Col Moore stated that Col Donald MacLeod, with twenty or so men, had got over the bridge, and were shot down on approaching the entrenchments.

J.P. Maclean, with Capt Alexander Maclean's narrative and Caruthers' book before him, copied and embellished them both. He deliberately read Alexander Maclean's narrative incorrectly, and made Col MacLeod challenge the sentry at the bridge, in Gaelic. He concluded by stating that, after the rush across the bridge, "a party of militia under Lieutenant Ezekiel Slocum, who had forded the creek and penetrated a swamp on the western bank, fell suddenly upon the rear of the royalists. The loss of their leader, and the unexpected attack upon the rear, threw them into confusion, when all broke and fled.

"The Highlanders lost about seventy killed and wounded, while the patriots had none killed and two wounded, one of whom recovered. The victory was complete, decisive and lasting, for the power of the Highlanders was completely broken." [13]

Col Caswell and Col Moore both reported that the Loyalists were routed, and C.Steadman wrote that the Loyalists broke and dispersed, but the Americans failed to follow up their dawn victory.

Capt Maclean wrote that "during the time of the fireing the most of the Country born Army began to run away & could not be made to stand their ground the Loyalists excepted, the people being away from the bridge and we retired with the Army to Camp, where when we arrived we found we had but two barrels of flour to serve the whole army, that the men were not to be kept together & that the Officers had no authority over the Men.

"A Council of War being instantly called it was proposed that the Army should retire to Cross Creek & there fortify themselves till Govr Martin's pleasure should be known ... which remonstrance had no weight. In short we found it needless to persist any longer in endeavouring to keep the Army together, therefore thought it most adviseable to destroy the Ammunition to prevent its falling to the Enemys hands." [8]

Capt Alexander Maclean may have considered that the Highland army could not be kept together, but others did. With the death of Lt Col Donald MacLeod, command of the army devolved upon Lt Col Allan MacDonald of Kingsburgh.

Kingsburgh wrote that "*Twelve Hundred Highlanders*, and *Three Hundred Regulators*, met and marched from Cross Creek, the one half of the whole not being armed, were (by accident) Discomfitted at Moore's Creek by General Caswell at the head of *Two Thousand* Rifleman, wherein a number of Highlanders were killed and wounded, and many made Prisoners. Your Memorialist ... had the honour of commanding that day, tho' unfortunate." [14]

Kingsburgh was in command, when the officers agreed to abandon the march to Brunswick, but he kept together a group of loyal officers and their men, who decided to march back towards their homes.

Flora wrote, many years later, that her husband raised the Highlanders, "This he and others did, to the noumber of 1600, — haveing no arms but 600 old bad firelocks, and about 40 broad swords the gentlemen had, and after marching 200 miles, and driveing the enemy from two different posts they had taken, made a night attack on General Caswell at the head of 3000 Congress troops, who were intrenched on the other side of Moors Creek, the bridge being cutt down except the two side beams, on which a noumber of the highlanders got over, but were bet back with considerable lose, the enemy haveing 3 piece of cannon planted in front close to the bridge, which forced the highlanders to retire back 12 miles, to the place from whence they marched the night before." [15]

Col James Moore reported that the Loyalists had abandoned their brigadier, but Thomas Jones wrote that they had defended him stoutly. William Purviance reported that "General Macdonald is taken Prisoner. He was drawn out of a lurking hole, where he had been concealed by a free Negro. The main body of Highlanders keep together, but are already almost destitute of provisions." [6]

Young Hugh MacDonald, on returning to the camp, found Brig MacDonald asleep in his tent, and being pursued, he fled. The remaining Loyalists were unwilling to face the enemy again. He wrote that "we were marched by Colonel Sampson's, and thence to Black Mingo."

Col Sampson's place was on Big Cohary Creek, 12 miles north of the courthouse, now Clinton. He gave his name to the county that was formed out of the western part of Duplin. Black Mingo Creek flowed into South river, near Dunn, sixty five miles north west of Moore's Creek bridge.

Hugh MacDonald stated that at Black Mingo "we were met by a party of cavalry, with buck's tails in their hats, who ordered us to club muskets, and those of us who had them were doing so, when a bold Scotchman, apparently nearly eighty years of age . . . struck one of them between the shoulders with all his force; but the man merely looked at him and said, 'old man, you are no object of my revenge.'

"This body of horsemen went with us, considering us as their prisoners, at Smith's ferry, where the flat being the other side of the river, we were detained until this small party of horsemen received a reinforcement of about five hundred, when our wagons and everything were taken from us, the men were searched, and their ammunition was all taken from them." [2]

Kingsburgh's little army marched ten miles a day. Glendale paid £6 "for provisions for the Provincial troops in their retreat from Widow Moore's Creek to Cape Fear at Alexr Smith's Ferry." [14]

Flora wrote that "the common highlanders then parting with my husband, Mr McDonald of Kingsborrow, and their other leaders, excepting about ninety faithfull followers, who with their leaders made their way back to Smiths Ferrie on the higher part of Cape fear, where Col: Martin with 3000 Congress men mett them, surrounded them & made them prisoners." [15]

Kingsburgh, with Flora's step-father, Hugh; Glendale and Cuidrach, had kept together at least 90, and perhaps as many as 350 men, a significant proportion of those who had marched to attack Col Caswell. They had their arms, ammunition and supply wagons. Kingsburgh avoided Cross Creek, which he knew was held, and marched by the old Indian trail, to Smith's ferry, the first ferry above the town, opposite Little river. The first Cumberland courthouse had been been built on the rise above the rivers. It was five miles north of Bluff church and the land that had been settled by Alexander Mac-Alester and his MacNeil and Campbell relations, and 20 miles up the Cape Fear river from Cross Creek.

Kingsburgh was captured at Smith's Ferry, on 9th March, ten days after the battle, according to his reckoning, and "was, with his son and three indentured servants among the Prisoners, being deprived of their Arms, Baggage, Horses, Money &c &c." [14]

Col Martin captured, and despatched to Halifax, Kingsburgh; "Colonel" Hugh MacDonald, who had been acting as a volunteer since resigning his command; "Colonel" Hector MacNeil; Cuidrach; Capt Alexander Morrison, and nine other captains; numerous lieutenants and ensigns; Kenneth MacDonald, aide de camp, and James Hepburn, secretary; Rev John Bethune; wagonmaster Aaron Vardy and "about three hundred and fifty Guns and Shot Bags, with about one hundred and fifty Swords and Dirks." [12]

An American wrote, on 10th March, that "parties of men are dispersed all over the Colony, apprehending all suspected persons, and disarming all the highlanders and regulators that were put to the rout in the late battle. The Conquerors have already taken 350 guns and shot-bags; about 150 swords and dirks; 1,500 excellent rifles; two medicine-chests fresh from England, one of them valued at 300 pounds sterling, a box containing half Joaneses and Guineas, secreted in a stable at Cross Creek discovered by a negro and reported to be worth 15,000 sterling; also thirteen wagons with their complete sets of horses, 850 common soldiers were taken prisoners, disarmed and discharged." [6]

The Highlander never had 1,500 excellent rifles, but Dr MacLeod did lose his new medicine chest, which had just arrived from England.

Glendale had been with Kingsburgh at Smith's Ferry, and wrote that he effected his "escape (after my friends were made prisoners) being obliged to secret myself in Woods for six weeks after, when I joined

Govr Martin at Cape Fear 18th April 1776." [14] By Glendale's reckoning, the Loyalists were taken on 7th March.

Capt Alexander Maclean, with some others, had left Kingsburgh, and arrived at Cross Creek to find it held by 2,000 Americans, "who were going on with all manner of irregularities." [8] He then made his way circuitously down to Fort Johnston, and managed to join the Governor.

Col James Moore, in his despatch to Cornelius Harnett, concluded that "thus, sir, I have the pleasure to inform you, has most happily terminated a very dangerous insurrection, and will, I trust, put an effectual check to toryism in this country." [8]

CHAPTER 17

Flora Abandoned in North Carolina

Being informed that her husband and friends were all killed or taken, contracted a severe fever, and was deeply oppressed, and stragling partys of plunderers from their army and night robbers, who more than once threatened her life, wanting a confession where her husbands money was. Her servants deserting her, and such as stayed grew so insolent that they were of no service or help to her. — Flora MacDonald.

The victory of Col Caswell's minutemen at the battle of Moore's Creek brought elation to the Americans. One enthusiast wrote that "It is inconceivable to imagine what joy this event has diffused through this province ... Since I was born I never heard so universal an ardour for fighting prevail and so perfect a union among all classes of men."[1]

The defeat of Brig MacDonald's army had a devastating effect upon the Loyalists. It was estimated that if the army had got through to Governor Martin, 10,000 people, who had remained doubtful, would have joined the royal standard, and with General Clinton and Lord Cornwallis, could have retaken North Carolina. But this was over optimistic. With feeling running so strongly against them, it seemed unlikely that the Loyalists could ever have reasserted themselves in the province.

News of the Loyalists defeat spread rapidly westwards. At Cheeks Creek all Flora's worst fears were realised. She wrote that "being all this time in misery and sickness at home, being informed that her husband and friends were all killed or taken, contracted a severe fever."

Flora suffered a physical collapse, and for the rest of her life she was to be ill, and prone to accidents, until her long last fatal illness killed her.

The plantation at Kingsburgh was immediately singled out for attention from the Americans, and Flora wrote that she "was deeply oppressed, and stragling partys of plunderers from their army and night robbers, who more than once threatened her life, wanting a confession where her husbands money was."

Even the care and concern that Flora had shown to her indentured servants was of no avail. She added that "her servants deserting her, and such as stayed grew so insolent that they were of no service or help to her." [2]

James Banks wrote that "The defeat of the loyalist army, and the capture of her husband at Moore's Creek, struck a knell of woe to the heart of Flora ... Flora remained a year or two at Killiegray, making frequent visits to Cross Creek, where she was always sure of receiving a hearty welcome." [3] Flora had never lived at Killiegray, and if she did visit Cross Creek, then she would not have been made welcome. The town was firmly in the hands of the Americans.

J.P.MacLean wrote, in an attempt to justify the lawlessness of the ascendant Americans, that "The district in which the Highlanders were settled was in tumult for some time after the battle of Moore's Creek. Colonel Caswell marched through the district, but allowed no violence, trying in all cases to be just. But there were independent parties who committed outrages, of which the legal officers were guiltless. These inhuman acts were deplored by all the better class, but owing to the disordered state of society, such things were often beyond their control." [4]

Capt Alexander MacLeod of Glendale later wrote that his property was "plundered and destroyed to a considerable amount; his wife (far advanced in her pregnancy) driven for refuge to a near relative's house 24 miles distant, and the children, who could not make a sufficiently expeditious escape, with their nurses secreted to the woods and those nurses, finding their determination was to carry off the Children (probably for Sale) had the Humanity to persist in declaring them their own. His Manservant was strangled almost to death in order to discover his Master's effects, which when found, were carried off to the extent of 1500 pounds." [5]

In the hurry of escaping, Ann MacLeod had been seperated from her children at Glendale. In desperation she rode 24 miles to the home of a near relative. Both Cheeks Creek and Mount Pleasant were about 24 miles away, but Ann's natural instinct would have made her go to her mother's house. But perhaps she went to her aunt Annabella MacDonald at Mount Pleasant, but there was no safety even there, for Cuidrach's house had been ransacked.

At Cheeks Creek the plantation was also stripped. Allan and Flora lost all their stock, about ten horses and fifty cattle; "a variety of Articles plundered out of his House", valued at £150, and all his "Books, Plate and Furniture plundered by the enemy," valued at £500, of which there was only £40 worth of effects "of Sundrie articles saved by Mrs McDonald." [5]

Even Flora's friends turned against her, and she wrote that "When she got the better of her fever, she went to visit & comfort the other poor gentlewomen whose husbands were prisoners with Mr McDonald, as they blamed him as being the author of their misery in riseing the highlanders, and in one of these charitable visits, fell from her horse and brock her right arm, which confined her for months, the only phishition in the collony being prisoner with her husband in Philadelphia Goal, haveing no comforter but a young boy her son, the older, Alexr, being prisoner with his father. She remained in this deplorable condition for two years, among robbers, and faithless servants." [2]

Depressed and ill, Flora felt abandoned in North Carolina. Hating everything around her, she continued to live at Cheeks Creek amongst robbers and faithless servants.

In May the Provincial Congress appointed commissioners to take inventories of the estates of prisoners sent out of the province, to prevent waste and embezzlement, and "to pay particular attention to the unhappy women and children to see that they do not want the common necessaries of life." Nothing was to be removed, except arms and ammunition, and the commissioners were to recover whatever had been taken from the prisoners and restore it to them. [6] But they arrived too late, for the homes of the Loyalists had already been looted. The families of the prisoners were, however, allowed some protection in returning to and remaining in their houses.

In the summer of 1777, Flora was summoned to appear before the Anson Court and required to take the oath of allegiance to the United States of America or to leave the county. Flora defended the authority of the King, and challenged the legality of the Court. A cousin wrote to Kingsburgh that "I am happy to hear of Mrs MacDonald's Welfare & Her Spirited behaviour when brot before the Committee of Rascals in North Carolina. I don't doubt but She & Other Gentlewomen there will be sorely oppressed by the Savage Cruelty of those Wretches who at present has the Upper hand of them." [7]

Kingsburgh's plantations on Cheeks Creek were confiscated. Nothing but the empty shells of the houses remained, but even they were taken away, with their lands and orchards. Flora was driven out of her home for a second time, not by economic failure, but by political force.

Kingsburgh described Flora as being "in a very sickly tender State of health, with a young Son, a Daughter, & four Grand Children." [8] Ann MacLeod had been reunited with her children and had given birth to a second daughter. Flora, with James, went to live with her daughter at

Glendale, or nearby on Kenneth Black's tract at Nick's Creek,[6] now near Southern Pines.

J.P.MacLean expanded the story and wrote that "Flora MacDonald was soon aroused to the fact that the battle was disastrous to her husband and her immediate countrymen, and that her husband, son, and her son-in-law were incarcerated in the jail at Halifax, North Carolina. Woes rapidly crowded upon her, all of which, in the spirit of a true heroine, she attempted to surmount. She was denied the privilege of visiting her husband and never saw him again in America." Flora and Allan were reunited in New York in 1778. Her son-in-law, Glendale, was not made a prisoner.

J.P.Maclean wrote that "there is no evidence that Flora MacDonald was ever bitter, vindictive, or unforgiving. In short, her character, from any viewpoint, is one to be admired." This was wishfull thinking. Flora's own account of her hateful days in Anson County was full of bitterness.

"True," wrote J.P.Maclean, "she was instrumental in bringing on the war, but she paid the penalty without a murmur and without a censure. The battle of Moore's Creek must have struck a knell of woe to her heart.

"The revolution around her was rapid and changing: plots and intrigues various; alarms constant, and every passing day placed her in a position where her mind hovered between hope and fear. Nor was this all. She was an object of suspicion, and her every movement was noted. Had she not been prominent in the rising of the MacDonalds? Had she not spoken words of encouragement to and exhorted the Highland army to be brave? Was it not reasonable to conclude that her interest and determination were still the same?

"It would be but reasonable to assume that Flora MacDonald should suffer for what she had done, when the war spirit was dominant. True, she was not arrested, nor imprisoned, nor, in person, was she molested." This was not true. According to her own account, Flora's life was threatened more than once.

"But the purported evidence against her was so great, that she was summoned before the Committee of Safety. True to her character, during the examination she is said to have exhibited a 'spirited behaviour.' She was permitted to return home in peace, but not so to remain, for war produces lawlessness. Irresponsible parties, taking advantage of the unsettled state of affairs, ravished her plantation and pillage her residence." Flora had returned to an empty house, for Kingsburgh had been pillaged a year before, soon after the battle.

"Her estate was confiscated by the Act of November, 1777, passed by the Provincial Congress at Newbern, when she sought a home at the plantation of old Kenneth Black. If any person was seen in her company it was sufficient evidence that the party was disloyal to the cause of America."[4]

J.P.Maclean then repeated the story that two of Flora's children had died and been buried at Killiegray. Flora had only seven children, and in 1776 they were all accounted for. The dead girl and boy buried at Killiegray were not Flora's children.

Flora was certainly unpopular with the Americans, for Rev Caruthers collected a bizarre story that, on having hurriedly to leave her house, one of Flora's servants had the small pox, and could not be moved. Rather than leave him to the mercy of a band of robbers, Flora was said to have taken a blanket and smothered him, before burying him and fleeing. This action was so out of character and preposterous, that it can only have been patriot propaganda. Perhaps one of Flora's servants did die of small pox, and was buried near her house, but the Americans used to incident to discredit Flora.[8]

Rev Caruthers, in recounting the story of an incident at Piney Bottom, and the arrival of American militiamen to seek vengeance, also wrote that Flora then lived nearby on Little river, on a plantation belonging to Kenneth Black. The Black family had had small pox, and Flora's two daughters came to visit, only to find the house full of soldiers. They were stripped of their gold rings and had their silk dresses cut off their bodies. Mrs Black told the raiders of the small pox, and the soldiers dropped everything and departed. Kenneth Black survived on this occasion, but was later killed.[8]

Rev Caruthers set the incident after Lord Cornwallis had marched through North Carolina in 1781. By then Flora had not lived in the State for three years. Unless Rev Caruthers had misplaced the chronology of the incident, Ann MacLeod could to have been present, since she too had departed. Her sister Fanny had never left Scotland.

Allan a prisoner

Allan MacDonald of Kingsburgh had marched the remnant of the Loyalist army away from Moore's Creek. He was made prisoner at Smith's Ferry on 9th March, ten days after the battle. He wrote that he was "stript of his Whole Property, including the clothes he then wore and marched from Gaol to Gaol through the country until he was at last lodged in the new Prison at Philadephia."[5]

Glendale, who had escaped capture at Smith's Ferry, stated that

"The cruelties committed by scourging & otherwise committed on the Lower Ranks of his fellow sufferers who fell into the Enemy's hands, and the Rigorous Confinement of the Officers, are well known to all those in this Country who are not determined to shut their eyes against the truth."[5]

From Smith's Ferry Kingsburgh was taken 100 miles to Halifax, on the Roanoke river, where the Provincial Congress was meeting. He was confined in the common gaol, which still stands, with his son Alexander. Old Hugh MacDonald was also taken to Halifax, but he was released and returned to Mountain Creek.

Some days later Kingsburgh was joined by Brig Donald MacDonald, who complained bitterly about his treatment. On 5th April the brigadier was allowed out on parole. Six days later the Provincial Congress took time "on consideration of the candour of Allan MacDonald and his being in a low state of health" to admit him to parole on the same terms as Brig MacDonald. Some days later Congress allowed Alexander to join his father on parole as well.

Later in the month the North Carolina Provincial Congress, in the "Halifax Resolves", became the first to recommend independence.

The Committee of Secrecy, War and Intelligence, while lamenting the fate of the families, agreed to send the 26 most important Loyalists to Philadelphia. The list included "1 His Excellency Donald McDonald Esqr Brigadier General of the Tory Army and Commander in chief in North Carolina. 2 Colonel Allen McDonald (of Kingsborough) first in Commission of Array and second in Command." The 26th prisoner was "Farquard Campbell late a delegate in provincial Congress — Spy and Confidential Emissary of Governor Martin."[1]

Farquhar Campbell, in the end, had been caught with the wrong side. His brother-in-law, Alexander MacAlester, was a member of the Congress, and had an uncomfortable time sitting in judgement over him.

On 25th April the prisoners began their journey to Petersburg, Virginia, travelling 50 miles in five days. Soon after arriving at Petersburg, Kingsburgh wrote to a friend thanking him for money, but complained that "Colonel Eliot ... Confined the General and me under a guard and sentries to a Roome; this he imputes to the Congress of North Carolina not letting Brigadier Lewes (who commands at Williamsburg) know of our being on parole by your permission while at Halifax ... I have also been depressed of the horse I held, and hath little chance of getting another. To walk on foot is what I never can do the length of Philadelphia."[1]

Kingsburgh, however, had to walk 120 miles to Alexandria on the

Potomac River; then 40 miles to Baltimore, and finally, crossing the Susquehanna River, 75 miles to Philadephia.

On 25th May the Committee of Safety of Pennsylvania informed Congress that the prisoners had arrived, and had been closely confined, with an officer to guard them. The New Gaol was on Sixth Street and Walnut. For all its fine appearance the prison was damp and unwholesome and ruled by despotic jailers. The Committee asked what allowances were to be granted to the prisoners. The Continental Congress, meeting in the State House, which had not yet become known as Independence Hall, granted the officers two dollars a week for board and lodging, to be repaid by the prisoners when they were released.

On 29th May Donald MacDonald wrote to Congress, stating that having surrendered himself to gen Moore, and been taken to Halifax, where he had been paroled, he asked "what crime he has since been guilty of, deserving his being recommitted to the jail of *Philadelphia*, with out his bedding or baggage, and his sword and servants detained from him . . . The other gentlemen prisoners are in great want for their blankets and other necessities." [6]

Congress eventually restored servants to Donald MacDonald and Kingsburgh and provided blankets and other necessaries, but throughout June much of its time was taken up in debate about independence.

On 4th July Congress agreed to apply for flints for the army in New York, and then resolved itself into a committee of all its members to vote on the Declaration of Independence, which had been prepared by Thomas Jefferson. As soon as the amended Declaration had been passed, Congress returned to flints. At the end of a long day, Congress resolved that Dr Franklin, Mr J.Adams and Mr Jefferson be a committee to prepare a device for a seal for the "United States of America", the first occasion on which this name was used officially.

The Declaration of Independence was read publicly on 8th July, and the prisoners across the square soon discovered why the bell was ringing so loudly. The Declaration was not signed until 2nd August.

Allan had been at Halifax at the birth of independence in North Carolina, and at Philadelphia at the birth of a new nation. Kingsburgh was about to receive some independence of his own.

On 28th June the Committee of Safety resolved that Kingsburgh, on signing a parole and word of honour, would be allowed to go the Reading, in Berks county. It also resolved "That such Prisoners from North Carolina as choose, may be permitted to write to their friends there; such letters to be inspected by this committee, and the jailer is to take care that all the paper delivered in to the Prisoners be used in such

Letters, or returned to him." [4] This was the first occasion, since arriving in Philadelphia, that Allan had been able to write to Flora.

On 9th July Congress resolved to allow Kingsburgh his parole, and six days later Alexander joined his father.

Reading, Pennsylvania, was a bustling little town, fifty miles up the Schuylkill river from Philadelphia. To the annoyance of the inhabitants, the town was used to house prisoners, especially Hessians, captured at Trenton. Kingsburgh and his son were the only paroled prisoners from North Carolina, but three MacDonalds had been sent by Gen Schuyler, as hostages from the Scots Mohawk settlement, in New York province.

In September, Allan, Alexander and their servant's weekly allowance totalling 5 dollars was paid. It had been outstanding for 21 weeks.

On 31st October a group of 16 Loyalist prisoners in Philadelphia petitioned Congress that "after a long separation of eight months from our Families and Friends ... think ourselves justifiable at this period in applying to your Honour for permission to return to our Families." [1] The petition failed, for amongst the group was Cuidrach and Alexander Morrison of Crosshill, who were not released until October 1779.

Brig Donald MacDonald was exchanged on 2nd December 1776, but Kingsburgh and his son spent the winter at Reading.

In April 1777, Kingsburgh wrote a petition to John Hancock, President of Congress, stating that "whereas your Petitioner and Son, are now nigh fourteen months Prisoners of War, and were above four months of those, in close confinement, removed from one Gaol, to another, and different places of confinement, in North Carolina Virginia, & Maryland, till they arrived in Philadelphia, from there — they were admitted on Parole, to reside at Riading, in the County of Berks, where they now are. From whence I am hopefull, it will be certified by his Excellency General Mifflin, Commanding Officer there and the County Committee, that they kept closs to their Parole, without giving the smallest offence to any person whatever.

"Your Petitioner begs leave further to observe, that Provisions — Drink, Lodging, Cloathing, and in short every thing, is so extravagantly high priced, that Prisoners must be in a very miserable State, Two Dollars, the common allowance pr Week, being greater service, ten Months before now, than Six this day.

"Your Petitioner expects, you will exchange him & Son for Officers of the like denomination, or order them to New York on Parole, till duly Exchanged." Allan had not received his allowance since 30th December. John Hancock referred the petition to the Board of War.

Kingsburgh's petition took time to be considered by the Board of War, but in May he was able to order from Alexander Bertram, merchant in Market Street, Philadelphia, two pairs of breeches "of wheat corded or plain stuff", material for two summer waistcoats and half a yard of scarlet cloth, with necessary furniture and buttons.[9]

In June, Congress proposed that "General Washington be directed to propose an exchange of Lt Colonel Allan McDonald and Lt Alexander McDonald for such officers of equal Rank as are entitled to a priority of Exchange."[4] Nothing came of the offer, because the British Army did not rate Kingsburgh as a lieutenant colonel.

In July Kingsburgh was still at Reading, but Gen Sir William Howe, having sailed round to Chesapeake Bay, was advancing upon Philadelphia. Allan wrote again to John Hancock that Col Lutes had been chosen for his exchange. From "the dispersed, and distress't state of my family, you will, at least sympathise with me, and pity my oppress'd mind. I am here with one Son Seventeen months a Prisoner.

"My wife is in North Carolina 700 Miles from me in a very sickly tender State of health, with a younger Son, a Daughter, & four Grand Children — two sons in our service of whom, I heard little or nothing, since one of them had been wounded at the Battle of Bunkers hill — And two in Britain, of whom I heard no accounts since I left it."

Kingsburgh's eldest son, Charles, had left the East India Company Service, and had joined the Royal Highland Emigrants in Nova Scotia. Ranald was serving with the Marines, and it was he who had been wounded, not at Bunker Hill, but earlier at Lexington or Concord.[10] The wound was to trouble him for the rest of his life. Ranald was promoted lieutenant two days after Bunker Hill, on the death of a fellow officer.

"Them in Carolina I can be of no service to in my present state, but were I Exchanged, I would be more of service to the rest if in life.

"Now Sir, let me further tell you, I am Captain in the Regular Service, & my Son a Lieutenant, I rank a Lieut Colonel in North Carolina; in this station I was made Prisoner, and I am convinced Sir William Howe will Exchange me in either of these Ranks — if not — I hereby binde my honour, my Character, & even my life, I, and my Son will returne."[4]

On 21st August Congress, in considering Kingsburgh's last petition and the report from the Board of War, resolved that "Allan McDonald, of Kingsbrough, North Carolina, a captain in the British regular service, be permitted to go to New York to negotiate an exchange for himself and his son, a lieutenant in the same service; he to give his parole not to convey to the enemy or bring back any intelligence whatever of a political nature, and to return in a certain time to be fixed by his parole or when called for, on behalf of the United States." [4]

Kingsburgh left Reading and travelled to New York. On 27th September he and his son Alexander were reduced from Governor Martin's corps of North Carolina Highlanders.

Kingsburgh did not find Gen Sir William Howe in New York. On 11th September the British Army had defeated the Americans at the battle of Brandywine, and on 26th September Lord Cornwallis entered Philadelphia. But Gen Sir William Howe's success was almost immediately to receive a severe setback, when Gen John Burgoyne surrendered his army to the Americans at Saratoga, in the Hudson valley.

CHAPTER 18

Flora and Allan Reunited

She remained in this deplorable condition for two years, among robbers and faithless servants, until her husband, and her son in law, Major Alexr McLeod obtained a flag of truce from Sir Henry Clinton and Admiral How, which brought me, my daughter, and her children from Wilmington in N Carolina to New York. — Flora MacDonald.

Major Alexander MacLeod of Glendale escaped capture at Smith's Ferry, on Cape Fear river, and, after many difficulties, he found his way to Fort Johnston on 18th April. Major Gen Henry Clinton had been with Governor Martin for more than a month, but Sir Peter Parker's fleet, carrying Lord Cornwallis' army, had still not arrived.

Governor Martin had seen his carefully cultivated plans crumble. At the end of February he had sailed in HMS *Scorpion* up to Wilmington, in the hope of meeting Brig MacDonald with the Loyalist army.

On 6th March the Governor learned that the Loyalist numbers had been reduced to 3,500 men, but that they would still make their way to the coast. He later added that the Loyalists "had been checked about 17 miles above Wilmington by the Rebels, in an attempt to pass a Bridge, on the 27th of February, and after sustaining the loss of Captain Donald McLeod, a gallant Officer, and near 20 men killed and wounded, had dispersed.

"This unfortunate truth My Lord, was too soon confirmed by the arrival of Mr McLean, Mr Campbell, Mr Stuart and Mr McNicole, who with infinite fatigue, danger and difficulty and by a vast effort made their way to the *Scorpion* Sloop or War, which lay at Brunswick. From these Gentlemen my Lord I have accounts very different from all my former intelligence.

"This little check ... I do not conceive My Lord will have any extensive ill consequences. All is recoverable by a body of Troops penetrating into this country, on the practicability of which I have given my very humble opinion to General Clinton."[1]

Gen Clinton later confirmed that "when Major Macleod joined me at Capt Fear, from the interior parts of North Carolina in 1776, he showed a zeal and readiness for promoting His Majesty's Interest in that Country which was highly commendable." [2]

Glendale set about reorganising the North Carolina Highlanders.

On 3rd May Lord Cornwallis arrived at Cape Fear but was unable to land his army. Several raiding parties went ashore, and on 12th May Brig Robert Howe's house, Kendall, not far from Brunswick, was burned. In the meantime the Continental Congress had elected James Moore, Richard Howe and William Alexander, Lord Stirling, to be brigadier generals.

Gen Clinton made a stirring proclamation but had no intention of penetrating into the back country. He abandoned the remaining Loyalists to their fate and returned to New York.

On 30th May Governor Martin promoted Alexander MacLeod of Glendale to be major commanding the North Carolina Highlanders, and appointed him to be the senior officer left at Cape Fear. The following day Lord Cornwallis and his army sailed south, with Governor Martin, to Charleston. Governor Martin abandoned his province and thought little more of the unfortunate Loyalists whom he had been proud enough to call out to provide him with a provincial corps.

After investing Charlestown for a month, Lord Cornwallis re-embarked his army and sailed north to New York.

In October Glendale left Cape Fear and went to New York. On 4th November Governor Martin wrote to Gen Sir William Howe, "It is due to Maj MacLeod, that I represent to your Excellency, he being an Officer in the King's Service of upwards of twenty year's standing; that he has pretensions to a Company in Lieut Col Maclean's Regiment, of which it will better become him than me to state to your Excellency the particulars, and that he exerted himself with the utmost zeal in North Carolina for His Majesty's Service, and by his influence among the Highland Emigrants in that Country, drew a considerable body of men to the King's Standard." [2]

Alexander MacLeod, a lieutenant of marines on half pay, had been named as senior captain by Governor Martin, in a provincial regiment the Governor proposed to raise, but then in July 1775 he had been named as captain in the Royal Highland Emigrants by Major Donald MacDonald. Alexander MacLeod accepted the latter commission, on condition that Governor Martin's regiment was not raised. Despatched to New York by Major MacDonald, Glendale had been detained at Fort Johnston by Governor Martin, and had returned to Cumberland County. There, in February 1776, in four days, he had raised 450 men, whom he commanded as a provincial major. After the battle Glendale had escaped to Cape Fear, where Governor Martin had promoted him major.

Glendale now discovered that, in his absence in North Carolina, his company in the Royal Highland Emigrants had been given to someone else. Glendale was indignant that he had been passed over.

On 24th November Governor Martin's North Carolina Highlanders were disbanded.

General Sir William Howe, with Lord Cornwallis, had driven General Washington off Long Island, and in November chased him across New Jersey to the Delaware River. The British army went into winter quarters, but General Washington crossed the frozen Delaware, defeated the British at Princeton and went into winter quarters at Morristown.

During all this time Glendale received no preferment, but he continued to serve in the army as a volunteer. In the summer of 1777 General Sir William Howe took his army by sea to Chesapeake Bay, and on 11th September the British defeated the Americans at Brandywine. Lord Cornwallis entered Philadephia on 26th September, and Congress fled to York. Glendale was a volunteer at Philadelphia.

Kingsburgh wrote that "In August, 1777, he was exchanged and sent to New York, having a Company given him in the 84th, or Royal Highland Emigrants. He had also the honour to command an hundred men, Gentlemen Volunteers, of good Property, from North Carolina, who were then in New York, in which command he continued, with the approbation of the Commander in Chief." [2] Kingsburgh later added that he had "raised a company of eighty six Volunteer Gentlemen from Virginia and Carolina, with whom he did duty, without pay." [2]

This was not strictly true, for Allan had received full provincial captain's pay from January 1776 to September 1777, when he was exchanged. He then discovered that his commission in the Royal Highland Emigrants entitled him to full captain's pay from June 1775. For 20 months Kingsburgh had received more than a lieutenant colonel's pay.

Flora stated that "my husband commanded a company of gentlemen volunteers, all Scotsh refugees from Carolina & Virginia. With them (all dressed in scarlet & blew) he and my son Alexr as Lieut. did duty under Generall James Robertson." [3]

Commanding an independent company of brightly dressed volunteers in New York, in the battle zone, was much more exciting than the prospect of joining the Royal Highland Emigrants at Halifax, Nova Scotia. Such a command was also potentially much more profitable, for it might lead to preferment and command of a regiment.

Alexander MacDonald of Staten Island had been a soldier for 31 years. In 1757 he had joined Col Archibald Montgomery's Regiment, the 77th, and had fought in the Seven Years, or French and Indian, War. "I have served my King & Country," he wrote in 1775, "now going on thirty one Years and have been in the most active Services during the last war both on the Continent of America and in the West Indies and was severely wounded, was reduced to Captain Lieutenant of the late 77th Regt." [4]

After the war Capt MacDonald had remained in North America and had settled on Staten Island. In 1775 Alexander MacDonald had left his home and had travelled up to the Mohawk Valley, in New York province, where he had recruited 200 Highlanders. He had "fled to Boston in the Nick of time when a parcel of low lived rebellious rascals were about to take possession of him and his house." [4]

Alexander MacDonald proposed to raise more men, but Lt Col Allan Maclean had already arrived with similar plans and a warrant from Lord Dartmouth to raise a regiment. Gen Gage promised that, in the Royal Highland Emigrants, Alexander MacDonald would be first, or oldest capt. Though William Dunbar was placed ahead of him, he was appointed senior capt of the 2nd battalion.

In August 1775 Capt Alexander MacDonald travelled to Halifax, Nova Scotia. In December he wrote to Major Small that the corps was to be moved to Windsor, where the fort was not fit for hogs. The regiment was constantly short of clothing, and at first had to make do with scarlet coats, white breeches, stockings and leggings. Eventually the regiment was clothed in Highland Dress of belted plaid, in dark green Government tartan, red and white cloth hose, scarlet coat with blue facings, and blue bonnet.

By April 1776 Capt MacDonald had 335 men under command. Also in Nova Scotia were 2 battalions of Marines and Col Gorham's Rangers.

On 18th October, 1777, Capt Alexander MacDonald wrote, from Halifax, to Kingsburgh, "Dr COUSIN: I am Extremely happy to hear that you & Yr Son were safe at New York. I hope to have the further pleasure of seeing you both soon here ... In Case you should have Occasion or be at a loss for want of money I send you Inclosed the State of your Accot. from wch you can see how much you may Venture to draw from."

Allan had been credited with £183 a year, since June 1775, and for 20 months had been paid twice that amount. From this he had to repay his allowance as a prisoner, and the expenses of raising his volunteer company.

"I dare say Ronald will write to you by this opportunity they are very happy at the thoughts of Seeing you soon & for Gods Sake don't Stay long Come to us before the Winter sets in & bring all the fine fellows you possibly can get along with you but dont venture in anything less than a frigate. Give my kind Compts to Sandy tho' a Stranger." [4]

Kingsburgh's third son, Ranald, had been commissioned 2nd lieutenant of Marines in 1773. He was in America in 1775, and had been wounded at Lexington or Concord, and in July, after Bunker Hill, he was promoted 1st lieutenant. In 1777 Ranald was stationed with two battalions of Marines at Halifax, Nova Scotia. In August Ranald had celebrated his 21st birthday.

Kingsburgh's eldest son, Charles, was also at Halifax. He had been commissioned in the East India Company service. In October 1775 Charles was in London and was still there in March 1776, when he wrote to Lt Col Allan Maclean about a lieutenancy in the Royal Highland Emigrants. Charles was in Halifax, Nova Scotia, in May 1776 and was promoted lieutenant on 18th May. His father later claimed that Charles had been wounded at Bunker Hill, but this was not correct. Charles was in India when the battle was fought near Boston in June 1775.

Sandy was Kingsburgh's second son Alexander, who had been a fellow prisoner at Philadephia and Reading.

On 30th November Kingsburgh wrote to Capt Alexander Mac-Donald, stating that he had been successfully exchanged, and with news from his wife, Flora, in North Carolina. From Halifax, Nova Scotia, Capt Alexander MacDonald replied on 31st December; "Nothing can give me greater pleasure than to hear of you & Your Son being Safe out of the hands of the Rebels. I am also happy to hear of Mrs Macdonald's Wellfare and her Spirited behaviour when brot before the Committee of Rascals in North Carolina. I don't doubt but She & the Other Gentlewomen there will be sorely oppressed by the Savage Cruelty of those Wretches who at present has the Upper Hand of them Tho' they may Sorely repent it before this War is at an End.

"I had rather you was here at the head of your own Company in our Regiment than Commanding a Compy of provincials wch as we have a great many Enemys may be made a handle of to hinder our Establishment. Major Small who goes by this Opportunity will talk to you more fully on this Subject." All newly raised regiments pressed to be established, or placed on the regular establishment of the army. This ensured that the officers would receive half pay, even if the regiment was later reduced.

"I would not advise you to venture here but in a man of warr as I assure you I think this part of British America the happiest Spot in it at present and would be very hapie to see you and all the othere officers of our Corpts here with all Cliver ffellows of recruits you can Bring with you we want about 85 to Compleat but Expect a Great Manney from Newfoundland and from your Endeavours.

"Your 3 oldest Sons are provided for Espetialy if this Regt will Establishd therefore has no right to Expect any more assistance from you, if you was worth ten thousand a year Except when a purchase Came their way." Kingsburgh's sons in Halifax wished to be promoted, and Alexander MacDonald hinted that Kingsburgh should spend money on purchasing more senior commissions.

"I am convinced Campbell with Rather Give up the Company for Nothing rathere than be obliged to joine, at lest would be Glad to take one or two hundred pounds for it ... I would not think Safe to pay above one years purchass for it." Capt MacDonald suggested that Kingsburgh should purchase a captaincy for his son Alexander, but that he should not pay more than one or two hundred pounds for it. A capt's pay for a year was £183.

"As your Son Ranald is going will be the Bearer of this I need not trouble you with any news to tell truth there are none, only he will Give you a Description of the place. He is a fine young ffellow and will make an Excellent Officer if he lieves.

"You tell me you have contracted a Great Deal of debt, I Darr Saie you must have lived Expensive but it is high time now my Dear Allan to Study Oeconomy." Allan was in debt again, despite amassing back pay. Kingsburgh's debt had resulted from his captivity in Philadelphia and Reading, but his smart new uniform of scarlet and blue, and the raising of his volunteer company had added to it.

"Pray for Godsake it is possible to gett Mrs McDonald & the othere poor women from N Carolina.

"I again wish we were alltogether as the more we are in one place the more respectable our appearance wishing you and all ffriends the complements of the Season and with Mrs McDonald's and my kinde wishes for every thing that can make you Hapy." [4]

On 12th January 1778, Capt Alexander MacDonald wrote again: "Dr COUSIN: Since my last of the 31st of Decemr ulto wch will be delivered to you by Your Son Ronald who from some hints I recd is going there not only wth Anxiety to see you but with some other Views to get you to lay out the little Money you have in my hands in purchasing a higher Commission for himself or Charles a Manuvre I wd highly approve of if you could afford it, but I have already given a hint upon this head & I again tell you that I think yr three sons extremely well provided for considering their Age especially if this Regt be Established as I hope it is by this time.

"Ronald is already in a very good corps & pretty far advanced & probably may have a Chance of a Company before this work is at an End." Ranald was 77th in the list of Marine lieutenants in 1778. By the following year he had jumped to 19th in the list, and on 1st September 1779, Ranald was promoted captain lieutenant, when the Marine establishment was increased from 55 to 135 companies. He was confirmed as full captain within a year.

"Charles is a fine young fellow for whom I have the Sincerest regard but the income of a Genral Offr wd be rather small for him, if he could get it, he is very Sensible & very Clever when Sober but rather unhappy when he is any ways disguised in Liquor but yr presence here might be the means of altering him & putting a Stop to it. These Circumstances are as galling to me to relate as they can possibly be to you to hear them but I think it my Duty from the Sincerest Friendship to acquaint you with them. Were so near Relations indifferent to me I might laugh as others do and pass it over in silence.

"I beg You wd not let Ronald or Charles know any part of this intelligence but with the power & authority of a parent Command Ronald at his peril to tell you the truth of all he knows Concerning Charles & his Behaviour. I have nothing earthly to lay at his Charge but wt the Effects of Liquor is the Cause of & a propensity to Extravagance wch I wish to God he was cured of As no man has a right to Spend more than his income & not even that it being much more honourable for a young Offr to have a Guinea in his pocket to lend to his Comrade than to be obliged to borrow one from him & I beg you wd keep a tight hand & learn them to live upon their pay Especially as you have other things to do with Yr money & other people to provide for. In Short I wish you was here for several good reasons.

"Wishing you a Speedy & Safe arrivale here wth great Good news from the Southward."[4]

Ranald had not seen his father since he had left Skye, six years earlier, to join the Marines. The most affectionate and caring of Flora's children, the meeting was not marred by Capt MacDonald's information on Charles's behaviour, for the letter had not been delivered by Capt Murdoch Maclean. Ranald returned to Halifax.

On 21st January Major Gen Eyre Massey, at Halifax, Nova Scotia, signed a muster return for the 2nd battalion of the Royal Highland Emigrants. Capt Allan MacDonald was listed as "lately exchanged & on his way to join." Kingsburgh's son, Alexander MacDonald, was listed as "still Prisoner & unexchanged."[5] Alexander was in New York on parole, but had still not yet been exchanged. Kingsburgh and his son had been reduced from the North Carolina Highlanders on 27th September 1777.

On 19th February Capt Alexander MacDonald wrote to Kingsburgh enclosing his earlier letter, which he had been unable to give to Capt Maclean. "Our worthy Major [Small] . . . left us the 27th of January & hope is now safe in London where he will insist upon the fate of our Regiment before he leaves it. So it is to be hoped that two months will Satisfy our Anxiety & curiosity." On 28th December 1778 the corps was established as 84th Regiment.

"I was obliged within these few days to Accommodate Charles with above £50 Sterg he has by the managemt of your Compy . . . wch is equal to £27.9 Sterg a year & £10 paid him out of your baggage & Forage Money by order of Major Small. If all this is not Suff[icient] to Support Char[le]s what will other poor Subalterns do who has not a farthing but their bare subsistance.

"I understand that Charles and Ronald are entirely agst your Joining the regiment. I dont know wt good reason they can have for it but One thing I am sure of it is absolutely necessary that you should be as near them as possible to overawe their Conduct & assist them with your good Advice & without you clearly see that you can do better for yourself by staying where you are I wd earnestly recommend it to you to Join the regt as soon as possible with all the Offrs & Recruits you can possibly bring.

"Bad as this place was always reckoned This certainly the Most peaceable Corner now in America & if you can by any Means obtain a safe Conduct for Mrs Macdonald & Mrs McLeod you might order them to follow you to this place."[4]

A flag of truce for Flora

Before Kingsburgh received Capt Alexander MacDonald's letter, however, Glendale had sailed in *Sucky and Peggy* for Cape Fear.

Glendale and Kingsburgh had been working all winter to secure freedom for their wives. General Charles Lee, who had been made prisoner by the British, had influence in obtaining a flag of truce from Gen Sir Henry Clinton and Admiral Lord Howe. It was counter signed by Commodore Hotham, and Gen Lee gave Glendale a letter of introduction. Richard Howe, now Admiral Lord Howe, was Capt Howe of *Baltimore*, whose taking of MacDonald of Boisdale on board to drink punch, had caused such concern amongst the Prince's followers, in June 1746.

Glendale sailed from New York, and on 20th February the sloop *Sucky and Peggy* arrived at Wilmington. To the alarm of the Committee of Safety, it was learned that Major Alexander MacLeod was on board, with a flag of truce. Lt Col Anthony Ward wrote to Governor Caswell, the victor at Moore's Creek, and now the first Governor of the State of North Carolina, that "There is a Flag of Truce arrived in our River from New York, which I stopt, and put a Guard on Board, and then sent to Genl Ashe, to acquaint him of it and he desired me to continue the same 'till he has orders." [1]

The next day John Ancrum and others also wrote to the Governor that "We must beg leave to acquaint you that Major Mcleod, who brings the Flag, was one of the principal acting officers in the Insurrection in this State, by the Highlanders and was himself in the engagement at widow Moore's Creek. We also enclose you these Depositions in regard to McLeod's going on shore at Brunswick, offering to purchase Cows &c &c &c of his being possessed of a large quantity of gold and silver. As he has heretofore been a traitor to this State, we are ignorant how far his views may be to renew a disturbance in the State." [1]

The Americans removed the sails from the ship. They had cause to be concerned about Major Alexander MacLeod, for Glendale had commanded the rump of the Loyalist land forces at Cape Fear from May to October 1776.

On 7th March Governor Richard Caswell, writing from Governor Tryon's Palace at New Bern, replied to John Ancrum that "the Despatches which Major McCleod sends to Mrs McCleod and Mrs McDonald must be perused by you in the absence of General Ashe." [1]

The Governor also wrote to Gen John Ashe that the Council "recommended to me to grant leave to Major McCleod to carry out with his wife and son, and Mrs McDonald and her four children with their Indented Female Servants. That he (Mr McCleod) have leave to send an express to any of their having leave to depart the State, and that the Governor direct the Guard to be continued while the vessel continues in this State, and also that the persons on board the Flag be not suffered to come on shore or have any communication with the people on shore." Glendale was to be told that only the persons mentioned in the letter could depart, and the sooner they got "away the greater satisfaction he will give the State." [1]

Gen Ashe was absent, and so it was John Ancrum who read Glendale's letters to his mother-in-law Flora, and to his wife Ann. Governor Caswell had confused the two ladies. Flora had the son and Ann had the four children. Glendale was expert at sending expresses, and within a few days his letters were carried the 110 miles to Glendale in Cumberland County.

Flora, her son James, Ann MacLeod, with her children Norman, Allan, Flora and Mary, had little enough to bring with them. Flora had managed to save only £40 worth of her possessions. The families also brought with them those female indentured servants that had remained.

Flora left behind in North Carolina friends, some of whom, she would never see again. Her stepfather Hugh had soon been freed from gaol in Halifax, and returned to Mountain Creek with his grandson, Donald, Cuidrach's son. Flora's half-sister Annabella had to be left behind with her daughters, for Cuidrach was still a prisoner. Flora's other half sister Flora remained in North Carolina with her son James MacQueen.

By the beginning of April, Flora and her son James, and Ann MacLeod, and her four children, were at Wilmington, reunited with Glendale. Flora later wrote that "she remained in this deplorable condition for two years, among robbers and faithless servants, until her husband, and son in law, Major Alexr McLeod obtained a flag of truce from Sir Henry Clinton and Admiral How." [3] Flora left the miseries of North Carolina thankfully. She had no intention of ever returning.

James Banks confused Allan MacDonald of Kingsburgh with Alexander MacDonald of Cuidrach. He therefore attributed to Flora, the trials and escape to Charlestown, South Carolina, of her half-sister, Annabella. [6]

J.P. Maclean copied and elaborated Banks' erroneous account, and then added that "It appears to be well established that in order to secure money to defray her expenses she sold her silverware. A silver tray, reputed to have been used for that purpose, was preserved in Wilson, North Carolina. Flora possessed a very large and handsome set of silver, probably presented her while a prisoner in London. While in Wilmington, perceiving she had not enough money for her journey, she was induced to part with it. This was purchased by Richard Quince. The waiter, bowl, ladle, and cream pitcher are now owned by Mrs E.J. Justice, of Greensboro. Several other pieces are owned by Mrs Brooke Empie, of Wilmington, and still others widely distributed." [7]

Flora saved only £40 worth of her family goods. Any silverware surviving in North Carolina, some of which was photographed earlier this century, had been plundered or stolen from her house at Cheeks Creek in 1776. When Flora arrived at Wilmington, Glendale had a ship waiting to take her to New York, and money. Flora had no need to sell her silver, even if she had any left. Richard Quince, described by Janet

Schaw as being "deeply engaged in the new system of politicks," was an unlikely purchaser of goods from Flora.

Flora wrote that the flag of truce "brought me, my daughter, and her children from Wilmington in N Carolina to New York in the dead of winter, being in danger of our lives for the most of the voyage by a constant storme." [3]

Flora and Allan had not seen each other since they had parted, with such high hopes near Cross Creek on 19th February 1776, more than two years previously. It was a happy and bitter re-union, for both Flora and Allan had suffered physically during their separation. Flora brought with her, her son James. Allan had not seen him for two years. At New York Flora may have seen her son Ranald, who had been transferred from Halifax to HMS *Alcide*. She had not seen him for four years.

Flora's eldest son Charles, was lieutenant in his father's company of the Royal Highland Emigrants at Halifax. Her second son Alexander, who had at last been exchanged, had joined Capt Ranald Mackinnon's 4th Light Company of the Royal Highland Emigrants, posted to New York. On "constant Light Infantry duty in New York &c." [2] Alexander had been wounded, and before June he travelled to Halifax, where Capt Alexander MacDonald wrote that "Lieut Alxr mcDonald lies very ill of his former ailment in his side, for which he has undergone an Operation." [4]

Flora and Allan had not heard any news of Johnny, at school in Edinburgh, or Fanny, who had been left in Skye.

Glendale was accompanied by his wife Ann, and their four children, and spent the summer in New York. Still without a rank in the army, Glendale worked away at recovering the commission promised him in the Royal Highland Emigrants. He obtained leave to return to Britain, and, with his family, sailed from New York to London in October 1778. Glendale carried despatches for Gen Sir Henry Clinton.

The British forces had suffered a major setback when, in October 1777, Major Gen John Burgoyne had surrendered his army at Saratoga. Gen Sir William Howe tendered his resignation, and in May 1778 departed for England. He was replaced by Lt Gen Sir Henry Clinton, and in June he promptly withdrew from Philadelphia. At the end of June Gen Washington attacked the retreating British Army at Monmouth, and though Gen Sir Henry Clinton hit back, he withdrew to New York. The two armies remained locked together for the remainder of the war, engaged in constant skirmishing.

Capt Alexander MacDonald was waiting for Allan and Flora to arrive at Halifax in June, where Lt Charles MacDonald "expects his parents every Day."[4] In August Capt MacDonald wrote that "If Capt Murd McLean or Capt Allan Macdonald Should be there [New York] tell them as I have said before it is very surprizing wt keeps them there that I will Certainly Stop their Credit from receiving any more money if they dont Join the Regt or Assgn Sufficient Reasons to the Contrary."[4]

Kingsburgh remained in New York, where he obtained a commission for his son, James, in the British Legion. The regiment had been formed in 1778 by Lord Cathcart, and James was appointed 2nd lieutenant in Capt James Stewart's company.

In the autumn Kingsburgh, threatened with having his credit stopped, prepared to travel to Halifax, Nova Scotia. He later wrote that "being exchanged, on his arrival at New York, raised a Company of eighty six Volunteer Gentlemen from Virginia and Carolina, with whom he did duty, without pay, for twelve months, and with General Robertson's approbation, delivered the Company to a young Gentleman whom he appointed to their Command; when your Memorialist joined his regiment of Royal Highland Emigrants in Nova Scotia."[2]

Flora added that "I remained for some time at New York ... until Mr McDonald was ordered to joyne the 84th Regt, in Nova Scotia, where he & his son had got commissions."[3]

Allan and Flora may have delayed in New York as long as St Andrews Day, 30th November, 1778, to celebrate the 21st birthday of their son James, 2nd lieutenant in the British Legion. Allan may have set off first, for Flora wrote that "I was obliged, tho tender, to follow, and was very nigh deaths door, by a violent disorder, the rough sea, and long passage had brought on. And at last landing in Halifax, were allowed to stay there for eight days on account of my tender state."

Kingsburgh's company was on detachment at Fort Edward, near Windsor, eight miles from the bay of Minas, and forty miles from Halifax.

"The ninth day sett off for Windsor, on the Bay of Minos, throw woods & snow and arrived the fifth day. There we continued all winter and spring, covered with frost & snow, and almost starved with cold to death, it being one of the wors winters ever seen there, a detachment of the regiment being there."[3]

Flora was once again reunited with Allan, and saw her son, Charles, for the first time since he had gone off to India, eight years before.

Fort Edward was a plain diamond shaped artillery fort, with four bastions, on a slight rise overlooking the Pisiquid River. This was the fort that Capt MacDonald felt was fit only for hogs. There was an accommodation block for officers and two for soldiers; a magazine, provisions store and bakehouse. The blockhouse, or guardhouse, just inside the fort's only entrance has survived, and bears a plaque commemorating Flora's stay in the fort.

Fort Edward was dull for young officers, who included Charles, who was extravagant and got drunk, and Alexander, who had been busy on military service in New York, and was still not fully recovered for an operation. Capt MacDonald wrote to Brig Francis Maclean in December that "Our young fellows are so fond of dancing and seeing the ladies at Halifax they are constantly plaguing me for leave to go down there and they'll think it hard when I refuse them." [4] He had given leave to Lts Charles and Alexander MacDonald, but asked that the brigadier send orders "that no officer Shou'd leave his post except where ordered on duty. I wish for this only out of regard for the Young Gentlemen's Interests as they have nothing but their pay to spend & they may have amusement enough here." [4]

On 18th January 1779, Capt Alexander MacDonald wrote that "The Annual Ships arrived here four or five days ago and brot a confirmation of the Establishmt of the Regimt by letters from Brig Allan McLean and Major Small." [4]

Next day, only a short time after Flora had reached Fort Edward, Capt MacDonald's wife, Suzie, died at child birth. The captain was grief stricken and wrote that "I have nothing now to trouble you with but the melancholy Acco[t] Mr[s] Macdonald's Death and lelft me behind a Miserable wretch with five children much at a loss wch way to turn myself to provide for them Shou'd God Spare my life to see them able to do for themselves." [4]

Capt MacDonald stopped copying his hearty, bluff, sometimes coarse letters into his letter book. [4]

Flora found herself looking after the three youngest children, and Charles, who wanted to get away to Halifax to see the ladies, and Alexander who was sickening. Alexander's wound, sustained during light infantry duties while in New York, had still not healed. In the summer he was sent to New York, with leave to return to Britain to convalesce.

The British seemed incapable of winning the war against the Americans. The Loyalists had become unpopular in Nova Scotia, and there were fears that there might be a revolt. Fort Edward was not a safe place in which to live.

Flora wrote that "by ane accedentall fall next summer I dislockated the wrist of the other hand, and brock some tendons, which confined me for two months, altho I had the assistance of the Regimental surgeon. When I got the better of this misfortune, I fixed my thoughts on Seeing my native country, tho in a tender state, and my husband obtained a birth in the Lord Dunmore, letter of mark ship of 24 guns. I and three young ladys and two gentlemen sett sail in Octr." [3]

Flora was weakened by illness and depressed by the thought of another cold winter in Nova Scotia. Even the prospect of being with her infirm husband, Allan, was not enough to keep her in Canada. It was a bitter parting, for Allan, through a sense of duty, and because he needed the money, decided to remained with his regiment. As Flora had been abandoned in North Carolina, so now Allan was abandoned in Nova Scotia. He still believed that Flora would rejoin him, after the war, and that they would settle in North America. But Flora had no intention of ever recrossing the Atlantic.

The grief of parting with Allan, and her son Charles, was mitigated by Flora's thoughts of returning to her native country again, and of seeing her younger children, Johnny and Fanny.

CHAPTER 19

Flora Returns to Skye

I stayed at Inverness for three days. I had the good luck to meet with a female companion from that to Skye. I was the fourth day with great difficulty at Raasay, for my hands being so pained with the riding. I have arrived at Dunvegan a few days ago with my young daughter, who promises to be a stout Highland "Caileag", quite overgrown of her age. Nanny and her family are well. — Flora MacDonald

Flora left Halifax, Nova Scotia, in October 1779, having lived five eventful, and latterly miserably unhappy years in North America.

"I fixed my thoughts," wrote Flora, "on seeing my native country, tho in a tender state, and my husband obtained a birth in the Lord Dunmore, letter of mark ship of 24 guns. I and three young ladys and two gentlemen sett sail in Octr, but, in our passage spying a sail, made ready for action and in hurreying the ladies below to a place of safety, my foot skipping a step in the trapp, fell and brock the dislockated arm in two. It was sett with a bandage over splints of wood, and keep my bed till we arrived in the Thames." [1]

William Chambers later wrote that on the homeward journey, "Flora insisted upon remaining on deck, where she endeavoured, by her voice and example, to animate the sailors. She was unfortunately thrown down in the bustle, and broke her arm; which caused her afterwards to observe, in the spirit of Mercutio, that she had now perilled her life in behalf of both the house of Stuart and that of Brunswick, and got very little for her pains." [2]

James Banks copied Chambers and concluded that "during the engagement Flora refused to go below, and remained on deck, urging the men to deeds of daring. Her arm was broken in the fight, and she was accustomed to say, that she had fought for the house of Stuart and for the house of Hanover, but had been worsted each time." [3]

J.P. Maclean copied the story, and could not resist improving it. [4] Chambers' tale, enlarged by Banks and Maclean was contradicted by Flora's own account. Flora never fought for the House of Stuart, though she did show warlike spirit in recruiting for the House of

Brunswick or Hanover in North Carolina. On the return voyage to Britain, Flora did not fight for the British monarch.

In great discomfort Flora arrived in London in December 1779. There was no repeat of the welcome that she had received as the Jacobite heroine, 33 years before. There was no record of where she stayed during the winter, but Ann, Viscountess Primrose had died in 1775, and Flora did not stay with Lady Margaret MacDonald, who had so resented Flora bringing the Prince to Monkstadt in June 1746. Lady Margaret was then living at Welbeck Street. Her son, Sir Alexander, now Lord MacDonald, had abandoned Skye and was also living in London.

Flora wrote that "to my great sorrow, on my landing, received the melancholy newes of my son Alexrs death, Lieut of Light Infantry, being lost in his way home, ane old wound constantly breaking out from the fatigue of the light-infantry service, brought him very lowe." [1]

Kingsburgh recalled that Alexander's "health was impaired by constant Light Infantry service in New York ... was afterwards lost in his passage going to England for the benefit of his health, being much reduced by active service under Sir Henry Clinton." [5]

Alexander, born in 1755, had emigrated to North Carolina, and in 1775 had been given a commission in the Royal Highland Emigrants. In 1776 he had marched away with his father to Cross Creek and had been captured after the battle of Moore's Creek. He had been sent as a prisoner to Philadelphia, and then had been paroled with his father at Reading. In August 1777 he had travelled to New York, where he was eventually exchanged. Alexander had joined the Light Infantry Company of the Royal Highland Emigrants, in New York, where he was wounded. By June 1778 he was on sick leave in Nova Scotia, but the following year he returned to New York, and set sail for Britain to convalesce.

Flora wrote that "a short time thereafter, got the accounts of the Villa de Paris being lost in her way home, where my beloved son Ranald was Capt of mareens haveing served in Lord Rodneys Ship, every where he was." Flora, in recalling her losses, ten years later, had telescoped events. Capt Ranald was not lost until 1782.

Flora wrote that "Those melouncholy strocks, by the death of my children who, had they lived, with Gods assistance, might now be my support in my declined old age, brought on a violent fitt of sickness, which confined me to my bed in London for half a year, and would have brought me to my grave, if under Gods hand Doctor Donald Munrow had not given his friendly assistance." [1] Dr Donald Munro was the son of Professor Alexander Munro of Edinburgh University, whose wife was the daughter of Sir Donald MacDonald, 4th Bt of Sleat.

Flora spent a wretched winter in London, separated from her husband and all her family. It was not until May 1780 that she was fit enough to travel to Edinburgh, where she stayed with her friend Mrs Mackenzie of Delvine. John MacKenzie, for so long the family's lawyer in Edinburgh, and the guardian and benefactor of Flora's son Johnny, had died in 1778. Flora saw Johnny, and that year he won a cadetship in the Bombay Infantry. He set out for India and started a career that was to prove to be the most successful of all Flora and Allan's children, though he was never to see his parents again.

In May 1780 Flora wrote to Donald MacDonald, merchant in Glasgow, that "Youl be surprised to be troubled wt a letter from one personally unknown to you. I am Mrs MacDonald late of Kingsborrow in Sky. I came lately from London to this place. I crossed to there from Nova Scotia. I have been during the winter in London & was in very bad health ... It is recommended to me my Physician to make all possible speed to the highlands for the benefite of the goat Whey. I mean to go to Sky by Inverness as being the most expeditious way. I propose to take up my residence in the Longisland — I have some things to be sent to that place." [5]

Flora left Edinburgh in June and travelled north. In July Flora wrote to Mrs MacKenzie of Delvine that "I arrived at Inverness the third day after parting with you, in good health, and without any accident which I always dread; my young 'Squire continued always very obliging to me." For all her winter's illness, Flora completed the journey of at least 120 miles in three days. The young squire, who accompanied her, was probably Flora's son Johnny.

"I stayed at Inverness for three days. I had the good luck to meet with a female companion from that to Skye. I was the fourth day with great difficulty at Raasay, for my hands being so pained with the riding . . . I have arrived here [Dunvegan] a few days ago with my young daughter, who promises to be a stout Highland 'Caileag', quite overgrown of her age."

It was 85 miles to the ferry for Skye and a further 20 miles to the ferry to Raasay. Flora went to Raasay to collect her daughter Fanny, whom she had not seen since 1774. John MacLeod of Raasay was a cousin of Flora's stepfather, and Raasay had married Jane MacQueen, a cousin of Flora's half-sister's husband. John and Jane MacLeod had a large family of three sons and nine daughters, three of whom were ages with Fanny.

"Nanny and her family are well. Her husband was not sailed the last account she had from him." Nanny was Flora's daughter Ann, and her husband was Glendale, who was preparing to return to North America.

"I have the pleasure to inform you, upon my arrival here, that I had two letters from my husband, the latter dated tenth May. He was then in very good health, and informs me that my son Charles has got the command of a troop of horse in Lord Cathcart's regiment. But alas! I have heard nothing since I left you about my son Sandy, which you may be sure gives me uneasiness; but still hope for the best.

"By public and private news, I hope we will have peace reestablished, to our great satisfaction, which as it is a thing long expected and wished for, will be for the utility of the whole nation; especially to the poor me that has my all engaged fond to hear news, but afraid to get it.

"I wait here till a favourable opportunity for the Long Island shall offer itself. Please direct to me, to Mrs McDonald late of Kingsboro', South Uist by Dunvegan." [6]

Flora's hope of peace in North America was a vain one.

Lord Cornwallis had already shown his flair, as a military commander, by defeating Gen Washington at the battle of Brandywine, and retaking Philadelphia. With the surrender of Major Gen Burgoyne, and the resignation of Gen Sir William Howe, Lord Cornwallis, however, became sickened by Gen Sir Henry Clinton's incompetence. He resigned his command and returned to Britain where he was promoted lt general, and was sent out to America again, with a dormant commission to replace Gen Sir Henry Clinton. After the commander-in-chief's withdrawal to New York, Lord Cornwallis eventually persuaded the cautious Sir Henry to open a second front in the Carolinas, in December 1779.

Meanwhile Glendale was still attempting to obtain a permanent preferment. In October 1778 he had left North America with his family and returned to Britain in December. He then travelled to Skye and installed his family at Dunvegan Castle. Alexander's nephew, Norman MacLeod of MacLeod, had allowed Glendale's family the use of the Castle while the Laird was away in the army.

In July 1779 Glendale returned to London, and petitioned for a preferment, and was given an allowance. He was ordered to return to North America with a recommendation to Gen Sir Henry Clinton that he should be given an appointment.

In December 1779 Gen Sir Henry Clinton sailed from New York and reached South Carolina in early February 1780. Amongst the regiments in the expeditionary force were the British Legion and 5 companies of the 2nd Battalion of the Royal Highland Emigrants, now the 84th Regiment. Flora's eldest son, Charles, lieutenant in the 84th, had purchased a captaincy in the British Legion, commanded by Lord Cathcart. His brother, James, was 2nd lieutenant in Capt James Stuart's company, and transferred to his brother's company. Kingsburgh's company of the 84th Regiment was not one of those that travelled south, and he remained in Nova Scotia.

In May Charleston was captured. Lord Cathcart resigned his command of the British Legion, and was succeeded by a brilliant, dashing young officer called Banastre Tarleton, who was only 25 years old.

Lt Gen Sir Henry Clinton retired to New York, but Lord Cornwallis took the initiative and marched inland. In August Lord Cornwallis defeated General Gates decisively at Camden. The British Legion was on the left of the line in Lord Rawdon's division.

In the summer of 1780 Glendale sailed from England to North America, and joined Lord Cornwallis at Wynnsborough, 25 miles west of Camden, in December. Despite a recommendation from Sir Henry Clinton, Lord Cornwallis could not find a preferment for Glendale, but he remained with the army as a volunteer.

Lord Cornwallis marched into North Carolina, and won a bloody victory at Guilford Court House. He decided to retire to Wilmington, and marched to Cross Creek and down to the coast. For the Highlanders left in western North Carolina, Lord Cornwallis had arrived five years too late.

Major Alexander MacLeod marched with Lord Cornwallis's army from Wynnsborough into North Carolina and was at Guilford Court House. He marched south east across Deep River passing close to Glendale, which he had left on 12th February 1776, and which still belonged to the Blacks; he passed by Mount Pleasant, where Alexander MacDonald of Cuidrach had lived and where his family had been so harshly treated before managing to escape to Charleston; he passed Barbecue church, where Flora had been a member. Hugh MacDonald, Flora's stepfather had died the previous year, at Mountain Creek, but Donald and Katherine Campbell of Scalpay were still alive, despite rough treatment. Hugh's grandson and Cuidrach's son, Donald, had remained in North Carolina but now joined the British Legion in Lord Cornwallis's army.

At Cross Creek Glendale proposed a plan to the Highland gentlemen for raising a Loyalist regiment. With no employment, Glendale got leave to return to New York.[7] In April 1778, Glendale had come to Wilmington to recover his wife and mother-in-law from the back country. Now Alexander MacLeod left North Carolina for the last time, having lost all his lands, his possessions, and even the commission promised to him.

In April 1781, Lord Cornwallis marched his army across North Carolina towards Virginia, reaching Yorktown in August. Lord Cornwallis began to fortify the town and sent an urgent despatch to Gen Sir Henry Clinton for reinforcements.

In August, Glendale left New York. He wrote that "From thence I was sent home by the Commander in Chief, to adjust with the Minister of the American Department, a plan for raising the Loyalists, which Sir Henry Clinton had approved. I was also charged with his despatches, which I delivered to Lord Germaine September last was twelve month. [1781] As nothing could be done in regard to plan for raising men, I had His Lordship's leave to come and stay with my family till called for." [7]

While Glendale was in America Flora and her daughter Fanny lived at Dunvegan Castle with Ann MacLeod. In the late summer Flora crossed the Minch to the Outer Hebrides, and visited her brother in South Uist. Flora wrote to her cousin Donald MacDonald of Balranald that "I had a few lines from Annie. She is always in a miserable state of health. By the last letter she had from her Husband he was not determined whither he cou'd come her length or not." [8]

Annie was Flora's daughter Ann. Glendale did get 'the length' of Dunvegan Castle in October 1781, and he brought the news of Hugh MacDonald's death and the harsh treatment that had been inflicted upon Flora's half-sister at Mount Pleasant, and Donald Campbell of Scalpay and his wife.

In November Flora was in North Uist staying with Margaret MacDonald of Kirkibost. Now widowed, she had been sent over to Monkstadt, on 27th June 1746, to warn Lady Margaret MacDonald that the Prince was about to arrive in Skye.

In December 1781, Flora was at Kirkibost when she wrote to her son-in-law, Glendale, that "I have scarce Power to write you the joyful News I received by this post from Ranald, dated from New York October the 10th of My dear Sandy that he is still in the land of the living — I shall give it to you in his own words — 'No doubt You will be surprised to hear that Sandy is still in the land of the Living. They were taken up at Sea by a Vessel from Lisbon & conveyed to the coast of Brasil.'

"So good news to be true. You are the only person fit to communicate this unexpected News to poor Anney. I Trust it does not have some bad effect upon her tender State of health." Poor Anney, was Flora's daughter Ann, who had become pregnant for the fifth time.

"He writes that General Clinton with 6 thousand Men was going to assist Lord Cornwallis who was blocked up by sea he had a letter from his Father in June. He said that He was in good health." [9]

On the same day, Flora also wrote to Balranald with the good news in Ranald's letter. "I have great reason to be thankful for all their preservation. He writs me that he got a letter from his father in June from Halifax and that he was then in very good health and that Charles and James was well, he regrets that his Brave Captain lost his Leg, his ship suffered greatly.

"This is two Letters I receiv'd from him within this ten days, he writs me that General Clinton with 6 thousand men was going to embark to assist Lord Cornwales, who was blocked up by the French fleet, they had 28 sail, the enemy 34 Sail of the line of Battle Ships. God send us good account of them. God bless him poor man he never refuses an oppertunity in writing to his Mother." [10]

Despite Capt Ranald's news of his brother, nothing was ever heard again of Alexander. Allan was at Halifax with the 84th Regiment. Capt Charles and Lt James were in South Carolina with the British Legion.

HMS *Alcide*, with Capt Ranald MacDonald on board, had returned to British waters. In November 1779 Ranald had been transferred to HMS *Shrewsbury*. While at Spithead, off Portsmouth, in March 1780, he had made his will. Admiral Sir George Rodney, given command of the Leeward Islands fleet, sailed across the Atlantic, later in the month. He bottled up the French fleet at Rhode Island, and returned to the West Indies.

When the Dutch joined the United States of America, France and Spain against the British, Admiral Rodney was ordered to attack St Eustati, in January 1781. This Dutch island was the depot for the trans-shipment of goods from Europe to the American fleet and privateers. Admiral Rodney took months disposing of the booty. Lt Ranald's share of the prize money may have been as much as £3,000.

Admiral de Grasse succeeded in slipping a French fleet across the Atlantic, and into the Chesapeake, and landed troops to support Marquis de Lafayette. Admiral Graves with Admiral Hood, sailed to the Chesapeake to prevent Rochambeau's army from landing. Graves had 19 ships to de Grasse's 24, but the battle, which began on 5th September, was not well managed. Ranald's ship, *Shrewsbury* came into action a little after 4pm, and was severely damaged. Capt Robinson was wounded in the thigh, and then lost his left leg. The first lieutenant was killed, and in a little over an hour *Shrewsbury* was ordered to retire. Hood's division, at the rear of the line, never saw action. Graves retired to New York, where *Shrewsbury* limped into the anchorage on 24th September. [11] It was from New York that Ranald wrote twice to his mother, with hopeful news about his brother Alexander.

On 28th September Gen George Washington and Marquis de Lafayette with the American army and Comte de Rochambeau with the French army, began to invest Yorktown and Gloucester.

On 17th October Admiral Graves, with Capt Ranald MacDonald on board *Shrewsbury*, sailed out of New York with 25 ships and Sir Henry Clinton's army of 6,000 men. Off the Virginia Capes Graves faced de Grasse with 36 ships, but then learned that on 19th October, Lord Cornwallis had been forced to surrender the second British army of the war to the Americans.

In 1779 the Trustees of the MacLeod estates had sold Harris to Capt Alexander MacLeod, of the Berneray family. Two years later the Trustees were forced to sell more land. Trumpan, in Waternish, was sold to Peter Nicolson; Skeabost was sold to James MacDonald, of the Heisker family, North Uist. James had married Emily, sister of Alexander MacDonald of Cuidrach and Mount Pleasant, and was a merchant in Portree. Lynedale was sold to Kingsburgh's cousin, Donald MacDonald of Balranald.

Kingsburgh wrote that "I do think Flory Judged right to take the world with so little trouble as posibly she can, and her plan of liveing will be as comfortable as Sandy and honest Peggie MacLeod can make it." Since Glendale's return to Dunvegan Castle, Flora had arranged to live with her sister-in-law, Peggy MacLeod, widow of Allan's brother James, and her son Alexander MacDonald, at Knocowe, near Kilmuir.

"I never received a line from my sister in law, tho I wrott about Sandy; But now I am glad he did not come out, as we expect very early in the spring to be besieged here. We have been fortifying all summer and harvest, and now in frost and snow. The Duty and King's works are very heavy, but the work must soon stop.

"I have desired my son Ranald to correspond with you, in case more of the [MacLeod] estate is to be sold. I am told his share of prize money will amount to three thousand pounds Sterling. I have heard nothing of Charly or Jamie since the 6th of June, that letter I have sent his mother and sister home, and so I doubt not but you may see it, if this and it arrives."

"My nephew Sandy McAlester was very lucky in getting that good girl and her money, and I think Ketty Mc Alester's marriage is a very wise and prudent one." Alexander and Catherine were two of the fourteen children of Allan's sister Anne and Ranald MacAlister of Skirinish. Alexander was the oldest son. In 1784 his younger brother John, who had died in India, left Alexander money to purchase the

Strathaird estate, and this he did, from Lord MacDonald in 1789. Catherine had married Peter Nicolson, who had just purchased Trumpan and Ardmore in Waternish.

"If I live for a year or two and goes home with a broken legg or hand, it will be a good place to live on so many young Lairds.

"I believe my two sons are in the Army in South Carolina. Ranald is in the fleet." [8]

In June 1782 Flora was staying with her brother at Milton. In July, she wrote to Mrs Mackenzie of Delvine thanking her for her letter and "the agreeable news about Johny's arrival, which relieved me of a great deal of distress, as that was the first accounts I had of him since he sailed. I think, poor man, he has been very lucky for getting bread so soon after landing. I had a letter from John which, I suppose, came by the same conveyance as yours. I am told by others that it will be in his power now to show his talents, as being in the engineer department. He speaks feelingly of the advantages he got in his youth, and the good example show'd him, which I hope will keep him from doing anything that is either sinful or shameful.

"I received a letter from Captain Macdonald, my husband, dated from Halifax, the 12th Nov. '81. He was then recovering his health, but had been very tender for some time before. My son, Charles, is captain in the British Legion, and James a lieutenant. They are both in New York."

Capt Charles and Lt James had not been made prisoner with the British Legion at Gloucester in October 1781, for they had been at Charleston with Lord Rawdon. From there they had made their way to New York. In March 1782, Lord Rawdon raised a Regiment of Foot, numbered 105th, and Charles was appointed second senior captain.

"Ranald is captain of Marines, and was with Rodney at the taking of St Eustati. As for my son Sandy who was amissing I had accounts of his being carried to Lisbon, but nothing certain, which I look upon, on the whole, as a hearsay; but the kindness of providence is still to be looked upon, as I have no reason to complain, as God has been pleased to spare his father and the rest." No more was ever heard of Alexander, and he was presumed lost.

Flora concluded her letter to Mrs MacKenzie of Delvine by stating that "I am now in my brother's house, on my way to Skye, to attend my daughter, who is to ly-in in August. They are all in health at present. As for my health at present, it's tolerable, considering my anxious mind and distress of times." [6]

Alexander and Ann MacLeod's fifth child had been conceived on his return from North Carolina, and was born at Dunvegan Castle in

August 1782. He was named Alexander for his father and his lost uncle. Flora attended the lying-in. Six years later a fourth son, John, was born.

In November 1781 Admiral Hood had sailed to the West Indies, with Capt Ranald MacDonald on board *Shrewsbury*. In late January 1782 the admiral attacked and outwitted Admiral de Grasse at St Christophers, retaking the harbour at Basterre. Hood rejoined Rodney and in April 1782 at the battle of the Saints, off Dominica, fought the biggest naval battle of the century. Rodney defeated de Grasse, capturing his 120 gun ship *Ville de Paris* and the admiral himself. *Shrewsbury* was in too poor condition to fight at the battle.

Ranald was sick, perhaps still suffering from the wound received at Lexington or Concord, seven years earlier, for in July, by order of Admiral Hood, he was discharged to hospital in Port Royal, Jamaica. In August Capt Ranald was sent home to Britain in a convoy that included the captured prize *Ville de Paris*, but died at sea in September. Ranald's will was proved in October 1783.[12]

Flora later wrote that she "got the accounts of the *Villa de Paris* being lost in her way home, where my beloved son Ranald was capt of mareens haveing served in Lord Rodneys ship, every where he was."[1]

Ranald, who had written so conscientiously to his mother, had been dearly loved by his parents. He had been with Admirals Rodney and Hood, later both created barons, but though he did not serve on *Ville de Paris*, he was a passenger on board, returning to Britain to recover his health. The ship foundered in heavy seas off Newfoundland on 9th September 1782, taking the beloved Ranald with it.

Flora and Allan lost their second son to the Revolutionary War, and the cold Atlantic.

CHAPTER 20

Allan Returns to Skye

The cast in both my arms are liveing monuments of my
sufferings & distressis, and the long goal confinement
which my husband underwent has brought on such
disorders that he has totally lost the use of his legs; so
that I may fairly say we both have suffered in our
person, family, and interest, as much if not more than
any two going under the name of refugees or loyalists,
without the smallest recompence.
— Flora MacDonald

In Nova Scotia, Capt Allan MacDonald of Kingsburgh continued to serve with the 84th Regiment. In the summer of 1781 the regiment had been employed in fortifying Halifax. The following year Kingsburgh was sent to defend Sydney harbour in Cape Breton.[1] In 1782 and 1783 he was back at Fort Edward, Windsor.

The war had ground to a halt in North America, and in Paris peace terms were being negotiated. On 3rd September, 1783, the United States of America, with her allies, France, Spain and the Netherlands, signed a peace treaty with Britain.

The 2nd battalion of the 84th Regiment was disbanded at Windsor, Nova Scotia, in October and November 1783, and the officers went onto half-pay. A grant of 105,000 acres of land had been made to Lt Col John Small, in trust for himself, his officers and men, in the districts of Nine Mile River, Gore and Kennetcock, now in the county of Hants, north of Halifax and north east of Windsor.

Kingsburgh, as a captain, received half-pay of £91 a year and a grant of 3,000 acres. No record of the exact location of the grant has survived, but there was reference to 700 acres which Allan had held on the Minas Basin and Cobequid Bay. Here Kingsburgh lived on his "Regimental Grant of Lands on the River Kennetcock, in Nova Scotia, where he has a neat little Hutt, and cleared a few acres."[2]

In January 1784, Kingsburgh was at Halifax where he submitted a claim to "The Commissioners appointed by act of Parliament to enquire into the Losses and Services of all such Persons who have suffered in their Rights, properties, and Possessions during the Late

Unhappy Dissentions in America in consequence of their Loyalty to His Majesty and attachment to the British Government." [2]

Allan stated that he had emigrated to North Carolina in 1774; had fought with the Highlanders at the battle of Moore's Creek; was captured and sent a prisoner to Philadelphia; was exchanged and went to New York, where he raised a company of volunteers; in October 1778 he had joined the 84th Regiment in Nova Scotia, where he remained until the Regiment was reduced in October 1783.

The "Account of losses sustained by him in consequence of the part he took in the late Rebellion, is as exact as he is now able to make it. That his sufferings and services are well known to Officers and others of the King's Servants and Subjects, and that the value of the Estates and Property which have been taken from him by the rebels, and the various Expenses he has put to in North Carolina for His Majesty's Service will, he trusts, be satisfactorily proved."

Allan claimed £1086 for his two plantations, grist mill, horses and cattle, household articles, and indentured servants. He sent his Memorial to London, where his agent, Alexander MacDonald, attorney, of Lombard Street, placed it before the Commissioners in March. [2]

Meanwhile at Dunvegan Castle, Major Alexander MacLeod of Glendale was summoned to appear in London before the Commissioners, in December 1782. He was unable to attend because of the ill health of his wife, but he did eventually travel to London in June 1783, but was back again at Dunvegan by the autumn.

In March 1784 a Memorial was presented to the Commissioners by 'Alexdr Macleod, Esquire, Commandant of a Corps of North Carolina Highland Emigrants,' in which he detailed his service and claimed £2280 in losses, being £1500 already submitted to the Board of Treasury in 1779, and £780 for supporting his family from February 1776 until they arrived in London in December 1778. The claim, already submitted to the Board of Treasury was for stock, farm implements, household goods, clothing and indentured servants taken to North Carolina.

The Commissioners considered Glendale's memorial and its extensive supporting evidence and noted that his present allowance was £200: that he had been deprived of £1500 of property by the rebels; that he had been compelled to leave by the rebels and had returned to Britain in 1779, and that he had certified accounts of military expenses and that Sir William Howe and Gen Fraser attested his loyalty and service.

The Commissioners decided that "It appears that this Gentleman went from Scotland to America in the year 1774, and says he carried out with him, money & effects to the amount of 1500 pounds, in order to settle there. When asked how he could think of going to settle in an Country which was at that moment in flames, he said that he did not know at that time that the troubles had grown to such a height. He was a Lieut of marines on half-pay when he went to America, which was 40 pounds per year, and which he lost by accepting a Captain's Commission in a Provincial Corps.

"It appears to us that Capt Macleod barely comes under the description of an American Sufferer. At all events however, we think his allowance is much too great in proportion to his property, but in consideration of his large family, we think it would be reasonable to allow him 100 pounds a year in the future." [2]

Alexander MacLeod, for all his loyalty and diligence was deemed not to have been an American sufferer. His allowance was halved to £100 a year and he was offered only £500 in compensation for the loss of all his possessions in North America. His case was typical of the parsimonious ingratitude of Commissioners, sitting safely in London, who had never known the deprivations and anguish of being uprooted from their homes.

Allan left Nova Scotia in October 1784 and travelled to London, on learning that he would receive a better award, if he presented his petition personally. He took lodgings in Clerkenwell Close, which was convenient for Lincoln's Inn Fields, where the Commissioners were sitting. Kingsburgh's son James was with him, and though he did not make a claim himself, James supported one made by his cousin, Donald, Cuidrach's son.

Governor Martin, Lord Cornwallis, Sir Henry Clinton, Lord Rawdon, Sir William Howe, Gen Simon Fraser and others were tireless in providing character references for the Loyalist claimants. Lt Col Donald MacDonald, who had commanded the Loyalist Army in North Carolina, was living in Highgate, and produced many affidavits. The Loyalists themselves gathered together, supporting each other in their claims — Kingsburgh, his son James, and son-in-law Alexander MacLeod; Cuidrach and his son Donald; Alexander MacDonald of Staten Island, Alexander Morrison of Crosshill, and many others.

In January 1785, Allan placed his second Memorial before the Commissioners. The sum claimed was increased to £1341 with a further £299 for military expenses incurred while raising the Highlanders in North Carolina. Allan concluded that the money expended and the value lost was by "an old, wornout officer in the service of his King and Country, lost the comfort and strength of his old age, his Estate; his all, and an old Wife, a Daughter and himself to support, with only a very small income, this money would contribute to make his living easy in his old age, and now in reduced and infirm state he is in, having neither Dwelling Place nor Abode but Regimental Grant of lands on the River Kennetcock, in Nova Scotia, where he has a little neat Hutt, and cleared a few acres last Summer, means soon to return, had he the Money to carry out his improvements which he was obliged to give up last October for want of cash." [2]

After a delay, Allan received only £440 in compensation. By then Allan had decided not to return to Nova Scotia. He was about 63 years old, and had been suffering from pains in his legs. He still had 3,000 acres in Nova Scotia, but he no longer had the energy to start life anew. And Allan was certain that Flora would not return to the cold winters of Nova Scotia.

Allan travelled to the Hebrides, where he rejoined Flora, whom he had not seen for five years. In the past nine years they had been together only in New York and Nova Scotia for a little over a year. Each weakened by illness, it was time for them to be together again; to love and to support each other in the declining years of their lives. Allan met his daughter Fanny, now aged eighteen, for the first time since leaving Skye in 1774.

It was a sad reunion, for Allan and Flora had no home of their own in which to live. William MacLeod was still the tacksman at Kingsburgh. There was a tradition in South Uist that Allan and Flora lived at Daliburgh, not far from Milton.

Allan and Flora's dreams of starting a new life in North Carolina and then Nova Scotia had crumbled into financial and personal ruin. They had only a small part of the money with which they had set out for America, and none of their possessions. They had both lost their health, and two sons, Alexander, and the much loved Ranald.

Flora bore her sorrows with Christian fortitude, for she had at last been reunited with her husband, and her children began to gather around her.

Alexander MacLeod and his wife Ann continued to live at Dunvegan until 1789, when the Laird of MacLeod returned from India and began improving the Castle. Alexander and Ann then went to live at Lochbay where a fishing village was being established by the British Fisheries Society. Ann MacLeod, 30 years later, claimed that "I raised the first Smoke in this village, and now I am the Oldest Settler." [3]

Alexander died in 1797, but his widow survived him for 37 years. In 1814 Donald Grant, the British Fisheries Society agent in Skye, wrote that "I cannot think of any one who is more Entitled to it [an allowance] than this poor Woman, or more in need, altho she saw many better days She lost her Three Sons in the Service of their

Country. Her Oldest son, was unfortunately killed in a Duel, being a Lieut in the line. Her second & only son, is now Lieut in the Company's Service in India. Her 3rd Son, a Lieut in the Company's Service was killed lately in India, by falling of himself & Horse. Her 4th Son a Lieut in the Company's Service was killed in battle in India, young Men of Superior Character and none of them lived to 29 years.

"She lost her ffour handsome Brothers all of whom, & Her ffather, & Husband were in the Service of their King and Country, and now lives upon an allowance from her only surviving Brother, Col John MacDond at London and the little pittance which you are about to draw for Her.

"I think whatever Success her other applications may have, That she should apply to the Compassionate Fund.

"Perhaps you will be Curious to know, that she is the only Daughter of the Famed Miss Flora Mac Donald, of whom so much is said in the History of the rebellion of 1745 — For accompanying Charles from the Island of South Uist to Sky." [3]

Alexander had received an allowance of £100 a year, a little more than captain's half pay, while he lived. Ann later noted that he was "a Married Subscriber to the Fund for the benefit of Marine Officers widows", and she received almost £20 a year from this fund.

Alexander and Ann's elder daughter Flora married a Mackay from Forres. Their younger daughter, Mary, lived with her mother at Stein, where she died in 1858. Both Ann and Mary met Rev Alexander Macgregor, minister at Kilmuir, and told him about Flora. Before she died, Mary bequeathed several artefacts associated with her grandmother to Dunvegan Castle, including a list of her children, written out in Flora's own hand, a lock of the Prince's hair and a set of stays that Flora had worn. These are now on display in the Castle.

Allan and Flora's eldest son, Charles, returned to Skye on a captain's half pay. In 1787 Charles married Isabella, the sister of Donald MacDonald of Balranald's wife. Balranald was a cousin of both Flora and Allan, and had purchased Lynedale in 1781. Charles and Isabella had no children and Charles died in 1795, aged 44.

Allan and Flora's second son, Alexander, and third son, Ranald, were lost at sea. After his will had been proved, his executor put forward Ranald's claim for prize money from the capture of St Eustati. After many delays some money became available. Ranald, Flora's favourite son, would have been pleased that his prize money became a support to his parents in their 'declined old age'.

Allan and Flora's fourth son, James, had served as a lieutenant in the British Legion and received half-pay. He took the tack of Flodigarry, where Allan and Flora had started their married life, and became known as Capt James of Flodigarry. He married Emily, daughter of James MacDonald of Heisker, who had purchased Skeabost in 1781. Emily's mother was the sister of Alexander MacDonald of Cuidrach and Mount Pleasant. One of James and Emily's great grandchildren, Major Ranald Livingstone, assumed the name MacDonald, purchased Flodigarry and built Flodigarry House, now an hotel. Capt James of Flodigarry died in 1807 leaving many descendants.

Allan and Flora's youngest son, Johnny, went out to India in 1780. In 1782 he was posted to Bencoolen, and the next year surveyed northern Sumatra. He was promoted captain and posted to Penang in 1786. He married Mrs Boyle, a widow and daughter of General Salmond, and had two daughters, Cecilia Flora and Nancy. The latter died in November 1786, and his wife soon afterwards.

In 1787 John wrote to his mother in South Uist that "I have ordered £100 to be given you immediately for your and Fanny's use and £40 for Anny. I have also ordered two thirds of the Interest of £1400 to be given to you annually and the other third to Anny — if Fanny marries with her parents' consent she is to have £100 — My child (handsome to the last degree) her Aunt Carries home this year — she will be better off with her than with any other person as she is rich and fond of her — In her mother I lost the best of women —" [4]

John's elder daughter Cecilia Flora died in June 1787, only a month after John wrote to his mother. In 1788 he returned to Sumatra as military and civil engineer, and in command of the artillery. He left Sumatra in 1796, and returned on leave to Britain, reaching England in January 1797. He retired from the East India Company service on half-pay, and in 1798 raised the Royal Edinburgh Volunteer Artillery. Next year he was appointed major in Lord MacDonald's Fencible Regiment of the Isles. Lord MacDonald was the Sir Alexander whose grasping regime had driven Allan and Flora from Kingsburgh. The Regiment of the Isles was posted to England.

While on leave, John married Frances, eldest daughter of Sir Robert Chambers, a judge in India. Sir Robert was President of the Asiatic Society, formed in 1800, of which John was one of the founding members. John was appointed lieutenant colonel of the Royal Clan Alpine Fencibles, raised for home defence in 1799. In 1802, the Fencibles were reduced.

John went to live in Exeter, where he wrote extensively on military matters, translating from the French *The Experienced Officer*, and other works, and compiling a *Telegraphic Dictionary*, with over 150,000 words, phrases and sentences. Lt Col John died in Exeter in

1831, leaving over £40,000 in his will. John and Frances had seven sons, one of whom was named Charles Edward Chambers, and one daughter, Flora Frances, who, as Mrs Wylde, wrote an *autobiography* of her grandmother.

Flora MacDonald Wylde's fanciful book about her grandmother, was the first to be published in Britain. It began the romantic cult of Flora and Bonnie Prince Charlie, which transformed the plain young woman from South Uist into a Victorian heroine, so beloved of romantic artists. A. Johnson painted a scene of Flora being introduced to the Prince in South Uist. J. Duncan depicted Flora watching over the Prince, as he slept in a cave. S. Joy painted the Prince parting with Flora at Portree, which now appears as an illustration on half the shortbread tins and boxes for sale to tourists.

In October 1789 Allan and Flora were living at Leabost, a pendicle or part of the tack of Penduin, on the shores of Loch Snizort, between Kingsburgh and Cuidrach.

Sir John McPherson, late Governor General of India, and Member of Parliament for Cricklade, had been in Skye and had asked Flora to write an account of her passage from the Uists to Skye, with Prince Charles, and of her time in North Carolina. Sir John was the son of Rev Martin MacPherson, minister of Sleat, who had married Allan and Flora at Armadale in 1750. Sir John had succeeded Warren Hastings as Governor General of India in 1785, when aged only 41, and had been created a baronet.

Flora dictated a letter to Sir John MacPherson.

"Honoured Dear Sir,

"Received inclosed the papers you was so very good as to desire me to send you I hope they are to the purpose, being exact truth; They are longer than I would wish, but Shorter I could not make them.

"My husband had a letter from John lately, he was very ill in his passage from Culcutta to Bencoolin for two months, but is now thank God well and on the surveying business need not desire you to mention his name to any of the Directors you are acquainted with.

"All friends in this Island are as you left them and with my husbands blessings who is always tender with his legs And my constant prayers to the Almighty to bliss, protect, and be your guide and director — I am ever Dr Sir, yours affectionately while able to Sign Flora mcDonald.

"Leabost by Sconcer, October 21, 1789

"I am always oppressed with the Rheumatism &c &c since I saw you. God bless you." [5]

Flora could manage to write only her name.

Written in another person's hand, the erratic spelling was not

Flora's. The memorial fell into two parts. The first started with "Miss Flora Macdonald was on a visit to her brother in South Uist, June 1746," and concluded, after parting with the Prince at Portree, that "Miss MacDonald proceeded next day to that to her mother's house." It was signed "Flora mcDonald."

The second part was the only account of Flora's life in North America. Possibly in a different hand, it was a bitter account of her later years, and began "Mrs Flora McDonald followed her husband to North Carolina", and concluded that "The Cast [crookedness] in both my arms are liveing monuments of my sufferings & distressis, and the long goal confinement which my husband underwent has brought on such disorders that he has totally lost the use of his legs; so that I may fairly say we both have suffered in person, family, and interest, as much if not more than any two going under the name of refugees or loyalists, without the smallest recompence." [5]

To the end of her life, the events of those exciting days in June 1746 remained in Flora's mind. She had never heard from the Prince, and now Flora knew that she would never meet him at the Palace of St James in London, and be rewarded by him for what she had done.

Prince Charles, after the splash that his return to France had made upon the European scene, waited impatiently for his ailing father and the sickly King George II to die. Neither did so for many years, and Prince Charles wandered, homeless, about Europe. He had two passionate love affairs with married women in Paris and later met up with Clementina Walkinshaw, who became his mistress, and by her he had a daughter Charlotte. After violent scenes, the Prince and Clementina were separated. The Prince settled in Italy, at Rome and then Florence, where he married Princess Louise Stollberg, but she ran off with her painting teacher. Prince Charles sank into a despairing torpor, but was eventually reconciled to his daughter, shortly before she died of cancer, and he himself died in 1788.

Flora died on 4th March 1790. Rev Alexander MacGregor, who mistakenly believed that Allan and Flora had returned from America to live at Kingsburgh, wrote that "Her death did not take place at her own residence of Kingsburgh, but at Peinduin, a friend's house on the sea coast, about three miles further north. She went thither in her usual health, to pay a friendly visit to the family of Peinduin, where she was taken suddenly ill with an inflammatory complaint, which refused to yield to all the medical skill available at the time. She possessed all her mental faculties to the very last, and calmly departed in the presence of her husband and two daughters." [6]

Flora was not living at Kingsburgh, but at Leabost, which was part of the tack of Penduin. The tack was held by Mrs MacQueen, the widow of Rev William MacQueen, minister of Snizort, who had died three years before. Flora had been seriously ill for some time.

Dr John Maclean was then living at Cuidrach, a few miles to the north. He had written out Allan and Flora's marriage contract, and had succeeded Allan as factor on the MacDonald estates. He wrote to his son Lachlan, in March, that "Nothing has occurred since I wrote you except the death of the famous Mrs Flora MacDonald, sometime of Kingsburgh. She suffered much distress for a long time in my neighbourhood at Peindoun."[7]

Alexander MacGregor stated that "Flora's remains were shrouded in one of the sheets in which the Prince had slept at the mansion of Kingsburgh. With this sheet she never parted in all her travels. It was religiously and faithfully preserved by her in North Carolina, during the Revolutionary War."[7] Both Flora and her sister-in-law, Anne, stated that Flora, Lady Kingsburgh, had been buried in both the Prince's sheets.

Alexander MacGregor heard the story of Flora's funeral from John MacDonald, who, as a young man, had carried the coffin. "Old John related to me very minutely the adventures of that night. He graphically described the storm, which was dreadful!

"At length the funeral day arrived. The procession started at an early hour, as the distance between Kingsburgh and the place of burial was about sixteen miles. The body was interred in the churchyard of Kilmuir, in the north end of Skye, within a square piece of coarse wall, erected in 1776, to enclose the tombs of the Kingsburgh family ... The funeral cortege was immense — more than a mile in length — consisting of several thousand of every rank in Skye and the adjacent Isles

"About a dozen pipers from the MacCrimmon and MacArthur colleges in Skye, and from other quarters, simultaneously played the 'Coronach', the usual melancholy lament for departed greatness."[7] There were pipers at Flora's funeral, but the MacCrimmon and MacArthur colleges had been closed for almost 20 years.

At Whitsun, in May 1790, only three months after Flora's death, her brother-in-law, Alexander MacDonald, formerly of Cuidrach and Mount Pleasant, received the tack of Kingsburgh, and went to live there with his wife Annabella and their son, Donald.

Later in the year Donald was married to Allan and Flora's younger daughter, Fanny, and they lived at Kingsburgh, where she had been born. Allan himself returned to Kingsburgh to live with his daughter, sister-in-law and his cousin Alexander. Donald and Fanny planned to return to Nova Scotia, but remained in Skye.

On 20th September 1792, Allan died at Kingsburgh, where he had lived as a young man, and later with Flora, before they had emigrated to North Carolina. Allan was buried at Kilmuir with Flora.

No memorial marked Flora and Allan's grave, inside the Kingsburgh burial chapel at Kilmuir. Their son, John, later erected a thin marble slab, within a sandstone frame, that stated that "In the family mausoleum at Kilmuir lie interred the remains of the following members of the Kingsburgh family, viz., Alexander Macdonald of Kingsburgh, his son Allan, his sons Charles and James, his son John, and two daughters; and of Flora Macdonald, who died in March 1790, aged 68 — a name that will be mentioned in history, and, if courage and fidelity be virtues, mentioned with honour. 'She was a woman of middle stature, soft features, gentle manners, and elegant presence.' So wrote Johnson." [4] The marble was cracked while being landed, and was soon removed in small pieces by curious visitors.

In 1871, after funds had been raised by public subscription, an Iona cross, 28 feet high, cut from Aberdeen granite, was placed over the graves, and the rough wall removed. Only two years later the cross was blown down in a December gale.

It was a song, however, that placed Flora in the pantheon of immortality. Based on a tune sung on the Isle of Soay, off Skye, the melody was recored by Annie C MacLeod. In 1879, while compiling a book of songs with Harold Boulton, they composed words to the tune while being rowed up Loch Ailort — 'Row us along, Donald and John, over the sea to Roshven' naming the two boatmen.

Boulton was so pleased with the melody that he later wrote that "with the tune ringing in my head I conceived the idea of making it the basis of a Jacobite song for our book. I originated the catchword, 'Over the sea to Skye', wrote the rest of the words, and called it the 'Skye Boat Song'." [8]

The air has become the most famous Jacobite song ever written, representing a romantic longing that "Yet, ere the sword cool in the sheath, Charlie will come again." And no matter that it was not an accurate account of the Prince's crossing, or that it was the Prince who watched over Flora's head, and not vice versa.

Rev Alexander MacGregor's biography of Flora kindled sufficient interest to have a new cross set up, at Kilmuir, similar to the first, with the inscription 'FLORA MACDONALD Preserver of Prince Charles Edward Stuart. Her name will be mentioned in history, and if courage and fidelity be virtues, mentioned with honour. Born at Milton, South Uist, 1722. Died at Kingsburgh, Skye, 4th March 1790.' [7]

Forty years later the cross had become loosened and the tablet detached. After a world wide appeal, in 1922, two hundred years after the birth of Flora, the cross was fixed more securely and a new plaque, with the old inscription, was attached to the monument. The refurbished cross was unveiled in the presence of Emily Livingstone, sister of Major Ranald Livingstone MacDonald of Flodigarry, and great-great-grand-daughter of Flora.

By 1922, after the publication of J.P. Maclean's *Flora MacDonald in America*, Flora had become a romatic heroine in North America as well.

One of the people on the platform at Kilmuir, when the memorial to Flora was rededicated in 1922, was Rev Charles Vardell, President of Flora MacDonald College, Red Springs, North Carolina, a Presbyterian college for girls. The College had been named for Flora MacDonald in 1914, and was later incorporated into St Andrews Presbyterian College, Laurinburg, North Carolina.

At Inverness a figure of Flora, scanning the horizon for the Prince, was placed on Castle Hill, with a legacy left by Capt Henderson MacDonald. In the Episcopal Church, Portree, a memorial window was dedicated to Flora, in 1896, by Fanny Charlotte, Mrs Henry, a grand-daughter of Col John of Exeter.

Mrs Henry's elder brother Augustus emigrated to New Zealand, and his son emigrated to America. In 1957 this son, Reginald Henry Macdonald, was recognised as, and received the arms of, Macdonald 15th of Kingsburgh. He wrote a book about the genealogy of his family. In 1960 Kingsburgh was present at the unveiling of a stone at Cheeks Creek, commemorating the home of Flora and Allan in North Carolina. Some years previously he had placed a new bronze plaque on his ancestor's grave at Kilmuir, and had been present at the unveiling of a cairn at Flora's birth place at Milton, in South Uist.

Flora MacDonald was now fully established as the Jacobite heroine in Scotland and North America. After Mary, Queen of Scots, Flora is Scotland's most famous heroine, remembered for saving Bonnie Prince Charlie by dressing him up in women's clothes and taking him 'Over the sea to Skye'.

Ironically, however, it is in North America, which she came to hate so bitterly, that Flora is most lovingly remembered. Some people believe that Flora is buried, with her 'children', in the grounds of the old Flora MacDonald College, at Red Springs, North Carolina. Every MacDonald in the state believes that they are descended from Flora. The Highland Games at Red Springs have been named to honour her. And more often than not, it is North American visitors who honour

Flora's name still, by seeking out her birthplace in South Uist, and by paying their respects beside her grave in Skye.

Flora had been born and brought up in South Uist, and it was there, at about midnight on 21st June 1746, that she took a decision which changed her life.

Capt Felix O'Neille wrote that he "had great difficulty to prevail upon Miss MacDonald to undertake being guardian to the Prince. She was not only frighten'd at the hazards and dangers attending such a bold enterprize, but likewise insisted upon the risque she would run of losing her character in a malicious and ill-natured world. The Captain was at some pains to represent to her the glory and honour she would acquire by such a worthy and heroic action, and he hoped God would make her successful in it.

" 'You need not fear your character,' said he, 'for by this you will gain yourself an immortal character.' " [9]

When Flora and Capt Felix O'Neille met again, as prisoners on board HMS *Furnace*, Flora told him that she feared that she would be taken to London, but he replied that "There you will meet with much respect and very good friends for what you have done. Only be careful to make all your conduct of a piece. Be not frighten'd by the thoughts of your present circumstances either to say or do anything that may in the least tend to contradict or sully the character you are now mistress of, and which you can never be robbed of but by yourself. Never once pretend (Through an ill-judg'd excess of caution and prudence) to repent or be ashamed of what you have done." [9]

It had been chance that had brought Neil MacEachen, Felix O'Neille and the Prince to the shieling at Unasary on the night of 21st June 1746, and yet it had been no chance that Flora had taken up the challenge with such courage. Her courage justly brought her immortality. Then, in 40 years of marriage, Flora had showed true fidelity to her husband and family.

Flora had lived a full and eventful life, bounded by adventure and tranquillity, fame and anonymity, success and failure, wealth and poverty, health and sickness, happiness and sorrow. Though turning bitter in her declining years, never once did she pretend to repent or be ashamed of what she had done.

There is no finer tribute to her, than that of Dr Samuel Johnson, who wrote that *Flora MacDonald*, was "a name that will be mentioned in history, and if courage and fidelity be virtues, mentioned with honour." [10]

References

Abbreviations:
BL — British Library, London. CDC — Clan Donald Centre, Armadale, Skye, *MacDonald* Papers. HL LO — Henry E. Huntington Library, San Marino, CA, *Loudoun Papers.* NCCR — *North Carolina Colonial Records.* NCDAH — North Carolina Department of Archives and History, Raleigh, NC. NLS — National Library of Scotland, Edinburgh. NLS CP — National Library of Scotland, *Campbell of Mamore Papers.* NLS DP — National Library of Scotland, *MacKenzie of Delvine Papers.* PRO — Public Records Office, London. PRO SP — Public Records Office, *State Papers.* RA CP — Royal Archives, Windsor, *Cumberland Papers.* RH GD — Scottish Records Office, Register House, Edinburgh. SHS — Scottish History Society.

Chapter 1 — South Uist. Page 1.
1 William Jolly, *Flora MacDonald in South Uist*, c1900.
2 Rev Alexander MacGregor, *Life of Flora MacDonald*, c1880.
3 Rev Robert Forbes, *The Lyon in Mourning*, SHS. 1895. Reprinted 1975.
4 James Boswell, *A Tour of the Hebrides*, ed F.A. Pottle and C.H. Bennett, 1936.

Chapter 3 — The Prince in South Uist. Page 13.
1 Duke of Cumberland to Duke of Newcastle, 5 June 1746, PRO SP 54/32.
2 Flora MacDonald, *Declaration* to Gen Campbell, 12 July 1746, NLS CP 3373/432.
3 Flora MacDonald, *Memorial* to Sir John MacPherson, 21 October 1789, NLS 2618, and H. Tayler, *A Jacobite Miscellany*, 1948.
4 Hugh MacDonald of Armadale to Lord Loudon, 20 June 1746, RA CP 16/215.
5 John Campbell to Sir Everard Faulkner, 11 June 1746, NLS CP 3373/396.
6 John Fergussone to Duke of Cumberland, 11 June 1746, RA CP 16/59.
7 Robert Jefferys to Sir Everard Faulkner, 14 June 1746, *ibid*, 16/122.
8 George Anderson, *Journal*, 3 July 1746, NLS CP 3375/406.
9 W.B. Blaikie, *Origins of the '45*, 1916. Reprinted 1975.
10 Ship's log of HMS *Baltimore*, PRO ADM 51/80.
11 A. and H. Tayler, *The 1745 & After*, 1938.
12 A. Tayler, *A Jacobite Miscellany*, 1948.

Chapter 4 — Flora meets the Prince. Page 21.
1 W.B. Blaikie, *Origins of the '45*, 1916. Reprinted 1975.
2 Felix O'Neille, *Declarations*, NLS CP 3735/400, 3736/416 & 464, and Rev Robert Forbes, *The Lyon in Mourning*, SHS, 1895. Reprinted 1975.
3 Flora MacDonald, *Memorial* to Sir John MacPherson, 21 October 1789, NLS 2618, and H. Tayler, *A Jacobite Miscellany*, 1948.
4 Rev Robert Forbes, *The Lyon in Mourning*, Vol II, SHS, 1985. Reprinted 1975.
5 A. Tayler, *A Jacobite Miscellany*, 1948.

Chapter 5 — The Prince's departure from Benbecula. Page 32.

1 Flora MacDonald, *Declaration* to Gen Campbell, 12 July 1746, NLS CP 3373/432.
2 Angus MacDonald of Milton to Gen Campbell, 16 August 1746, NLS CP 3736/452.
3 John Maclean to Gen Campbell, NLS CP 3736/448.
4 W.B. Blaikie, *Origins of the '45*, 1916. Reprinted 1975.
5 Rev Robert Forbes, *The Lyon in Mourning*, SHS, 1895. Reprinted 1975.
6 Felix O'Neille, *Declarations*, NLS CP 3735/400, 3736/416 & 464, and Rev Robert Forbes, *ibid*, Vol I.
7 George Anderson, *Journal*, 3 July 1746, NLS CP 3375/406.
8 John Campbell to Lord Albemarle, 24 July 1746, NLS CP 3736/447.
9 John MacLeod of Talisker to Lord Loudoun, 24 June 1746, RA CP 16/276.
10 Lady Margaret MacDonald to Delvine, 27 June 1746, NLS DP 1309/26.
11 Lachlan MacMhurrich, *Declaration*, 12 July 1746, NLS CP 3736/429.
12 Duncan Campbell, *Declaration*, 3 August 1746, NLS CP 3736/460.
13 A. Tayler, *A Jacobite Miscellany*, 1948.
14 Flora MacDonald, *Memorial* to Sir John MacPherson, 21 October 1789, NLS 2618, and H. Tayler, *A Jacobite Miscellany*, 1948.

Chapter 6 — Flora and the Prince on shore on Skye. Page 43.

1 Flora MacDonald, *Declaration* to Gen Campbell, 12 July 1746, NLS CP 3373/432.
2 Rev Robert Forbes, *The Lyon in Mourning*, SHS, 1895. Reprinted 1975.
3 W.B. Blaikie, *Origins of the '45*, 1916. Reprinted 1895.
4 Flora MacDonald, *Memorial* to Sir John MacPherson, 21 October 1789, NLS 2618, and H. Tayler, *A Jacobite Miscellany*, 1948.
5 H. Taylor, *Ibid*.
6 MacAlister MSS, NLS, and Archibald MacDonald, *Memorial of the '45*, 1908.
7 D.W. Stewart, *Old and Rare Tartans*, 1890.

Chapter 7 — The Prince and Flora part at Portree. Page 55.

1 Flora MacDonald, *Declaration* to Gen Campbell, 12 July 1746, NLS CP 3373/432.
2 Rev Robert Forbes, *The Lyon in Mourning*, SHS, 1895. Reprinted 1975.
3 Flora MacDonald, *Memorial* to Sir John MacPherson, 21 October 1789, NLS 2618, and H. Tayler, *A Jacobite Miscellany*, 1948.
4 H. Tayler, *ibid*.
5 Charles Macnabb, *Declaration*, 9 July 1746, NLS CP 3736/420.

Chapter 8 — Flora arrested. Page 61.

1 Felix O'Neille, *Declarations*, NLS CP 3735/400, 3736/416 & 464, and Rev Robert Forbes, *The Lyon in Mourning*, SHS, 1895. Reprinted 1975.
2 George Anderson, *Journal*, 3 July 1746, NLS CP 3375/406.
3 Lachlan MacMhurrich, *Declaration*, 12 July 1746, NLS CP 3736/429.
4 Rev Robert Forbes, *ibid*, Vol I.
5 Unnamed *Journal*, undated, NLS CP 3736/543.
6 Lady Margaret MacDonald to Delvine, 27 June 1746, NLS DP 1309/26.
7 Rev Alexander MacGregor, *Life of Flora MacDonald*, c1880.

8 Rev Robert Forbes, *ibid*, Vol II.
9 John MacLeod of Talisker to Lord Loudoun, 8 July 1746, RA CP 17/144.
10 MacAlister MSS, NLS, and Archibald MacDonald, *Memorial of the '45*, 1908.
11 Alexander MacDonald of Kingsburgh to Gen Campbell, 11 July 1746, NLS CP 3736/428.
12 David Campbell to Gen Campbell, 11 July 1746, NLS CP 3736/427.
13 John MacLeod of Talisker to Lord Loudoun, 10 July 1746, HL LO 12111.
14 Donald MacDonald of Castleton to Gen Campbell, 12 July 1746, NLS CP 3736/433.
15 Donald MacDonald to Sir Alexander MacDonald, 11 July 1746, RA CP 17/248.
16 Caroline Scott to Col Napier, 13 July 1746, RA CP 17/257.
17 Flora MacDonald, *Declaration* to Gen Campbell, 12 July 1746, NLS CP 3373/432.
18 Duke of Cumberland to Gen Campbell, 10 July 1746, RA CP 17/184.
19 Sir Alexander MacDonald to Duke of Cumberland, 12 July 1746, RA CP 17/247.
20 Duke of Cumberland to Gen Campbell, 13 July 1746, NLS CP 3736/434 and RA CP 17/250.
21 Duke of Cumberland, *Proclamation*, 12 July 1746, NLS CP 3736/431.
22 John Campbell to Duke of Cumberland, 13 July 1746, NLS CP 3736/436.
23 Duke of Cumberland to Duke of Newcastle, 17 July 1746, PRO SP 54/198.
24 John Campbell to Lord Albemarle, 24 July 1746, NLS CP 3736/447.

Chapter 9 — Flora a prisoner. Page 75.

1 Rev Robert Forbes, *The Lyon in Mourning*, SHS, 1895. Reprinted 1975.
2 *Culloden Papers*, 1815.
3 Lady Margaret MacDonald to Delvine, 27 June 1746, NLS DP 1309/27.
4 Flora MacDonald, *Declaration* to Gen Campbell, 12 July 1746, NLS CP 3373/432, and Rev Robert Forbes, *ibid*, Vol II.
5 John Campbell to *Duke of Cumberland*, 13 July 1746, NLS CP 3736/436.
6 W.D. Simpson, *Dunstaffnage Castle*, 1958.
7 *Inventory of Ancient Monuments: Argyll*, Vol 2, Lorn.
8 John Campbell to Lord Albemarle, 4 August 1746, NLS CP 3736/462.
9 Lord Albemarle to Gen Campbell, 6 August 1746, NLS CP 3736/463.
10 John Campbell to Lord Albemarle, 8 August 1746, NLSa CP 3736/465.
11 Lord Albemarle to Gen Campbell, 11 August 1746, NLS CP 3737/466.
12 Rev Alexander MacGregor, *Life of Flora MacDonald*, c1880.
13 Angus MacDonald of Milton to Gen Campbell, 16 August 1746, NLS CP 3737/469.
14 John Campbell to Lord Albemarle, prisoners, 4 August 1746, NLS CP 3736/463.
15 John Campbell to Lord Albemarle, 4 August 1746, NLS CP 3736/462.
16 Ship's log, HMS *Furnace*, PRO ADM 51/379.
17 Ship's log, HMS *Bridgewater*, PRO ADM 51/411.
18 Rev Robert Forbes, *ibid*, Vol II.
19 Lord Albemarle to Duke of Newcastle, 23 September 1746, *Albemarle Papers*, 1902.
20 Catherine Stewart to Miss Mercer, 31 Oct 1746, Dalguise Papers, RH GD 38/2/7.

21 Duke of Cumberland to Duke of Newcastle, 5 June 1746, PRO SP 54/32/20.
22 Lord Albemarle to Duke of Newcastle, 27 October 1746, *Albemarle Papers*, 1902.
23 Charles Knowler probably to Gen Campbell, 30 November 1746, NLS CP 3736/511.
24 Ship's log, HMS *Royal Sovereign*, PRO ADM 51/.
25 Donald MacDonald to Lord Loudoun, 23 November 1746, Loudoun Papers, HL LO 11873.
26 Allan MacDonald to Duncan Forbes, 27 November 1746, *More Culloden Papers*, Vol V.
27 Rev Alexander MacGregor, *Life of Flora MacDonald*, c1880.
28 Anon, *The Female Rebels*, published by J. Drummond, 1747.
29 James Boswell, *Tour of the Hebrides*, 1936 edition.

Chapter 10 — Flora in Edinburgh. Page 94.

1 Rev Robert Forbes, *The Lyon in Mourning*, SHS, 1895. Reprinted 1975.
2 A.R. MacDonald, *The Truth about Flora MacDonald*, 1938.
3 *Albemarle Papers*, Vol II.
4 Lady Margaret MacDonald to Ranald MacAlister, 1747, CDC GD 221/394.
5 Rev Alexander MacGregor, *Life of Flora MacDonald*, c1880.
6 Dr John Burton, *Narrative of Several Passages of the Young Chevalier*, 1749.

Chapter 11 — Flora marries Allan MacDonald. Page 107.

1 *Scots Magazine*, January 1751.
2 Samuel Johnson, *Journey to the Western Isles of Scotland*, 1775.
3 Rev Alexander MacGregor, *Life of Flora MacDonald*, c1880.
4 Original marriage contract at Abbotsford House, Melrose. A.R. MacDonald, *The Truth about Flora MacDonald*, 1938.
5 Rev Robert Forbes, *The Lyon in Mourning*, SHS, 1895. Reprinted 1975.
6 A.R. MacDonald, *ibid.*
7 MacDonald Estates Judicial Rental, 1733, CDC.
8 Flora MacDonald, hand written list at Dunvegan Castle.
9 Letters to John MacKenzie of Delvine, NLS Delvine Papers, 1309 and 1310.
10 James Boswell, *Tour of the Hebrides*, 1936 edition.
11 Samuel Johnson, *ibid*, 1775.

Chapter 12 — Following their friends to America. Page 123.

1 Letters to John Mackenzie of Delvine, NLS *Delvine Papers*, 1310.
2 Unnamed to Sir Alexander MacDonald, 13 June 1770, CDC GD 221/420.
3 A.R. MacDonald, *The Truth about Flora MacDonald*, 1938.
4 Rev Robert Forbes, *The Lyon in Mourning*, SHS, 1895. Reprinted 1975.
5 *Scots Magazine*, March 1772.
6 Thomas Pennant, *Tour of Scotland & Voyage to the Hebrides*, 1772.
7 Edinburgh *Courant*, July 1773.
8 James Boswell, *Tour of the Hebrides*, 1936 edition.
9 Samuel Johnson, *Journey to the Western Isles of Scotland*, 1775.
10 Alexander MacLeod, *Loyalist Claims*, PRO Audit Office Papers; copies in

NCSA and printed in Rassie Wicker, *Miscellaneous Ancient Records of Moore County, NC.*
11 Rassie Wicker, *ibid.*
12 James Banks, *Life of and Character of Flora MacDonald*, 1857.
13 Flora MacDonald, *Memorial* to Sir John MacPherson, 21 October 1789, National Library of Scotland 2618, and H. Tayler, *A Jacobite Miscellany*, 1948.
14 Brunswick Port of Entry Book, NCDAH.
15 Crowe, Catherine. *The Nightside of Nature*, 1848.

Chapter 13 — Flora and Allan in North Carolina. Page 137.

1 James Boswell, *A Tour of the Hebrides*, 1936 edition.
2 [Janet Schaw], *The Journal of a Lady of Quality*, 1922.
3 James Banks, *Life and Character of Flora MacDonald*, 1857.
4 F.X. Martin, *History of North Carolina from the Earliest Times*, 1829.
5 Duane Meyer, *The Highland Scots of North Carolina*, 1957.
6 Rev Henry Foote, *Sketches of North Carolina*, 1846.
7 J.P. Maclean, *Flora MacDonald in America*, 1909.
8 B.J. Lossing, *American Historical Record*, Vol I pp 1-9-10, March 1872.
9 Rassie Wicker, *Miscellaneous Ancient Records of Moore County, N.C.*
10 J.E. Purcell, *Lumberton River Scots*, 1941.
11 Josiah Martin to John Burnside, 10th July 1775, PRO Audit Office 13/117/360. Copy in NCSA in John Burnside, *Loyalist Claims.*
12 St Andrews Presbyterian College Records, Laurinburg, NC.

Chapter 14 — The Highland Gentlemen remain loyal. Page 149.

1 [Janet Schaw], *The Journal of a Lady of Quality*, 1922.
2 Alexander MacAlester, *Letter Book*, printed in Paul Green, *The Highland Call*, ed D.S. Clark, 1976.
3 NC Colonial Records.
4 Rassie Wicker, *Miscellaneous Ancient Records of Moore County, NC.*
5 J.P. Maclean, *Flora MacDonald in America*, 1909.
6 Elizabeth Vining, *Flora MacDonald – her Life in the Highlands and America*, 1967.
7 Flora MacDonald, *Memorial* to Sir John MacPherson, 21 October 1789, National Library of Scotland 2618, and H. Tayler, *A Jacobite Miscellany*, 1948.
8 NC Department of Archives and History.
9 Alexander MacDonald, *Letter Book*, New York Historical Society, 1883.

Chapter 15 — The Loyalist attempt in North Carolina. Page 163.

1 NC Colonial Records.
2 Rassie Wicker, *Miscellaneous Ancient Records of Moore County, NC.*
3 NC Department of Archives and History.
4 Rev Henry Foote, *Sketches of North Carolina*, 1846.
5 Rev Eli Caruthers, *Interesting Revolutionary Incidents, and Sketches of Characters Chiefly in the Old North State*, 1856.
6 Flora MacDonald, *Memorial* to Sir John MacPherson, 21 October 1789, National Library of Scotland 2618, and H. Tayler, *A Jacobite Miscellany*, 1948.
7 J.P. Maclean, *Flora MacDonald in America*, 1909.

8   Samuel Johnston to James Hewes, 10 March 1776, *Hayes Collection*, NC Department of Archives and History.

Chapter 16 — Moore's Creek. Page 178.
1   Rev Henry Foote, *Sketches of North Carolina*, 1846.
2   Rev Eli Caruthers, *Interesting Revolutionary Incidents, and Sketches of Characters Chiefly in the Old North State*, 1856.
3   B.J. Lossing, *American Historical Record*, Vol I, March 1872.
4   J.P. Maclean, *Flora Macdonald in America*, 1909.
5   James Banks, *Life and Character of Flora Macdonald*, 1857.
6   NC Colonial Records.
7   *Journal A,* Treasurer's Account for 1775-6, NC.
8   Alexander Maclean, *A Narrative of the Proceedings of a Body of Loyalists in North Carolina*, in letter to Gen Howe to Lord Germain, 25 April 1776, PRO. Copy in NC Department of Archives and History. Printed in Rassie Wicker, *Miscellaneous Ancient Records of Moore County, NC*.
9   NC Department of Archives and History.
10 *American Archives*, 4th Series, Vol V, p61.
11 C. Steadman, *History of the Origin, Progress, & Termination of the American War*, 1794.
12 F.M. Hubbard, *Who Commanded at Moore's Creek Bridge?*, NC University Magazine, 1857.
13 *New York Packet*, 28 March 1776.
14 Rassie Wicker, *Miscellaneous Ancient Records of More County, NC.*
15 Flora MacDonald, *Memorial* to Sir John MacPherson, 21 October 1789, National Library of Scotland 2618, and H. Tayler, *A Jacobite Miscellany*, 1948.

Chapter 17 — Flora abandoned in North Carolina. Page 193.
1   NC Colonial Records.
2   Flora MacDonald, *Memorial* to Sir John MacPherson, 21 October 1789, National Library of Scotland 2618, and H. Tayler, *A Jacobite Miscellany*, 1948.
3   James Banks, *Life and Character of Flora MacDonald*, 1857.
4   J.P. Maclean, *Flora MacDonald in America*, 1909.
5   Rassie Wicker, *Miscellaneous Ancient Records of Moore County, NC.*
6   *American Archives*, 4th series, Vol V.
7   Alexander MacDonald, *Letter Book*, New York Historical Society, 1883.
8   Rev Eli Caruthers, *Interesting Revolutionary Incidents, and Sketches of Characters Chiefly in the Old North State*, 1856.
9   Pennsylvania Historical Society, Library MS.
10 *Leicester & Nottingham Journal*, 17 June 1775.

Chapter 18 — Flora and Allan reunited. Page 203.
1   NC Colonial Records.
2   Rassie Wicker, *Miscellaneous Ancient Records of Moore County, NC.*
3   Flora MacDonald, *Memorial* to Sir John MacPherson, 21 October 1789, National Library of Scotland 2618, and H. Tayler, *A Jacobite Miscellany*, 1948.
4   Alexander MacDonald, *Letter Book*, New York Historical Society, 1883.
5   Returns of 84th Regiment, PRO WO 17/205.

6   James Banks, *Life and Character of Flora MacDonald*, 1857.
7   J.P. Maclean, *Flora MacDonald in America*, 1909.
8   R.D. Bass, *The Green Dragoon*, 1957.

Chapter 19 — Flora returns to Skye. Page 217.
1   Flora MacDonald, *Memorial* to Sir John MacPherson, 21 October 1789, National Library of Scotland 2618, and H. Tayler, *A Jacobite Miscellany*, 1948.
2   William Chambers, *History of the Rebellion of 1745-6*, 1827.
3   James Banks, *Life and Character of Flora MacDonald*, 1857.
4   J.P. Maclean, *Flora MacDonald in America*, 1909.
5   A.R. MacDonald, *The Truth about Flora MacDonald*, 1938.
6   Rev Alexander MacGregor, *Life of Flora MacDonald*, c1880.
7   Rassie Wicker, *Miscellaneous Ancient Records of Moore County, NC.*
8   Archibald MacDonald, *Memorials of the '45*, 1908.
9   Flora MacDonald to Alexander Macleod, BL ADD 45524.
10 Elizabeth Vining, *Flora MacDonald – Her Life in the Highlands and America*, 1967.
11 Ship's log, HMS *Shrewsbury*, PRO ADM 51/905.
12 Ranald MacDonald, Will, PRO PROB 11/1109/206.

Chapter 20 — Allan returns to Skye. Page 227.
1   Archibald MacDonald, *Memorials of the '45*, 1908.
2   Rassie Wicker, *Miscellaneous Ancient Records of Moore County, NC.*
3   British Fisheries Society Papers, RH GD 9/217/10.
4   A.R. MacDonald, *The Truth about Flora MacDonald*, 1938.
5   Flora MacDonald, *Memorial* to Sir John MacPherson, 21 October 1789, National Library of Scotland 2618, and H. Tayler, *A Jacobite Miscellany*, 1948.
6   Rev Alexander MacGregor, *Life of Flora MacDonald*, c1880.
7   See *The Times*, 4 June 1991, letter from Gen Sir Patrick Palmer.
8   Donald Mackinnon, Manuscript biography of Flora MacDonald.
9   Rev Robert Forbes, *The Lyon in Mourning*, SHS, 1985. Reprinted 1975.
10 Samuel Johnson, *Journey to the Western Isles of Scotland*, 1775.

Other sources:
Anon, *Alexis or the Young Adventurer*, 1746.
Anon, *Ascanius or the Young Adventurer, A True History*, 1747.
Ashe, Samuel A., *History of North Carolina*, 1925.
[Birt, S.], *Letters from a Gentleman in the North of Scotland*, 1754.
Blaikie, Walter, B., *Itinerary of Prince Charles Edward Stewart*, Scottish History Society, 1897, reprinted 1975.
Bristol, Nicholas M., *Hebridean Decade, 1761-1771*, 1982.
Bumstead, J.M., *The People's Clearance*, 1982.
Chambers, Robert, *Jacobite Memoirs of the Rebellion of 1745*, 1834.
Connor, Robert D.W., *The History of North Carolina*, 1919.
Daiches, David, *Charles Edward Stuart*, 1973.
de Mond, Robert, *Loyalists in North Carolina during the Revolution*, 1940.
Douglas, Hugh, *Flora MacDonald – The Most Loyal Rebel*, 1993.
Duke, Winifred, *In the Steps of Bonnie Prince Charlie*, 1953.

Duncanson, J.V., *Rawdon and Douglas: Two Loyalist Townships in Nova Scotia*, 1978.

Elcho, David, Lord, *A Short Account of the Affairs of Scotland, in the Years 1744, 1745, 1746*, 1907.

Forster, Margaret, *The Rash Adventurer*, 1973.

Gibson, John S., *Ships of the '45*, 1967.

Grant, Isobel F., *The MacLeods – The History of a Clan*, 1959.

Haddow, Alec, *History and Structure of Ceol Mor*, 1982.

Haldane, A.R.B., *New Ways through the Glens*, 1962.

Haldane, A.R.B., *The Drove Roads of Scotland*, 1971.

Home, John, *History of the Rebellion in the Year 1745*, 1836.

Johnson, Stanley C., *A History of Emigration: From the United Kingdom to North America, 1763-1912*, 1913.

Jones, Thomas, *History of New York during the Revolutionary War, and of the Leading Events in the Other Colonies at that Period*, ed Edward F. de Lancey, New York Historical Society, 1879.

Knox, John. *A Tour through the Highlands of Scotland and Hebride Isles in 1786*, 1787.

Lee, Lawrence, *Lower Cape Fear in Colonial Days*, 1968.

Lefler, Hugh T., and Newsome, Albert R., *North Carolina: The History of a Southern State*, 1954.

Lenman, Bruce P., *The Jacobite Risings in Britain, 1689-1746*, 1980.

Linklater, Eric, *The Prince in the Heather*, 1965.

MacDonald, Revs Alexander & Archibald, *Clan Donald*, 1906.

Macdonald, Reginald H., of Kingsburgh, *Notes on the Kingsburgh Family*, 1962.

MacKenzie, Compton, *Prince Charlie and his Ladies*, 1934.

Mackinnon, Donald, *Flora MacDonald*, unpublished and incomplete MS.

Maclean, Alasdair, *A. MacDonald for the Prince*, 1982, 1990.

Maclean, Alasdair, and John S. Gibson, *Summer Hunting A Prince*, 1992.

McLean, Angus W., *History of the Scotch in North Carolina*, unpublished MS, NCDAH, Raleigh.

Maclean, James N.M., *Reward is Secondary*, 1963.

Maclean, Fitzroy, *Bonnie Prince Charlie*, 1988.

Maclean, John P., *An Historical Account of the Settlements of Scotch Highlanders in America Prior to the Peace of 1783*, 1900.

Maclean, Lorraine, of Dochgarroch, *Indomitable Colonel*, 1986.

MacLeod, Finlay, *Togail Tir, Marking Time*, 1989.

MacLeod, R.C., of MacLeod, *Book of Dunvegan*, 1938, 1939.

MacLeod, Ruairidh, *Independent Companies of the 1945 Rebellion*, Transactions of the Gaelic Society of Inverness, Vol LIII.

McLynn, Frank, *Charles Edward Stuart*, 1988.

Marshall, Rosalind, *Bonnie Prince Charlie*, 1988.

Martin, Martin, *Description of the Western Isles of Scotland*, 1703.

Menary, G., *The Life and Letters of Duncan Forbes of Culloden*, 1936.

Morrison, Alick., *Harris Estate Papers*, Transactions of the Gaelic Society of Inverness, Vol XLV.

Morrison, Alick., *The MacLeods – the Genealogy a Clan*, 1975-88.

Newsome, A.R., *Records of Emigrants from England and Scotland*, NCHR, Vol XI.

Pinkerton, John, *A General Collection of the Best and Most Interesting Voyages and Travels in All Parts of the World*, 1832.

Prebble, John, *Culloden*, 1961.

Quynn, Dorothy M., *Flora MacDonald in History*, NCHR Vol XVIII.

Rankin, Hugh F., *The Moore's Creek Bridge Campaign, 1776*, NCHR, Vol XXX.

Seton, B.G. and Arnot, J.G., *Prisoners of the '45*, 1928.

Smyth, John F., *A Tour in the United States of America*, 1784.

Swain, David L., *A Revolutionary History of North Carolina*, with Hawkes, F.L. and Graham, W.A., ed Cooke, William D., 1853.

Terry, John S., *The Forty Five*, 1922.

Whitaker, Ian R., *The MacPhersons of Skye*, Scottish Genealogist, 1954.

Williamson, Margaret, *The Real Flora MacDonald*, Lady's Realm, 1897.

Wylde, Flora MacDonald, *The Life of Flora MacDonald*, an autobiography, 1870.

Index

Suck Creek, NC, 145
Sucky & Peggy, ship, 210-11
Sydney, Cape Breton, 227

Tarleton, Col Banastre, 221
Thames, River, 83, 87
Tobermory, Mull, 17-18
Touchstone, Caleb, NC, 146-7, 175
Trotternish, Skye, 38-9, 46, 62, 66-7, 106, 110-12
Trumpan, Skye, 224-5
Tryal, HMS, 18

Ulysses, ship, 135
Unasary, South Uist, 21, 26, 76, 238
Union, cutter, 18, 83
Upper Cape Fear, NC, 141, 152, 157, 159

Vatersay (Watersound) Bay, Barra, 62
Vardell, Rev Charles, 237
Vardy, Aaron, NC, 176, 191
Ville de Paris, French ship, 218, 226
Vining, Elizabeth, 152

Wads Creek, NC, 145
Waternish, Skye, 38-40, 64-5
West Indies, 136, 223, 226
Wiay, Isle, Benbecula, 15, 32, 39
Wicker, Rassie, NC, 146-7
Windsor, Nova Scotia, 206, 214, 227
Williams, Samuel, NC, 156
Wilmington, NC, 134, 139-40, 153-8, 161, 176, 180-2, 203, 211-13, 221
Wynne, Sir Watkin William, 90, 126

York, England, 94, 101, 104